SANGREAL CEREMONIES AND RITUALS

Sangreal Sodality Series

Western Inner Workings, Volume 1

The Sangreal Sacrament, Volume 2

Concepts of Qabalah, Volume 3

Sangreal Ceremonies and Rituals, Volume 4

SANGREAL CEREMONIES AND RITUALS

Sangreal Sodality Series
Volume 4

William G. Gray

SAMUEL WEISER, INC.
York Beach, Maine

First published in 1986 by
Samuel Weiser, Inc.
Box 612
York Beach, Maine 03910

Copyright © William G. Gray, 1986
All rights reserved. No part of this publication may be reproduced or transmitted in any form or by any means, electronic or mechanical, including photocopy, without permission in writing from the publisher. Reviewers may quote brief passages.

ISBN 0-87728-583-7
Library of Congress Catalog Card Number: 85-51169

Typeset by Positive Type
Printed in the United States of America

Publication of this series was made possible by the Sangreal Foundation, Inc.

Contents

Introduction ix

Part I: Preparing for the Sangreal Ritual
1 An Overview of Ritual 3
2 A Sangreal Catechism 21

Part II: Progression of the Soul Through the Sangreal
3 The Stations of the Sangreal 41
4 The Sangreal Nomination Service 59
5 The Wedding Service of the Sangreal 79
6 The Act of Last Annointment 97
7 The Rite of Release 107
8 The Sangreal Funeral Rite 113

Part III: Calling Upon Deity
9 The Healing Service of the Sangreal 129
10 Sangreal Exorcism of Evil 147
11 The Rite of Rejection 175
12 The Service of Commination 185
13 The Rite of Reproach 203
14 The Sangreal Rosary 217

Part IV: Celebrating the Sangreal Year
15 Sangreal New Year Service 223
16 The Seasonal Rituals 251

Appendix: The Office of the Holy Tree of Life 329

*To the memory of Carr P. Collins, Jr.
May he meet with Perfect Peace Profound.
So mote it be.   Amen.*

Also by Wm. G. Gray

Inner Traditions of Magic
The Ladder of Lights
Magical Images of the Tree
Magical Ritual Methods
An Outlook on our Inner Western Way
The Rite of Light
The Rollright Ritual
The Sangreal Sodality Series
   (in four volumes)
Seasonal Occult Rituals
A Self—Made by Magic
The Talking Tree
The Tree of Evil

About the Author

Wm. G. Gray was born in Middlesex, United Kingdom, at 2:10 p.m. on the 25th of March, 1913. Astrologically this gave him: Sun in Aries, Moon in Scorpio, and Leo rising.

On his father's side, Bill Gray comes from a long line of churchmen with his grandfather being an Anglican rector and his heritage extending back to Archbishop Walter de Gray of York. His mother was Scottish-American and in mid-life became a prominent astrologer. This was young Bill's first introduction to the occult and through his mother was able to meet many members of the Golden Dawn and other esoteric groups.

He joined the British Army as a communications technician and served several years in Egypt where he came into contact with additional material relevant to the *Inner Tradition*.

Shortly after his return home, England became involved in World War II and Bill's military outfit was immediately transferred to France where he was in action until evacuated during the Dunkirk disaster. It was at this time that he swore to devote the remainder of his life to the Western Spiritual Way of Life. After the holocaust, his health broke and he was invalided from the British forces.

For a short period, Wm. G. Gray was a member of the Society of the Inner Light. This organization was founded by Dion Fortune, the author of many books on the Western Tradition which had been of great help to him in his early occult studies. Bill Gray's own especial mentor was a Rosicrucian associate of "Papus," Dr. Gerami Encausse. To this advanced initiate, Bill Gray attributes his own psycho-spiritual development.

Wm. G. Gray did not commence writing until the late 1960's when he wrote an essay on Qabalah purely for the benefit of a few close associates. They were so enthusiastic about the article that he was encouraged to expand it into what is now one of the classics of Qabalistic literature, *Ladder of Lights*. When Israel Regardie was asked to read the manuscript, he was full of praise in acclaiming it both unique and original. Since that time Wm. G. Gray has written eight more books about the Qabalah and the Western Tradition before undertaking the present Sangreal Sodality series.

Wm. G. Gray is married to an ex-service woman who, like his mother, is a professional astrologer. He established himself as a Chiropodist in the West Country of England and there has devoted his free time to the study and advancement of the Western Inner Tradition.

• • • • • • • • • •

SANGREAL SODALITY chapters are being organized throughout the western world. If you would like information on organizing your own group, please write:

Wm. G. Gray
c/o Samuel Weiser, Inc.
P.O. Box 612
York Beach, Maine 03910

Introduction

With the inception of a Western esoteric movement termed the "Sangreal Sodality," a kind of "blood-brotherhood" relating all Occidental souls who follow their inherited way of inner life and light, it seems only natural that some formalized method of working together be found which would present the Sangreal concept to its active adherents in the most practical and modern manner.

A nucleus of this has been achieved by the psychodramatic ceremonies collected in this book. This volume of ceremonies and rituals consists of the Services Section for Sangreal Sodality. These rituals are new to the modern world even though many are based on worship in the ancient mysteries with occasional similarity to Rites in the Judeo-Christian tradition. Since this work is the fourth and final volume in the Sangreal Sodality Series, the reader will note the omission of certain important rituals already contained in other volumes: the Sangreal Mass and Seeking the Sangreal are to be found in Volume 2 of this series, *The Sangreal Sacrament*. The rituals contained here consist principally of the "Rites of Passage" marking the stages of life as we pass through this world, such as nomination, marriage, and death, plus a shared communion with spirit through a sacramental service which condenses every essential faith. Additionally, there are many auxiliary exercises which augment the practices of most faiths. Healing, Blessing, exorcism and other formalized acts of the self's relationship with Deity will be found in this unusual book, which is not so much an official publication for some elitist and exclusive "Church" as an open invitation to everyone feeling an affinity with Western Inner Ideology to adopt and adapt its contents freely for their own purposes.

The style of many of the ceremonies will surely arouse interest among modern-minded ritualists. They are often in a sort of dialogue form, alternating between a priest who prays directly to Deity concerning whatever point has been reached, and a preceptor who comments on it in an explanatory fashion. Thus both mind and soul combine their faculties in a common act of worship.

Although the rituals in this work are fundamentally religious in character, none could be fairly described as strictly sectarian. It is true they assume beliefs in a directional Deity, the immortality of individual life, and an integrative connection between souls which amounts to a spiritual blood relationship leading eventually to a coexistence with Divine Consciousness itself, but such ideas are basic for most esoterically inclined people. None of the Rites are considered obligatory or inflexible, and there is no reason why they may not be adapted or altered if there should be real necessity for this. Alteration for its own sake alone would be most unwise, however, since every ritual has been most carefully assembled and constructed by experienced practitioners.

Some of the Rites may be strange or startling to those unfamiliar with the ideology involved. The idea of "Commination," or directing retributive energy toward deserving wrongdoers, is obviously an instance. So may be a ritual of reproach for humans who feel exasperated beyond endurance by their unsatisfactory state of relationship with Deity. Yet such was commonplace in olden days and translates well into contemporary terminology. A reliable means of catharsis is a sadly lacking element in most official religions, and here we find it in an almost classical form which has considerable literary and spiritual significance. These rituals are considered to be more beautiful, more meaningful and more powerful than similar ceremonies previously available.

It is never for a moment claimed that these rituals comprise a complete liturgical collection, and it is sincerely hoped that future authorship will add to or even improve their present format. They are designed to fill a current urgent need, and not to constitute a rigid ruling for all time. Though they are primarily intended for the use of those who consider themselves capable of constituting a Sangreal Sodality throughout our Western world, these rituals are being published to provide interested people with information concerning the ideology of the entire Sangreal concept and its implications.

There is nothing secret or in the slightest sense subversive about these ideas. They signify no more than the soul of Western esotericism (or "Wesotericism"), awakening to another stage of development in its most modern, yet fundamentally oldest, form of faith. That is what it *is*. These rituals are what some of its most recently awakened members actually *do* in order to celebrate their present state of awareness. Such is virtually the whole story to date. May subsequent history complete it with a maximum of honor and service to the Holiest Spirit enlivening us all.

The entire sense of the Sangreal can be compressed into its motto: I SEEK TO SERVE. These psychodramatic services are intended to show a style in which the Sangreal ideal can be served by modern mortals. They should be regarded as an example of that style only. There are many other styles and methods of service in this world. It is for everyone to find their own styles for themselves. Many may decide that formalized rituals and preset patterns of behavior do not suit them and they would prefer not to participate in any regular rituals or ceremonial occasions. They might not be able to give any cogent reasons for this attitude other than "It doesn't appeal to me," and that would be quite true if not explicatory of why this should be so.

Therefore, among those who care enough to constitute themselves part of the Sangreal Sodality within our Western world, there should never be the least disagreement between any of them concerning the ceremonies presented here. They are for participation in by whoever has need for them, and should never under any circumstances be considered either obligatory or in the slightest sense compulsory. It is natural that there will be people who love ceremonies and those who don't or perhaps never will. That is no reason why the two distinct types of soul should not "agree to differ" amiably and work perfectly well together because they are bound by a common conceptual ideal which they seek to serve in quite different ways.

Ritual is not for everyone, and there is no reason why it should be. Neither, for that matter, is sport, athletics, science, art, or any other specialized human activity for everyone. The Sangreal Spirit of service, however, applies to every area of life, and should be understood accordingly. We may be reminded of the famous line, "They also serve who only stand and wait." But like all truisms, it is only an often repeated accuracy. There are as many ways of serving in a Sangreal style as there are humans alive to follow them. Each soul is unique, but all can *unite* in a special concept of spiritual service among each other, because we are all in this world for the same reason: to evolve beyond its boundaries altogether in the course of Cosmic time.

Therefore all ceremonial procedures are purely temporary according to the century and epoch we happen to live in regardless as to how far back we can trace their principles. The present construction of Sangreal rites may change completely before another century has passed. However useful they may be now there must always be room for improved alteration. At the same time, there should never be change for the sheer sake of change itself. That would be counterproductive and stupid. The sensible thing to do is take the rites as they are and then discover what may be done with them as they are experienced. Some people may need others, and other people may need none. As they stand they are simply a sincere contribution to our overall experience as Wesoterics and it is most earnestly hoped that they will expand and improve that Inner Awareness which is so sorely needed in this sad world.

Surely it is about time we forgot the futilities of senseless pseudo-spiritual rituals aiming at personal power and profit which will have to be paid for in terrible terms anyway at the end of existence. What would be the sense of trying to gain a whole world at cost of existence itself? That would be as idiotic as trying to steal a million dollars in a suitcase which would explode a nuclear device when opened. Why bother with unreasonable rites reputed to bring instant riches, gratify all sex demands, and make "powerful talismans" absolving anyone from every personal responsibility or efforts in life, and all the rest of such ridiculous rubbish?

What we need most in the way of psychodramatic procedures are those which are most likely to alter our characters for the better and contact higher than human consciousness before it becomes too late to alter anything in this threatened world. Most of all, we need to reach and touch whatever God may be in us and let That loose around ourselves for the benefit of whoever is able to absorb the least trace of It. However such a service is accomplished, it will be of the utmost value in a world which seems to be losing all sense of values. Sangreal services of the type we have been dealing with should at least offer such an opportunity for anyone able to work with them, and those who are not ought to show understanding towards their brethren who are attempting their utmost in the style they feel suits them best.

Anyone of even minor intelligence alive today has some kind of instinct that the spiritual situation of our planet becomes more and more perilous with every passing period. Only the most drastic changes in human characteristics can possibly avert the worst events this world is likely to experience. That much is obvious. Man cannot cause those changes by himself alone. Therefore he must call on consciousness originating on other levels of life altogether. When driven to desperation, humans demand the intervention of Deity by any name they can think of, and that is what the Sangreal amounts to in the end: our very lifeblood crying out for the holiest help we can ever hope for. May we indeed be heard in time.

· Part I ·

Preparing for the Sangreal Ritual

• 1 •

An Overview of Ritual

Rites develop from behavior patterns, and these come from adaptation and adjustments on inner levels between individuals or groups, and from the various energies affecting them. It depends entirely on those concerned how they react, and consequently, the type of rite they evolve varies enormously according to their nature, even though fundamental principles are the same for all. If individuals are illiterate and without resources, their rites will consist mainly of open air gatherings spent in primitive activities. Literate people of fair means need rituals of artistic and cultural merit. The ideal in occult ritualism is that everyone should become the priest of their own Temple, and work their own rites within it. For "Temple" read the body, for "priest," the soul, and for "rites" read the actions of one within the other.

First and foremost in ritual making, it is necessary to know what particular system is most suitable for the practitioner, then to ensure that the rite or rites are constructed strictly within that framework and none other. There must be no haphazard mix-up of divergent pantheons or incongruous activities. Rites are built up not unlike a theatrical production, each aspect calling for specialist treatment. Rites have a script or score, ballet or mime, wardrobe, and "special effects" besides "props." These all have to be put together so that their "outworkings" will facilitate their "inworkings." Whether they are very simple and inexpensive, or elaborate and costly, each should be a good sound species of its kind.

It is fairly simple to classify rites according to the Three Ways: Hermetic, Mystic, and Orphic. Hermetic rites are mainly intellectual ones, calling for temple conditions and sophisticated types of ritual. Mystic rites are more of the Spirit than the body, very largely contemplative in nature, needing few physical adjuncts, but a degree of devotional ability very much beyond most human participants. Mystic rites are usually worked in physical solitude. Orphic rites operate very broadly along emotional lines, using a great deal of dancing, music, and natural means of expression. It will be seen that any particular system (such as Qabalistic, Rosicrucian, etc.) could operate rites of all these three sorts for members of differing temperaments. On the whole, it seems generally accepted that Hermetic types of rite appear most suitable for the average Western worker, and to some extent the Hermetic Tradition carries the other two within it.

To compose a rite of any kind means working with many media toward a common purpose. Here we are concerned with the intellectual medium of contrived wordage which must also provide emotional and spiritual links. We must find the best words as vehicles for the will within. This is a truly magic task. It may not be easy to select a thought here, a suggestion there, a name somewhere else, and a framework elsewhere, recast these into appropriate form and come up with a workable mystical rite, yet this is precisely what has to be done. Of course, we cannot do this without help from inside, and when we start producing practical rites which seem to come together almost of their own accord, we shall realize that inner help is being duly given. Phrases we would not have thought of on our own, or even names, will "pop into our minds" quite suddenly and surprisingly. We shall get the feeling that "someone is looking over our shoulders" at what proceeds from our pens, and suggesting what to write or correcting what has been written.

Whether or not we receive assistance with what we compose, the responsibility for it will be our own and no one else's.

While one hand holds the pen, the other must be firmly kept on the controls. There must be no scribbling of endless rubbish and pointless meandering without purpose. Rites have to be composed of definite components in a definite circuit. Otherwise, neither rite nor device will work. Most of the rules are covered by those of good literary composition and poetic license, but a few points in particular deserve to be borne in mind.

Since we are involving body, mind, soul, and spirit in our rite, we should decide what links with which, so that these may be worked on their own levels. On a broad basis, this is approximately:

BODY is involved in a rite verbally by material allusions such as: "I shall hunger and thirst for Truth." "Take my left shoulder and direct my ways, etc." References to the body generally have such higher inferences, so that bodily functions or material assets serve spiritual ends rather than vice versa.

MIND comes into a rite largely by means of problems and intellectual presentations. Queries and answers are mainly mental, and so are the majority of visual symbols needing interpretation through understanding. A large percentage of modern rituals is mental, and there is a tendency to overbalance on this level.

SOUL enters a rite principally through emotional appeal and empathetic suggestions such as, "As Thou lovest me, so fill my heart with love for..." or "Let not grief prevent us from..." etc. All that connects with feelings of any kind involves the soul.

SPIRIT is brought into a rite through pure principles, such as the determination of right from wrong, recognition of Divine powers, dedication to purpose, devotion to duty, etc. God Names, Words of Power, Declarations, and Calls express the Spirit of a rite which forms its nucleus. Consecratory formulae and benedictions are vehicles of Spirit.

The question immediately arises as to ideal proportions for combining these. There can be no absolutely hard and fast answer because so much depends on the type of rite being constructed. But for general purposes, we might consult a glyph of the four geometrical symbols for the levels of being, and see how they relate to each other.

The rough proportions, if we accept the oval of Spirit as one unit, are:

SPIRIT	1
SOUL	2
MIND	3
BODY	4
	10 Units

This seems a very fair distribution of ritual energies for most purposes. It indicates we should base our rites on the purely Spiritual content as a nucleus, double this in references to soul, triple it in those of mind, and quadruple it for those of body. In the whole body of a rite, this makes for three-quarters of that amount mind, half of it soul, and a quarter of it Spirit. It is rarely possible in practice to observe such exact proportions, but at least we are provided with some kind of a guide. Reflected inwardly, of course, the proportions inverse. Body leads into mind, mind into soul, and soul leads into Spirit, folding backwards as it were, until all is compressed in Spirit.

Next, we must bear in mind the Three Rings of Limitation: Time, Space, Events. A given number of things (Events) have to be done in specific conditions (Space) within a calculated period (Time). Some things therefore will take a little or a lot of Time-Space, some conditions will be crowded or empty, and some periods be brief or lengthy.

A ritual is a very precise and properly ordered construction indeed, but unless it is worked in the correct spirit, it will amount to no more than amateur theatrics. Even in that case it may still have value for all providing their intentions are rightly directed.

The most wonderful ritual in the world will be of no use to those for whom it proved only a meaningless amount of uninteresting noise, or just a lot of boring words repeated in a dull, unattractive voice. To ensure enough of the right reactions by participants in carefully constituted rituals, we must either find means to avoid reliance on words altogether, or else discover ways of relating ourselves successfully through them with the necessary inner energy to work our Will in the Word uttered.

Ritualists would be well advised to build their rites chiefly from sonic rhythms, significant movements, and associative visual and olfactory stimuli.

Those committed to the use of verbal symbology in ritual practice should consider very carefully their capabilities of bridging the inner distance between the elemental life energies and the perimeter of their outer awareness by means of words.

Direction of Intention

Every genuine Mystery Rite should have built into it some factor or other which is designed to lead its practitioners ultimately out of it into even better, nobler, and much finer forms of ritualism beyond any practice confined to purely human consciousness.

Somewhere within the structure of a rite there ought to be a direction of intention towards a more perfect expression and vehicle of inner energies put into patterns of power. A few words, a gesture, or a mutely offered prayer will do. Anything practical which makes the ritualists realize their necessity for rising above and beyond their present position on the Path is an essential in all Magical Rites which deserve to be considered "white," or beneficial to human spiritual progress.

Unless there is a true feeling of their worthwhileness and a really deep satisfaction obtained by carrying them out, no rites are likely to be of much value to those engaged with them.

If occult rites were entirely dramatic presentation and nothing more, pace and pressure could only be maintained by keeping audience interest captivated. Though there is some truth in this, especially during the early stages of initiation, the main pressuring factor of a rite is keeping in constant contact with the Inner linkages behind it. This is the personal and collective responsibility of those taking part. Those unable to keep up the necessary concentration and inner awareness for sufficient periods should not be allowed to participate in rites requiring such ability. It is for this reason that genuine occult schools insist on so much meditational training work before anyone is allowed to take part in even the smallest rite. This at least ensures that participants in the rites of that school have proved their ability to maintain Inner contacts for working periods. By and large, the rule should be that if people are to participate in any rite, they should be able to hold purely meditational contacts for the same length of time.[1]

It is quite futile to expect anyone who cannot hold an inner meditational contact for even five minutes to take a useful part in a rite lasting over an hour or more. If their intention can be held by nothing but an hypnotic alteration of events, they are no better than television watchers, who, possibly without being consciously aware of it are held in thrall more by the ultra-rapid flicker of the screen itself than the subject matter presented on it. This can be a very nasty mind menace in fact, and serious ritualists might be well warned to cut television viewing to a minimum if they cannot avoid it. The flicker frequency of the television screen is a formidable modern agent for captivating and controlling the mass mind. Dedicated seekers on occult paths who are aware of this set up their own safeguards.

A major reason for the failure of ritual practices is sheer inability to hold contact with the inner content to any workable degree. The faculty for doing so can be developed from within ourselves through sustained meditational exercises. There are *no* "instant techniques" for acquiring this ability, just as there are none for instant plant growth or instant adulthood. Before embarking on any ritual workings, therefore, it must be ascertained whether or not they are within the concentrational competence of those who

---

[1] The reader will notice that this volume contains no rites specifically for children—there is no infant baptism, no equivalent to the Jewish bar mitzvah or Christian confirmation. These rituals are not intended to be children's affairs, and participants should ideally be at least 21 years of age. These rituals require a high degree of self-consciousness, devotional ability, direction of intention, and, as I've just mentioned, the ability to hold an inner meditation contact.

would work them.[2] Rites will not give such abilities, but only occasions for using them. It is far better to design short rites which may be worked well, than long ones few can follow. At least we provide ourselves with a standard for rite-making, which is that the Time ring must not exceed the ability of the participants to remain actively engaged in inner meditational pursuits.

In such a way, everyone can work out their rite rating as to a Time constant with the help of any watch or clock. It is only necessary to go into meditation and see how long this can be kept up without drift or distraction. An average of, at the very least, ten such experiments gives the rating value in minutes (at first) for the individual. Once this is known, it will be a simple matter for the individual to choose, or be chosen for, their most suitable rite workings. It is important for such time tests that the meditation must come wholly from within, and not be evoked in any way by external suggestions such as vocal or musical leads. Nor should it consist of daydreaming or trying to keep a blank mind. The type of meditation needed for this purpose is preferably a coherent involvement with inner living for some definite issue. The subject of meditation is immaterial, so long as it is developed consistently with the adopted style.

Probably the best practical way to safeguard the continuity of any rite and maintain its inner pressures is to cast it in metrical form. There is no reason why the meter should be the same for the whole of a rite, and indeed its rhythm ought to vary according to need as the human heart or breathing does, but the meter and rhythms of any rite must be a recognizable feature of it. Usually this is of more importance than the actual words themselves. It is hard to overemphasize the importance of meter in magic. Ritual and rhythm are inseparable. Every child who dances round a circle to an invented chant knows this well enough, and our most sophisticated rites are but developments from such beginnings. In primitive and earthly rites, it is the drum rhythms which keep pressures going to a

---

[2]Reread Chapter 1, "Contemplation," in *Sangreal Sacrament*, Volume 2 of this series, to sharpen your concentration skills.

virtually wordless throaty accompaniment. Those risen above such levels are faced with the same problems in need of answer in a different fashion.

Invocation and Evocation

The much quoted "Words without thoughts, never to Heaven go" is perfectly true, though it should be counterbalanced with "Thoughts without words, cannot to Kingdom come." We have attached formulated consciousness to sonic sequences on earth, but if we want to project those beyond the limits of physical matter, we shall have to do so along carrier waves of insound.

To invoke means literally to voice inside or call inwardly, and that is precisely what we must do if we are aiming to make contact with higher intelligences through the collective unconscious. External wordage and sounds are only useful as material to be converted to inner sonic energy, which alone is capable of reaching the contacts we seek. Invocation means using our inner voices to reach those able to hear them in ourselves and other human beings when we are speaking spiritually rather than physically.

Evocation means calling out of. It signifies that we are calling upon our inner contacts to approach more closely toward our outer terms of consciousness. If we evoke, we ask the inner ones to come out of us so that we may meet them as nearly as possible at material level. For this to be effective in any way means we should have to provide our inner guests with at least a mental semblance of humanity and all the limitations of intelligence and speech that this implies. We cannot expect to be met by Divine Ones in human guise, using human language, without allowing for the distortions and errors of which we are capable. If we insist they confine their consciousness to human phraseology, then we must accept the shortcomings of our language and the degree to which we understand it.

Invocation or evocation only forms part of ritual procedure. A great deal of it is concerned with effects in the minds and souls of the participants. They are being encouraged to think, feel, and undergo experiences aimed at processing their consciousness for various reasons. This needs skilled psycho-physiological techniques.

There is a close relationship between sonic patterns and consciousness on all levels. The sole problem ritualists are concerned with is the selection and use of specific sonic arrangements for operations of consciousness outside the range limited to material manifestations. We may use the word psycho-sonics if it helps. How do we translate human speech into energies that make meaning in other states of being? How to reverse this force-flow so that we can make sense of what we receive from elsewhere? How shall we arrange sound-effects physically to cause definite reactions from our minds, souls, and spirits?

Divine Names

The God names are intended to cover every aspect of inner being in a definite number of categories reachable by human consciousness divinely inspired. When we intone the name, we link ourselves with that category or type of God-ness. The archangel names are to link us with the creative intelligence of that sphere, while names of angels or spirits are for individualizing our contacts even more toward our human limits until we reach our instant of time-place-purpose. Each name brings the original energy closer to our humanity, and puts us in touch with its own category of inner awareness.

It is advisable to retain the God names in their archaic forms of Hebrew, Latin, Greek, or other derivation, for several reasons. First, because this allows us to use them for ritual purposes alone, and they will not trigger off responses at impractical times or places during everyday life. Second, because they are thus less likely to be profaned or treated with the familiarity that does indeed breed contempt or sheer lack of interest. Third, because the old formulae have links that go right back to early times, and have made channels in our deep collective consciousness forming natural conductive paths for the energies we are dealing with via ritual. If we train ourselves in their sonic use, we can modulate them with whatever inner adaptions we are capable of.

Inflame with Prayer

To *inflame oneself with prayer* should mean more than just becoming word-intoxicated, yet that is exactly what happens if control is lost during the process. What should happen instead is a steady lifting up of consciousness while keeping on target the whole while until this inflaming is reached inwardly. It is difficult to describe the exact inner technique for applying this control, but the broad outlines below will give enough information for the rest to be developed through personal practice.

The major factor behind this process of upliftment is the production of a constant vibrato in not only the voice but the whole body and inner being also. This means not simply a vocal resonance, but a double, or resonated resonance. We may achieve this physically by sounding off a resonant note and then shaking the body so that the note shakes accordingly. To make this a magical practice, it must be reversed so that the note is not shaken by the body, but the body shaken by the note. Once this is possible, a vibrato is set up which must be kept going consistently, while being modulated into words or utterances by the lips and larynx. We shall be virtually turning ourselves into an organ producing a single tone which becomes notations by manipulating the keyboard.

A good deal depends on the poise of the body in the first place, so that it is not unlike a spring which will vibrate when given a flick with a finger. One most useful stance is with legs together, right foot behind left with its instep to the left heel in the "square" or tau cross position. Most of the body weight is shifted slightly forward toward the ball of the left foot. Arms should be raised to the "prayer" position, palms of hands facing outwards about level with shoulders. This will place the body in a nicely balanced state, ready to respond when sonic energies move it.

Conditions for Ritual

Rites are workable under almost any reasonable conditions, providing sincere efforts are made to cover the principal points, with appropriate symbology connecting inner and outer essentials.

An Overview of Ritual • 13

For instance, while it may not always be possible for the ritualist to be properly robed, they might at least make an attempt to wear something in keeping with the occasion, even if colored cords, sashes or ribbons are all they can manage. It is the pattern and purpose of the rites which matter above all else, and the details of how to arrange the physically symbolic representations rest entirely with those who work them. Expensive equipment is no guarantee of a successful rite at all, but only more fun for those able to enjoy them.

If possible, some kind of ceremonial clothing ought to be worn by the officers, the Priest, and Preceptor. The main consideration is color, and the secondary one is style. Rules of plain good taste should decide this issue, and exotic or fantastic creations reminiscent of fancy dress balls are only likely to invite laughs at the expense of the wearer. Failing any special design requirements, the conventional habit or gown makes a reliable basic robe, and girdles with other additions may be suitably colored.

Mantles or flowing draperies are not recommended for practical reasons. Nothing, in fact, that is likely to catch on anything or trail around is advisable in rites of this nature. Care should especially be taken to wear nothing whatever of an inflammable kind.

For any rite, it is a good standard practice to write out a list of every possible item which will be needed in physical form, and make it the responsibility of one official, usually the Cord, to be sure everything on the list is present and properly placed before the rite begins. Read through the ritual and all its instructions *before* you begin! Find out what's necessary—a gong? bread? a sword? rods?—and make sure it is all together before the ritual begins. That way participants will not have to go scrambling about at the wrong time trying to gather things up. This still does not absolve individual officers from checking their own necessities. Even in the event of any item being forgotten or failing in function, *once the rite has started, it must continue until the end without the circle being broken.* Any deficiency should be gotten around in the most practical way, as part of the rite itself. This is a universal rule.

Decide also, before you begin, who will be in charge of what. You will note the rituals contain instructions in brackets such as "horn blow" and "gong sounds." Usually these instructions are carried out by whoever is closest, but you may want to delegate these responsibilities beforehand. These rituals are spare in terms of encumbering stage direction so that the *flow* of the ritual text itself can remain intact. For each ritual, rely on your common sense and, most importantly, what feels right.

Outdoor rites are subject to many hazards calling for all sorts of countermeasures and so, before being decided on, they should be very carefully considered. In the unlucky event of a rite being unavoidably broken off in mid-course due to weather, for example, if must be postponed for not less than a day, nor more than a month, and without fail worked through completely and correctly, even if this has to be done by a single companion of that circle on his own. Somehow or other the rite must be carried out once it has commenced its emergence into earthly expression.

Ceremonial Dress and Robing

Traditional ceremonial dress consists of an inner and outer robe, sandals (usually slippers nowadays), girdle, pectoral or collar, and cap or headgear. Adjuncts such as rings, stoles, or other ornamentation will depend very much on the nature of the Rite being worked. All these robes may be simplified down to an apron with symbolic embellishments worn over ordinary clothing, or more simply still an appropriately colored cord worn round waist or neck. What matters is that something physical is assumed to represent an actual nonphysical change of appearance and personality for some particular magical purpose. This inner change must take place in fact, and constitutes the real "robing up." It is an exercise in its own right and must be treated as such.

We propose to change ourselves to suit the occasion. Our ordinary everyday selves are inadequate for the task before us. Somewhere in our own depths we really are the sort of person who is able to perform our proposed ritual, and it is this individual we must now become. We can bring that aspect of us to the surface and link it with the symbolic clothing of its proper appearance. These are the clothes of our souls which we wear quite apart from our bodies, and this is how we look when our bodies will no longer be wrapped round us. Strictly speaking, we propose to remove the garments of flesh, and assume the robes of spirit. We intend to shine forth in our own true colors, and let our heavenly beings appear through our earthly counterparts. For this reason the inner robe of glory is worn beneath the outer robe of concealment.

These are the type of thoughts to prepare us for robing. They can be summarized into a prayer or statement-formula if required for it is quite necessary that some such approach be made to the robing procedure. The realization must not be "I am going to change my garments," rather "I am going to change myself, for the purpose of so and so." Then we set about actually making this change while we assume the physical robes.

One of the principal reasons why many working ritualists wear white robes is because white combines all colors and reflects them equally. Black, on the other hand, absorbs all colors and neutralizes them. Thus the use of both black and white vestments signifies an absorption of the unwanted portions of the spectrum, and a radiation of the selected light frequency. Ideally, a magical Operator should wear the color of whichever sphere is being worked with, or whatever colors are appropriate for the reason or subject of working. No amount of external color, however, will compensate for lack of internal light which must provide the real colors of any ritual. External colors of lights, robes, or other accessories only serve as reminders and guides for inward activity. There is no use putting on the most colorful or gorgeous robe if you do not put on inner colors to match it.

Since robing up for ritual is basic to the Rite itself, some practice in the art is called for. Robing should never be done carelessly or casually as if putting on fancy dress for fun, or hurriedly cramming oneself into some dubious disguise. The whole purpose of robing up should be to make the necessary inner adjustments for tuning the Operator to exactly the right pitch for the forthcoming Rite. Properly done, robing will accomplish exactly this when practiced sufficiently to make it effective.

The types of robes worn vary enormously with the system worked and the resources of the wearer. Most magical workers favor a cassocklike garment with close sleeves that are unlikely to knock candlesticks over or catch in other equipment. There may or may not be a hood attached to this robe. Hoods are not primarily worn to make the wearer mysterious, but to assist concentration by excluding side views, and also for the practical reason of keeping the head warm during open air workings. Hoods are quite a useful aid during meditation, since they also muffle distracting noises and give the sense of being "wrapped up in the subject." If an outer cloak is worn, the hood is often attached to this instead of the inner robe.

There is a proper sequence for robing if we are to get the most from the exercise. First come the sandals or slippers. A dedication or affirmation should be made at each stage of robing, and we might say for instance: "Firmly have I set my feet upon this path of righteousness, nor shall I falter from it til my present purpose is accomplished."

The phrasing of such affirmations will vary to suit the user. Every step we take in them will carry us nearer our aim, and every inch of the journey be crammed with meaningful events. These noble shoes will take us the whole way.

Next comes the inner robe of glory. This may be either white or golden. With the robe, we must "turn on the inner light" as strongly as we can. Breathing exercises will help. Here we should try to feel as light as possible, shining and rising with the light of glory pouring out of us. This is our garment of light in which we live apart from our physical bodies, and we should pray that when we attain the reality behind this symbol, we shall indeed be amongst the shining ones.

Now follows the controlling symbol of the girdle. It forms the immediate circle into which we are bound by our own wills, and its free ends connect with all other links which join us up with divine and human entities. The girdle must be tied tightly enough so that we can feel its grip, and the knot is usually a "reef knot" which cannot slip: right over left, then left over right. This knot is the hexagram, and carries the symbolic meanings thereof. As the girdle is tied, we should feel ourselves being tied in with all others who follow our particular Paths. It is the umbilical cord attaching us to the Great Mother, and its color or design should accord with the general intent of the Rite. If we are working on the left pillar, then the ends will hang on our left sides, if the right pillar is being used, our cords will hang on the right, and for the middle pillar the girdle will be central, hanging down in front of us.

The stole follows the girdle, and is tucked behind it to keep the ends in place. As we assume the stole, we should realize it indicates our limits of action in breadth as the second of the rings. In effect it is the right and left pillars, between which we have to keep an exactly middle course. It should give us the feeling of defining our path precisely. The stole and symbology embroidered on it provide us with the necessary ideas for keeping ourselves between the bounds of our present purpose, and defines the edges of the portal we intend to enter. Once the stole hangs over our shoulders, we should feel as if we were supported on our right and left by guiding angels whose responsibility is to keep us upon our appointed way. Invocations may be made to such angels if required.

The pectoral may take a number of forms. It hangs upon the breast suspended from either an ornamental chain or a cord of whatever color harmonizes with the Rite being worked. The pectoral itself may be an ornate piece of jewelry or some very simple glyph. If it is square and flat with engraved designs, it is usually called a lamen. If the wearer happens to be a Christian, it would probably be a cross or crucifix, if a Jew, the Star of David, or if a Qabalist, the Tree of Life. Otherwise the pectoral symbol must bear some design which indicates the nature of the operation being undertaken and the confidence of its wearer in the whole affair. The fundamental principle of the pectoral must be that it expresses as concisely as possible the faith pattern of its wearer. It must represent whatever we believe in with our whole hearts, and will stand by with our very souls. The pectoral shows what we proclaim ourselves to be before everyone else, and what we will defend with all our might. Without this quality of belief no effective Rite would be possible.

As the pectoral is assumed, we should realize we are bringing the entire structure of our faith to bear upon the purpose of the Rite to be worked. We must think "This is what I am in myself, and this is what I intend to do." The pectoral symbol and its cord fulfills the third ring of being, and completes the limiting principles. Our robing pattern begins to reveal itself. We first manifested motion with the slippers, then became light with the inner robe of glory. After that we applied the three rings of limitation by means of the girdle, stole and pectoral. We are creating our new personality according to the esoteric laws behind creation itself.

The next process in robing is the cloak or mantle, otherwise called the outer robe of concealment. It signifies all the externalities surrounding our purpose and ourselves, in the midst of which we have our inner being. The mantle is the body in which we live, the matter which spirit animates, and everything extraneous to the essence of the Rite in which we are engaged, yet which will prove necessary for its fulfillment. It is the outside of the inside we have been creating; and as it settles on our shoulders, we should feel the full weight of our responsibilites and burdens in bearing the consequences of all our actions. Putting on the mantle should give us the experience of aligning ourselves with the objective part of our subjective inner world. Ideally it should be the color suited to the operation, but otherwise it can be a true purple which is an exact balance of red (justice) and blue (mercy). Between its openings in the front, we should try and radiate the color needed for the Rite.

Now comes the headdress. Qabalists will adopt a plain square cap not unlike a biretta without its top adornments. Others may use some metallic circlet or fillet. It should fit the head firmly so its pressure can be felt without any particular discomfort. The whole purpose of the headdress is not to decorate ourselves or look important, but to symbolize and signify the higher consciousness to our own under the direction of which we must place ourselves in order to evolve spiritually. Spiritually we must open ourselves to the consciousness of those superior intelligences who seek to lead us along the Path of light if we are able to accept what they offer. They do not command us, but expect us to command ourselves. Our assumption of the headdress means that we are willing to open our inner minds to the wisdom that comes from contact with such beings.

The headdress is therefore held above the head with both hands, and slowly lowered into position. We may think of our headdress inwardly as being like a receiving apparatus tuned into our spiritual directors who transmit truth towards us. Qabalists may choose the four great Archangel intelligences to line up with the four sides of their cap.

Finally comes the ring. It should be worn on the right forefinger, and signifies our own "marriage" with the Eternal One. We must literally put our hand out towards God with perfect faith that it will be taken hold of and we shall be led in the best way for us. The action is not unlike that of a child holding up a finger trustingly for an adult to grip while the child tries to walk. The ring is held above the head with the left hand, and with eyes closed, the right hand with extended forefinger is raised slowly towards it. It should be felt that we are reaching as far as we can out of ourselves toward the Highest Power while we ask to be "taken in hand" and guided aright in the path we have chosen. As the ring slides down our finger, it should seem like the answering grip of the Divine Hand.

Providing the whole robing procedure has been properly done, it will prove a most uplifting experience to prepare the practitioner for whatever Rite may follow.

· 2 ·

A Sangreal Catechism

Introduction

Strictly speaking, there should be no need for an introduction to any catechism since it is in itself an introduction to whatever subject it deals with. A catechism per se is nothing more than a comprehensive set of questions with appropriate answers formulated to cover each query. Obviously, they have been carefully chosen by the formulators to present their own particular beliefs or opinions in as favorable a light as possible and therefore could be considered an attempt to indoctrinate or influence new readers accordingly.

In the case of the Sangreal Catechism, that is only minimally true. Its primary purpose is to supply information concerning the beliefs included in the Sangreal concepts. Readers may take or leave the Catechism as they please. Whether they believe it as it stands or not is their own concern. What matters is that they know what is sincerely believed and practiced by those to whom the concept is both a life guide and a constant source of spiritual inspiration. Though the principles involved may not be acceptable to many people for various reasons, that does not mean they need not be known and understood as applying to others. Just as a devout Buddhist or Jew may study Christianity purely for the sake of understanding fellow humans in a more comprehending light, so does this Catechism deal with the Sangreal concept as a system of study for all interested enough to approach it in an enquiring frame of mind.

By its own admission it is far from complete and purports to be nothing else than a lead in to deeper investigations. Yet how else could such an ideology be presented in a concise, informative, and practical way? That is why it should be studied first before the remainder of the psychodramatic ceremonies are tackled, and preferably be read and digested in conjunction with other Sangreal material such as *An Outlook on our Inner Western Way*[3] and *Western Inner Workings*.[4] A catechism is but a beginning. Actual attainment of the ideals it contains is an end. To reach any end in life its beginnings must first be grasped. Here they are.

A SANGREAL CATECHISM

1. Question: What is the Sangreal?

    Answer: It is our Occidental concept of a principle for people to pursue in search of inner spiritual truths. This pursuit confirms their discernible relationship with Deity itself.

2. Question: What does the word "Sangreal" mean?

    Answer: It is a composite word meaning Blood Royal. *Sang* = Blood, and *Real* = Royal, old Franco-Latin derivation.

3. Question: Why Blood?

    Answer: Because blood was seen as a common life-bearing medium that communicated our characteristics through every distinct human generation. Thus, it was a living link between the beginning and end of our existence as a special species of being.

---

[3]Also by William Gray, published by Samuel Weiser, Inc., York Beach, Maine.
[4]This is Volume 1 in the Sangreal Sodality Series.

4. Question: Why Royal?

   Answer: Because the term royal formerly indicated superlatively fine and splendid qualities meaning the very best of human capabilities, especially when allied with good spiritual influences.

5. Question: How did this all originate?

   Answer: Esoteric teaching says that it began with interbreeding between anthropoid humans and a far superior race from another solar system many millennia ago.

6. Question: With what results?

   Answer: With ever-widening dissemination and development of "Sangreal strain"[5] among its peoples on this planet. This has considerably influenced our state of civilization and culture for the better.

7. Question: What is peculiar about this Sangreal strain?

   Answer: It inculcates an unusual element of true self-sacrifice among its human holders for the sake of spiritual immortality and ultimate identity in Universal Entity.

8. Question: Have all humans this strain in them?

   Answer: It was once regarded as exclusive to certain noble families, but long ago was known to have become extremely widespread, albeit in varying degrees in different individuals.

9. Question: What distinguishes such degrees?

   Answer: Self-sacrifice of life itself at one end of the scale, and minor beneficences at the other, always motivated altruistically and spiritually.

---

[5]The "Sangreal-strain" is the individual blood factor that carries instinctual consciousness of the Sangreal implications within it.

10. Question: What was supposed to be the end effect of this?

    Answer: It was hoped we would evolve beyond bodily incarnation altogether into states of very superior spiritual life in terms of existence and energy.

11. Question: Is this connected with the old-time Divine King sacrificial customs?[6]

    Answer: Directly so, though they became debased and ultimately useless due to much misunderstanding and unfortunate abuse.

12. Question: How?

    Answer: Because unwilling victims were butchered and unsuitable substitutes were offered in the place of an original oblation.

13. Question: Was that not allowable?

    Answer: Not in the original idea. The slightest suspicion of compulsion or coercion would invalidate the sacrifice entirely. A sacred sacrificial victim must be absolutely voluntary, and even eager, for the act to be a valid one.

14. Question: Is such a sacrifice required today?

    Answer: By no means. We are now expected to live active lives devoted to the service of Divinity within ourselves and other humans.

15. Question: Why was a substitution sacrifice invalid?

    Answer: If it was another, yet inferior human, that would be regarded as an insult to the "Gods." Only a symbolic sacrifice could be considered in exchange.

---

[6]The reader is referred to Volume 2 of this series, *The Sangreal Sacrament*, Chapter 8, for further reading on the Divine King sacrificial customs.

16. Question: What was that?

    Answer: In olden times an animal that might be eaten anyway. Nowadays some commonly held symbol which signifies sacrifice.

17. Question: Something in the nature of an IOU?

    Answer: Virutally, yes. A pledge of promise and performance on our parts.

18. Question: And would that be sufficient as a Sangreal obligation?

    Answer: Yes, because it is the intention of the will which counts as consecrating factor.

19. Question: Why would anyone decide to devote themselves entirely to Divinity?

    Answer: Because It is eternal and important, whereas we are ephemeral and relatively insignificant as humans. It is therefore in our interests to remain with what *remains as a reality*.

20. Question: Do most humans realize such a relationship?

    Answer: Mostly those that sense some aspect of the Sangreal in themselves.

21. Question: Has it an especial influence with any particular people in this world?

    Answer: Although it is essentially the spiritual "salvation factor" in mankind, it seems to be specifically associated with the Western section of this world.

22. Question: Why should this be so?

    Answer: Because we have held the Sangreal pattern of salvation for so long and semiconsciously, it has become intrinsically hereditary as a custom of our culture.

23. Question: What is that pattern?

    Answer: That a God must die for man to live, good must deliver evil, the best of blood be shed to redeem the worst, and this sacrificial cycle of salvation be perpetuated through our people till the end of time.

24. Question: How is this traceable?

    Answer: As a religious culture-current dating back to ancient Sacred Kings, eventually epitomized as basic Christianity, thence extended through esoteric channels like the Holy Grail and Rosy Cross movements into modern times.

25. Question: Can this be symbolized?

    Answer: Yes, initially as light behind blood to signify illumination by our inner spiritual sources.

26. Question: Is there a spoken summary of the Sangreal?

    Answer: It is expressed by its motto: "I seek to serve."

27. Question: What does that mean?

    Answer: It means that the salvation of mankind depends on mutual service gladly given for the sake of spirit shared amongst us all.

28. Question: What is this "salvation?"

    Answer: It is the transmutation of our faulty human nature into an eventually satisfactory state of spiritual entity.

29. Question: Why should this be necessary?

    Answer: Because it is the major mission of mankind on earth to save our species from destruction and decay, and further to develop it towards Divinity.

30. Question: How would the Sangreal help us here?

    Answer: It is the spiritual quest for best within the West that motivates us in perpetual pursuit of *Perfect Peace Profound*.

31. Question: What is meant by that?

    Answer: It means the ultimate "perfection point" where human nature ceases altogether as we "unify with God" or are absorbed entirely in the Absolute.

32. Question: Does the Sangreal extend beyond that point?

    Answer: It does not need to, since it is something in our blood that makes us think of spiritual things and urges us to their achievement. When these are gained in God the Sangreal's mission is accomplished.

33. Question: What sort of Spirit is the Sangreal?

    Answer: It has become our Folk Soul, or a collection of our Occidental consciousness that seeks relationship with the Supreme Creative Spirit from our special angle of approach and outlook.

34. Question: What kind of relationship is that?

    Answer: We believe it is the spiritual equivalent of blood relationship, however distant from Divinity each individual degree might be.

35. Question: What does this imply?

    Answer: It implies we should regard ourselves as being related to each other by a spiritual bond of blood much deeper than its purely physical counterpart.

36. Question: What should this signify?

    Answer: It signifies that we who recognize this should behave according to its natural law and love each other in the light of our beliefs.

37. Question: How is this defined?

    Answer: By believing we belong to the same Blessed Blood, then caring for each other by a confident and competent compassion shared with the same Spirit which created us by Love within itself.

38. Question: Why "Blessed" Blood?

    Answer: The term derives from an old English word *bloedesan*, denoting sacrificial blood scattered from an altar over an assembly to prove their participation and agreement with the sacrifice. Therefore, it signifies the blood we bear and share, together with the sacrifices we will have to make because of that.

39. Question: How is this symbolized?

    Answer: It is symbolized by the mystical Mass of the Sangreal Sacrament.

40. Question: What is a sacrament?

    Answer: It once signified a solemn oath of obligation but has since become a sharing of belief by means of symbolism proper for the spiritual intention.

41. Question: How is the Sangreal Sacrament celebrated?

    Answer: By the symbols of shared bread and wine with prayers and worship.

42. Question: What does the bread mean?

    Answer: It means our bodies which we sacrifice in service through the Sangreal to the will of the Supreme One working in us.

43. Question: What does the wine mean?

    Answer: It signifies our blood we also offer so that we may share the selfsame Spirit of eternal light and life.

44. Question: What do bread and wine together signify?

    Answer: The spiritual sum of ourselves we dedicate to Deity by means of this mystical Mass.

45. Question: Why is this called "Mass?"

    Answer: Because it is an actual a*mass*ment of our energies in search of Entity.

46. Question: How is this accomplished?

    Answer: By purposeful prayer which has its climax in a common union or communion with the Spirit it invokes.

47. Question: What Spirit is that?

    Answer: Since there is only One Supreme Life-Spirit, we invoke whichever aspect of it seems appropriate to our intentions.

48. Question: If there be but one Deity, is not all mankind equal before It?

    Answer: Only so in the sense of existence as entities; otherwise we are classifiable into categories each with some specific function to fulfill as a special duty to that Deity.

49. Question: Is the Sangreal such a category?

    Answer: We see it in that light.

50. Question: How does it appear?

    Answer: It appears to us as the equivalent of blood within the body of God, which is creation as a whole, or Cosmos.

51. Question: How do humans relate with this?

    Answer: By becoming as individual cells within that bloodstream and fulfilling the equivalent of such a function.

52. Question: How?

    Answer: By serving Deity as our blood serves our human systems.

53. Question: What way is that?

    Answer: Mainly as an agency of healthy harmony and most effective energy in every part of our anatomy.

54. Question: How can we accomplish this?

    Answer: By a constant conscious recognition of our finest function, coupled with a firm resolve to follow it with faith.

55. Question: How should we know what to do?

    Answer: In ourselves we have no knowledge, but the blood we bear does know and this is the intention of Divinity in us which should be sought and served.

56. Question: How?

    Answer: By sensing it within ourselves, seeking it through symbols, and then living as we are enlightened by our codes of conduct aimed at bringing out the best in us.

57. Question: What are those?

    Answer: They should be instinctive in us, but they have been frequently defined by every Western system of belief in spiritual living.

58. Question: Is there a special Sangreal code?

    Answer: So far as may be said it is the common code of chivalry.

59. Question: What is that?

    Answer: Briefly, to behave with courtesy and courage as good Companions of right and light against wrongs and wickedness within this world.

A Sangreal Catechism • 31

60. Question: How are these principles presented to us?

    Answer: In general as the Mythos of the Holy Grail, a mystical objective achieved by means of disciplined devotion to Divinity. This devotion proceeds from our beliefs in all we value better than ourselves.

61. Question: Is this not a purely Christian concept?

    Answer: Far from being so. It is deeply rooted in our oldest faiths, but was later Christianized for the convenience of poetic presentation and to conform with current customs and official outlooks.

62. Question: Does the Sangreal deny Christianity?

    Answer: To the contrary. It supports the spiritual principles involved completely.

63. Question: Then why did the Church declare it an heretical belief?

    Answer: On policy grounds alone since it did not support ideas of Church supremacy and its exclusive claims or other dogmas that permitted an ecclesiastical authority alone to represent our rights to Universal Deity on earth.

64. Question: Is the Sangreal against the Church?

    Answer: Not in the least. It simply says that humans should be free to find a formal faith according to the inborn instincts of their natural nobility.

65. Question: Can this not be found in Christianity?

    Answer: Of course it can, though not exclusively.

66. Question: Which is the best form of faith to follow?

    Answer: There is neither best nor worst, but only suitability for every soul involved, and close compatibility with individual states of spiritual consciousness.

67. Question: Is it possible to belong with the Sangreal and also a Church?

    Answer: Perfectly, since the Sangreal is an inherent state of spirit, and a Church is a humanly organized collection of people dedicated to a common fellowship of faith which could be compatible with Sangreal ideology.

68. Question: Has the Sangreal a Church of its own?

    Answer: Only insofar as people seek to formalize their faith in it and so combine their consciousnesses by participating in religious rituals and practices that honor it specifically in special ways.

69. Question: Then is there anything to join officially?

    Answer: Only if an operative grouping opens to include another active individual among their constituted company.

70. Question: Can any soul belong with the Sangreal yet not to such a group?

    Answer: Certainly. The only difference is between collective and coordinated recognition, and an individual awareness of the concept by an independent contact with it.

71. Question: Which is preferable?

    Answer: That depends entirely on the nature of the soul concerned and its circumstances. Most work best in bodily communication with others, yet some call for seclusion to intensify and integrate their spiritual sensitivity.

72. Question: What *is* the work of the Sangreal?

    Answer: To cooperate consciously, intentionally, and intelligently with the Divine Will that we trace through our blood.

73. Question: Can we do otherwise if we choose?

    Answer: We can repudiate, reject, or otherwise oppose it altogether if we will.

74. Question: Why should anyone do this?

    Answer: To gain short-term temporal profits rather than evolve more slowly into an eternal entity of spirit. This once was known as selling a soul to the Devil.

75. Question: What happens to those who so oppose the Sangreal in themselves?

    Answer: The same as with an ordinary blood cell in the case of a disease. It is eventually eliminated altogether from existence by a self-correcting Cosmos.

76. Question: What happens then?

    Answer: The individual ceases when reduced to elemental energy which is then recycled into other forms of life.

77. Question: What does this imply?

    Answer: Put into childish terms it means do we want to live with God or die with the Devil, the decisive factor being our own individual wills.

78. Question: Is that what is meant by the saying: Do what thou wilt?

    Answer: Among alternative meanings—yes.

79. Question: How is the Sangreal involved?

    Answer: It is the main means of our distinguishing between a purely personal and Divine directed will within ourselves.

80. Question: Why?

    Answer: Because though we inherit both good and bad characteristics from our forebears, the Sangreal alone accounts for all our best inherencies.

81. Question: Therefore the stronger the strain the better we are?

    Answer: So we believe.

82. Question: Can the strain be increased in individuals?

    Answer: Yes, with each incarnation.

83. Question: How is this?

    Answer: If we maximize the blood potential we were born with in each human life, we will become reborn with improved spiritual status.

84. Question: Can this be done apart from definite religious faiths?

    Answer: Certainly. It calls for alterations of a natural character which are in keeping with a betterment of actual being according to the highest code of conduct.

85. Question: So could the Sangreal be served by ethical behavior only?

    Answer: To a considerable degree until enlightenment enlarges and expands an outlook.

86. Question: Do any organized religions recognize the Sangreal?

    Answer: In principle, yes. Christians by insistence on self-sacrifice, Buddhists by the Great Renunciation, and Jews by the flesh-blood Covenant of Circumcision.

A Sangreal Catechism • 35

87. Question: How are these connected?

    Answer: They are all human offerings made by man in hopes of gaining Godhood. Other faiths have their equivalents which show the Sangreal in action.

88. Question: How can the Sangreal be briefly summarized?

    Answer: It is an implicit belief that by our blood we have inherited enough natural nobility to gain whatever Grail we might expect as an immortal end.

89. Question: Does this account for ancestor worship?

    Answer: People of the past did not worship ancestors; they respected and revered them.

90. Question: Is this necessary?

    Answer: No, but it could be helpful if reviewed in the right light.

91. Question: What light is that?

    Answer: Simply as a linkage leading back to light itself.

92. Question: Suppose an ancestry is both unknown and of some common origin?

    Answer: All ancestry is common, and objective knowledge is not necessary. Faith in it is a sufficient factor if assisted by appropriate actions.

93. Question: What can faith do?

    Answer: Eventually everything, providing it persists in a sufficient strength.

94. Question: Is faith alone enough?

    Answer: Not unless accompanied by service as the Sangreal in us requires.

95. Question: What might this be?

    Answer: Its immediate aim is the improvement of our people as a spiritual species, and this starts with an improvement in each individual.

96. Question: How does this begin?

    Answer: By dedication of the self unto Divinity, then following the blood-belief, or our inherited beliefs, direct. This was considered as the Quest of the most Holy Grail.

97. Question: Was that not for knights exclusively?

    Answer: The degree of natural nobility alone confers the Knighthood of the Grail, but whether it is claimed or not depends entirely on the individuals concerned.

98. Question: How is a selfstate of Knighthood acquired?

    Answer: By serving without thought of rank or seeking an unjustified authority.

99. Question: We keep hearing about service. What is it?

    Answer: It is firstly the plain duty that we owe each other ordinarily as human beings, secondly the generosity we give because of blood companionship, and lastly for the sake of purely spiritual Love alone.

100. Question: Does anything special distinguish this service?

    Answer: Yes. It must be freely offered and accepted, never forced in any way at all, because it should be altogether sacrificial.

101. Question: Can such service be bought?

    Answer: The only permissible payment is for services by which anyone makes a legitimate living as a trade or profession.

102. Question: Then where does the sacrifice come in?

    Answer: A sacrifice is offered for the joy of its acceptance only, so that being itself is better for the doing, and a contribution has been made to the continuance of Cosmos.

103. Question: What does this mean?

    Answer: Simply that we should improve our quality of life by learning how from higher levels.

104. Question: Shall we learn this through the Sangreal?

    Answer: If we treat it as a sacred trust that we have inherited in order to improve and hand it down through our descendants so that we shall rejoice when we return to claim it from them once again.

105. Question: Who is "we?"

    Answer: Anyone of blood belief, but in particular people of the Western Way of inner life who have distinctive dealings with the Spirit working through our special culture, customs, and our consciousness.

106. Question: Should we feel superior to other cultures because of the Sangreal?

    Answer: Most certainly not. It should mean nothing more than suitability and singularity.

107. Question: Then what are the advantages of the Sangreal to us?

    Answer: If forms a basis of belief beyond all argument: that we hold something of a special spiritual significance in us which is worthwhile enough to find and follow with the firmest faith.

108. Question: Is this all we need to know about the Sangreal?

    Answer: It is but the briefest of beginnings. All the rest should come from study, research, and the Love of living it.

109. Question: How should anyone be taught to take the Sangreal?

   Answer: As an integral part of their inner selves which may not be denied with any more authority than anyone can claim an absence of all ancestors.

110. Question: Where do we go from here?

   Answer: Back again to the beginning of the Sangreal cycle, and approach it from another angle altogether, so that we shall renew ourselves with it in perpetuity until we reach our ultimate in *Perfect Peace Profound*.

Part II

Progression of the Soul Through the Sangreal

· 3 ·

The Stations of the Sangreal

Introduction

This "Stations of the Sangreal" Service is designed so as to supply a means of making an imaginary devotional journey from commencement to completion of human spiritual development by a minimum of ten successive stages or "Stations." Each consists of a stop made before a symbol suggestive of the subject in question, a passage read which is relative to it, then an orison made to the Deity aspect which refers to that stage. During progression from one stage to another, either one verse of a suitable hymn is sung, or appropriate music is played. This is optional, but makes for a pleasant progress. It is suggested that the chorus of The Sangreal Hymn would be useful here. There are of course preparatory and closure prayers to the entire proceedings.

It is intended that the descriptive sections should be read by all or any particular participator, while the orisons are read by the Pontifex or Preceptor. If only two people are present, they could be taken by one as Pontifex and the other as Responsor.

The "mysto-mechanics" of this Service are normally the displaying of the Stations around the walls of the temple. Progress is made from one to another starting from the altar and finishing there. Alternatively the symbols for the Stations can be displayed at the altar position one after another while the service progresses.

Strictly speaking visual symbols are not really needed, provided everyone is familiar with the subject under contemplation. If required, a short pause for meditation may be made after each Station has been duly made.

The appropriate symbols can be anything whatever, concrete or abstract, which adequately set forth visual suggestions conveying the entire significance of the subject. Music and incense can be used appropriately as well.

The intent and purpose of this exercise is to condition consciousness for the entire cycle of Grail-gaining, so that when actual events of life occur which are connected with the topics, there will be a preconditioning already associated with them in the participator's awareness.

It should be noted that the cycle commences with a normal level of consciousness, descends to and through the deepest depth of emotional experience, then climbs back up and past the starting point in an opposite direction until the heights of attainment are reached, and there held in mind at the end. In the Grail process only those capable of descending to "Hell" can possibly "Ascend to Heaven." Hence the frequently forgotten episode of the "Harrowing of Hell" in Christian doctrine—the three days Christ spent in Hell before Resurrection. It was and is an essential part of progress and should never be shirked. Those unable to understand this vital point should never be allowed to partake in this particular Service. Its message is essentially: "The way to Heaven is through Hell." A lot of the text is self-explanatory on this issue.

There is no real reason why this Service should not be curtailed by selecting specific Stations for single meditations, or expanded by addition of rosary prayers (see page 217 for a description of the Sangreal Rosary), or possibly an address or other appropriate matter. Indeed the whole 10 topics could be dealt with as meditational subjects for two rosaries. To sum up the subjects again:

1. *Glimpse of the Grail.* Inspiration and encouragement to start the Quest.
2. *Determination of Direction.* Ideas of how and where to search.
3. *Encountering the Enemy.* First indications of difficulties and problems of the path.

4. *Stress of Struggle.* A reminder that spiritual progress means endless effort.
5. *Depths of Despair.* The very worst thing experienced on earth in search of spirit.
6. *Hints of Hope.* Beginnings of encouragement to continue with the Quest.
7. *Signs of Success.* Real encouragement and conviction of spiritual certainties.
8. *Wonders of Winning.* Realization of what this would mean to everyone.
9. *Perception of Perfection.* Encouraging view of possibilities and probabilities ahead.
10. *Gaining the Grail.* Realization of glories and responsibilities involved.

THE STATIONS OF THE SANGREAL

Preparatory Prayer

In the name of the **Wisdom**,
      and of the **Love**,
      and of the **Justice**,
      and of the Infinite **Mercy**,
      of the One Eternal **Spirit**,
                  Amen.

We who seek our Sangreal spirit here devote ourselves unto the Deity whose consciousness is the containing cup of all creation.

As we embark on this, an emblematic and arcane adventure, questing for our highest Holy Grail through substitute symbology, may its complete contents be really roused and mediated in our souls because of the sincerity with which we work on this occasion.

We ask this by the Blessed Bond of Blood because of our affinity with all its mystic meanings and the true significance of what it always stands for in our firmest fundamental faith. Amen.

PRECEPTOR: Let us start by glimpsing our most glorious Grail.

RESPONSOR: With all our will. Amen.

1st Station

Glimpse of the Grail

What is it that impels us on our inner pathways of progression? Surely something in ourselves we neither can deny nor yet dismiss from our concern with conscience. It is indeed the need for an ennoblement and hallowing of human nature, an improvement of our individualities, and universal uplift of our souls toward a spiritual ultimate beyond our bodies altogether in the Absolute.

We believe this urge originates with our best blood and is inherent in those humans who seek sure salvation from their fallibilities of flesh by turning to the strength and sustenance of Spirit. Hence we have adopted as our special symbol of this impulse in us, the immortal

Sangreal or most illustrious royal blood of our redemption. This idea, contained and compassed by our consciousness, inspires us unto its achievement through our aspirations and our actions.

Here then, we will commence our Quest, and sally forth on it with faith, a sanguine spirit, and the highest hopes of gaining this most Holy Grail wherewith we shall survive and at the end of everything participate in *Perfect Peace Profound*.

PRECEPTOR: O Divine Director of our wandering ways in every world existing, we who are aware of thine intentions in us while we do not know their details, offer up ourselves as agents of thy working will and ask acceptance of this voluntary vow and obligation. Lead us through life so that we may become as thy most Blessed Blood and thus attain true immortality when we will live as an identity in Thee forever and forevermore. Amen.

PRECEPTOR: Let us continue on our Quest.

RESPONSOR: With all our will. Amen.

> [First verse of hymn sung while proceeding to next Station.]

2nd Station

Determination of Direction

In which direction are we drawn to gain our Grail? Since we are westerners by birth and spirit why not work that way to find fulfillment of our faith? There is our own tradition of those truths which must be found and followed by all men and women of this world in search of spiritual certainties. Each distinct division of humanity has an appointed way of working for achievement of this universal ultimate. Within those ways are once again a multiplicity of methods, each entirely suitable for some especial sort of soul.

Since ours is termed the Sangreal system, pointing in a westerly direction to Divinity, we will duly take that track towards our truth. Therefore through our old and trustworthy tradition shall we seek the Sangreal as our special share of spiritual work in this our world. Let the roseate rays of sunset lead us on to light that knows not darkness nor defeat. Come with confidence and courage on our holy quest and claim companionship with all belonging with the blood. Let our watchword be: "We will be one within our blessed bond of brotherhood." Forward in this our Sangreal sign of faith.

PRECEPTOR: O Protector of our people, guide us graciously towards the Grail of thy most generous goodness. Make manifest the royal road toward the goal we are to gain. Show us straightforwardly our favorable paths of progress and encourage our endeavors to pursue them peacefully.

Grant us glimpses of the Grail when we would otherwise be overwhelmed with opposition. May we never deviate more than a minimum from our direction forward, and also may thy might and mercy send us safely on a joyous journey through the many wonders we will meet with on our Western Way. Amen.

PRECEPTOR: Let us continue on our Quest.

RESPONSOR: With all our will. Amen.

[Second verse of hymn sung while all proceed to next Station.]

3rd Station

Encountering the Enemy

Whoever would expect that everything was easy, safe or simple on our Sangreal search? Here we have all kinds of conflicts and contentions, doubts and difficulties to disperse, dangers to be dealt with and antagonisms answered as seems suitable. Trials, troubles and temptations throng by thousands to attack and aggravate us. Is the Sangreal a sort of magic magnet that attracts adversity?

Indeed it is. Such is a certain sign of its involvement with our world. Coincidentally it gives us grace and sends the strength to counter and survive these struggles of our souls. It is impossible to gain the Grail without such striving, which could be considered in this light of learning. They are an offered opportunity for fighting opposition and so change our characters that we become the better for that battle.

No wonder seekers of the Sangreal were once considered knights, or those who could control their chargers symbolizing sheer instinctive strength and inclination to impulsive action. Only that discipline demanded of a trained and trusted warrior will win against adversity which we are likely to encounter on these earthly levels of our lives. Each knight must fight for right to live in light. Our Sangreal is only to be earned by strenuous struggles and our efforts at endurance through the strictest tests a human soul may be subjected to with honor for the sake of its inherent faith.

PRECEPTOR: O Highest Helper of our humankind created by thy consciousness, be Thou our present benefactor with the problems which we bring to thine attention hoping for a helpful answer. How will we realize the Sangreal is reliable? What will prove its presence and convince us it is capable of aiding us against adversity? To what degree is it dependable? How will we experience its energy and feel its forces working in this world? We need to know and trust it totally. Provide us with some evidence of its essential power, and bless us as we battle in thy cosmic cause. Amen.

PRECEPTOR: Let us continue on our Quest.

RESPONSOR: With all our will. Amen.

> [Third verse of hymn sung while all proceed to next Station.]

4th Station

Stress of Struggle

Surely the stress of our belonging with the Holy Blood is far too heavy for a human being to bear with any happiness? Nobility of nature does indeed impose its obligations on whoever claims it conscientiously. Far from bestowing generous gifts and all advantages upon its bearers, it often offers only poverty and perils as the price of its possession. Why should such difficulties and disasters seem to find and follow those that seek the Sangreal? Have we no hope of our escaping or eluding these events? Are we always to endure them as an earth experience? Is it part and parcel of some spiritual pattern planned for us by a bewildering fate which is indifferent to our futile importuning and interested only in its own affairs? How can we hold any confidence in Cosmos when we feel neglected in necessity by its supposed Supreme Creative Spirit?

    This is why we call our conduct a continual Quest, because there are so many awkward questions to decide and disentangle. That of itself is hard enough to handle and endure. How long can this continue, and how difficult or damaging may all its many perils prove?

PRECEPTOR: O Lord of Life, such surely was the reason we were sent into this world and still remain here? We are requested to redeem our race and save our species from the horrors human nature has in it. Alteration of an animal existence into evolutionizing sentient souls that seek thy spiritual sanctuary.

    This takes time. Then we must mediate these things through an experience of what they mean, connecting them with consciousness into improved conditions as our generations gather an inheritance of ingenuity and capability of coping with incarnate living. Grant us the grace to work thy will within us if indeed we are intended to accomplish it in action. Amen.

PRECEPTOR: Let us continue on our Quest.

RESPONSOR: With all our will. Amen.

> [Fourth verse of hymn sung while all proceed to next Station.]

5th Station

Depths of Despair

    This is the end of everything! Darkness and despair surround our souls, and we are almost overcome by our opponents. Horror heaps on horror, Hell is here, and it looks as if all light is lost and wickedness has won at last.

We are too few for fighting against such awful spiritual odds alone, and only far too fallible. We have been weakened with exhaustion and expect no help from any hand. We are also wounded badly and we bleed. Our precious blood is perishing and gushing to the ground.

Hear how the forces we are fighting howl with horrid laughter at our losses. See how they sneer and mock maliciously at our attempts to break their overbearing opposition. Shame adds to our sufferings. Humiliation is so hard to bear with bravery. Let us die dishonored and disgraced if need be, but we never shall survive in slavery or subjugation. Why should we submit to such, or be beaten into bondage by a host of human spiritual savages? What is the worst we have to lose except our expectations of incarnate life, which would not be worth living anyway if our antagonists were mortal masters of this perishable planet. Let us sacrifice those lives to save our souls for better states of being in our universal ultimate. Salutations Sangreal. We are on our way.

PRECEPTOR: Lord of Light, prevent the triumph of the powers of darkness and destruction. Send swift aid and all assistance to those faithful few that struggle for survival in a world where wrongs and wickedness seem so successful. Turn this trend towards an inclination to investigate our higher hidden faculties and forces. Help us to transmute our human natures into something moved much more by spiritual than material motives. Move quickly with thy might to save all questers of the Sangreal. Haste with every help available. Find us fast and send us strong support. Delay not for a single second but deliver and defend us. Amen.

PRECEPTOR: Let us continue on our Quest.

RESPONSOR: With all our will. Amen.

[Fifth verse of hymn sung while all proceed to next Station.]

6th Station

Hints of Hope

Have we any hopes at all that our conditions can indeed improve and alter to far finer circumstances? It seems we still survive with fewer fatal casualties and considerably less chances of close conflict or of individual injuries. Have we had some special help from Heaven? It certainly might seem so by this momentary halt from full hostilities.

Now that we have had this brief but blessed rest in which we could recuperate, we can renew and reassess our spiritual situation. It may not be as bad as many might suppose. Although outnumbered, we are not outclassed nor altogether outcast and abandoned. Perhaps we have been practicing a poor approach, or are we to adopt another angle of attack? We could well afford to change our tactics for a far superior form of strategy.

That is what we will in fact decide to do. Gather round our Grail and concentrate our consciousness inside its castle of impregnability. Evil cannot enter there, nor anything adverse contaminate its inner atmosphere. Behind its battlements we shall be safe from spiritual siege and human harassment. From the fighting field therefore we will go forth and garrison the hospitable fortress of the Holy Grail. That is where we should assemble and await our call for future conflict.

PRECEPTOR: O Powerful One in whom all human hopes are placed, we give Thee gratitude for favorable aid in time to take us out of trouble. Let us learn to live so that we dare to die because we feel for sure we shall exist as spiritual beings beyond our merely mortal bodies. Show us how we are the Sangreal itself and share its whole identity because its Blessed Blood becomes the living line of our immediate immortality. This hope is all we have to cling to as a cord connecting us with Cosmos. Hold Thou its other end eternally and offer us the opportunity of an ascension. Amen.

PRECEPTOR: Let us continue on our Quest.

RESPONSOR: With all our will. Amen.

[Sixth verse of hymn sung while proceeding to next Station.]

7th Station

Signs of Success

At last the long due signs of some success are evident as an encouragement. We have collected in our castle and are living in the light of common consciousness combined with everything investing inner life with mystic meaning which provides a sense of spiritual purpose.

Now we see our Sangreal by the light of blood because of Love that none but those belonging to it would believe. It is unique to us, and absolutely certain to succeed in its intended end as an essential part of inner progress on this planet.

It signifies our spiritual and our cultural contributions to the wealth of this whole world in terms of total truth: our outpoured offering of all we are as sincere souls that only seek to share ourselves with others who are willing to accept what we are able to afford. We have so much to make mankind more healthy, happy, and harmonious, and yet we would not force this upon anyone that was not free to take it.

The Sangreal has to be beneficence held out as a glad gift and open for acceptance both by God and man alike. Such should be our occupation with it in this world and otherwise. That is our task which we will hold in honor as a duty designated by Divinity and duly blessed by the blood we are particularly privileged to bear.

One sighting of our Sangreal for a single second is worth all the watching and the waiting which accompany its welcome advent.

PRECEPTOR: O Thou Greatest Guardian of our Grail, make it more manifest to we that work and suffer for its sake within this world. We would have evidence on earth of its existence in the highest Heaven.

We may be weak, but we are merely mortal, be Thou patient with us Blessed Power. Sometimes we want firmer facts than faith alone affords for an assistance to support our spiritual struggles. Send us a sight or so on rare occasions that reveal the Sangreal but for the very briefest vision. That should be sufficient to sustain us through prolonged and painful periods. Amen.

PRECEPTOR: Let us continue on our Quest.

RESPONSOR: With all our will. Amen.

[Seventh verse of hymn sung while proceeding to next Station.]

8th Station

Wonders of Winning

What would happen to humanity if we once won the glorious Grail? A warless world without the worries of continual conflict for the first of many marvels. Providence made practical for men to share with a sufficiency enjoyed by everyone. The best of our beliefs brought into being as an everyday experience of ordinary events.

Thus lives the legend of the Grail that gives whatever preference which each partaker asks expectantly shall be supplied out of a common cup. Also the feeling of a free and friendly fellowship in which each individual unites with everyone through his uniquity and natural nobility. Links of Love conjoining consciousness around creation as a blessed bond between all beings. A whole humanity in whom both happiness and holiness are welded into one as an idea of individuation.

Fears will fade into forgotten instincts, and all that we might ask for will be made available if it improves us or is likely in the least to lead us lightward. It will be a wondrous world and state of our society beyond belief, but possible to be procured by human beings who are determined to deserve it.

Behind such benefits are spiritual actualities advancing us through evolution as embodied entities up to the top of our especial tree. May all these Blessings and much more be manifested unto mankind together with the golden gift of understanding.

PRECEPTOR: O Mighty Maker of mankind and every marvel manifest or not in nature, incline our instincts and intelligence to seek the Sangreal in all its aspects however they are hidden from us for whatever valid purpose of protection.

Surely it is time to send our Sangreal back to earth as an experience for us to undergo because we are entitled to its presence in our present problems and predicaments. May we be made most worthy to uphold and undertake that change of consciousness which will attrack it here again among humanity. Amen.

PRECEPTOR: Let us continue on our Quest.

RESPONSOR: With all our will. Amen.

[Eighth verse of hymn sung while proceeding to next Station.]

9th Station

Perception of Perfection

What would we be like as perfect people? No one knows, since such exist not on this earth. They would surely be another species altogether, existing as accumulations of an active energy, and if they focused into forms at all, it would be what was willed.

Conditions of creation would be made by means of direct consciousness determined by the true degree of sheer divinity those superpeople held in their equivalents of human hearts. They would certainly construct the best and brightest style of spiritual structure possible in their perception.

Only people of an almost perfect nature could exist as entities in those conditions. That is how a Heaven automatically excludes all evil. It is an absolutely different dimension formulated so that ill-intentioned individuals simply will not fit its framework nor could ever enter its environments however hard they sought admission. Only if they altered all they were essentially and so eliminated evil in themselves that they were changed completely in accordance with acceptibility would they be welcome as celestial citizens.

So does the Sangreal define its Circle of collectiveness. It presents the proper place where everyone entitled to admission should assemble and so is an actual environment to enter and experience. Who would be more welcome than the many who could claim companionship with those that gain the Grail.

PRECEPTOR: Look, Lord of Love, on we who seek the Sangreal, and make it manifest for us within our midst. Since its collective symbol is the cup, we offer up ourselves to be completed by its blessed contents.

Pour into us thy power that we may meet perfection in thy presence. Join with us in joy and energy without an end. Express thyself through us as entities who are thine agents anywhere. Dispose of us as thy Divinity decides. We are thy willing workers, issue us with thine instructions, O Thou Overlord of Order. Speak unto us thy servants as we gather round our gracious Grail. Amen.

PRECEPTOR: Let us continue with our Holy Quest.

RESPONSOR: With all our will. Amen.

[Ninth verse of hymn sung while all proceed to next Station.]

10th Station

Gaining the Grail

Our Grail is gained! We are beyond all battles, past all pain, free at long last from fetters of flesh. We are above all agonies and without worries, fears, or fallibilities forever. We have won our way to holiness and life in light. There is no longer need to live on earth in order to obtain experience eventually exempting us from incarnation. Blessed by bliss and held by heavenly happiness, what might be wished or wanted more than that?

We may have been delivered from the fatal doom of death, but still our sacred blood continues to connect and bind us to our erstwhile brethren on earth. Those ties of truth are knots that never will be loosened while the weakest links with life continue calling on us as Companions in a common Cosmos.

As souls we are superior to incidents of incarnation or events of evolution, yet as selves we cannot be considered as complete until we ultimate and are united all together in the Absolute.

Therefore they that gain Grail are always bound by blood to help their human confreres all they can, because this benefits themselves in terms of truth, and also is a free fulfillment of their obligation oaths which last as long as life itself on every level.

So the Sangreal ends as everything we should have been from our beginning as the blood of being itself which is the individuality of every one of us consolidated in the consciousness of our Creator.

PRECEPTOR: O Life of Lives in whose most blessed body we are simply cells, yet each invaluable as an individual being, receive our recognition and return us a reply. We will wait with faith for contact and for confirmation of it in our own opinion.

Be Thou the best of all we bear within our blood, and sensitize the Sangreal in our souls so that it will infallibly direct us unto thy Divinity where we will ultimate eventually into our appointed everlasting end in *Perfect Peace Profound.* Amen.

PRECEPTOR: Let us conclude our Holy Quest.

RESPONSOR: With all our will. Amen.

> [Tenth verse of hymn sung as all proceed back to altar or to previous places.]

Final Prayer

PRECEPTOR: At the end of our adventure let us learn to live so that the Sangreal indeed becomes that blessed bond among us all, uniting us into a fellowship of faith and summoning a strength of spirit far beyond the power of anything to break, or possibility of perishing by apathy, abatement, or attrition.

May the maximum of meaning possible in this imaginary pilgrimage induce a mystically indelible impression in the hidden hearts and secret souls of everyone endeavoring to seek enlightenment within our Western Way. Blessed by the blood be whoso follows far enough to earn emancipation from self-servitude and so find a fuller freedom in the highest grace of our most Holy Grail.

> In the name of the **Wisdom**,
> and of the **Love**,
> and of the **Justice**,
> and of the Infinite **Mercy**,
> of the One Eternal **Spirit**,
> **Amen.**

• 4 •

The Sangreal Nomination Service

Introduction

           The Nomination Rite, or Service, is the Sangreal equivalent of a Christian baptism and confirmation combined. It has the elements of purification, nomination, anointing, communion, and illumination in it. Of special and unusual interest is the use of a "Containing Cord," a long, blood red cord passing around and behind the whole Circle so that all are contained therein during the important parts of the ceremony. It represents the Sangreal linking everyone by blood. It is usually kept as a ball, and unwound as it is passed from one to another around the Circle; the cord is either draped on the backs of chairs or laid on the floor. It may also be borne around by a single bearer, but should be at least touched by everyone present.

    The Candidate should enter accompanied by Sponsor who may prompt throughout the Rite. The Candidate should not be told the new name given by the Companions, nor should they know what the Candidate has chosen. Names if possible should indicate perceptions of the Candidate's nature or individual characteristics. Thus the first name is the Candidate's own estimation of him/herself, while the second is the Circle's (or select few Companions') notion of their new member. The blood specimen is best taken by whoever is experienced at this. In general, it is taken by binding the left thumb round the middle tightly for a few moments, then stabbing smartly but not deeply with a sterilized needle. A guard may be fitted to regulate the depth like an acupuncture needle, and the thumb is squeezed to expel blood. The first drop is mixed with the wine, and the remainder taken up with a fine brush to paint in the special Sangreal symbol, afterwards retained by the temple for contact. The symbol may also be signed by the Candidate with his/her real and Sangreal names.

Responsibility for checking everything in advance is usually the Preceptor's, but may be done by anyone reliable. Officers are: Preceptor, responsible for the procedural side only and all specifically non-religious passages. Priest, responsible for all direct prayers involving approaches to spiritual powers, consecrations, and specifically spiritual sayings. Responsor, which may be the Preceptor or anyone. Sponsor, who is customarily the same sex as the Candidate, but not necessarily. All means everybody must say it.

The general positioning, apart from the congregation who occupy a perimeter around the temple, are the Candidate in the East with the Sponsor on the right, the Priest on the South, and the Preceptor on the North. It is usually a good idea to have all appurtenances handy on side-stands which can be quickly moved to required positions by those appointed specially for the task. Everyone should know their places in advance and be properly rehearsed. The action takes place centrally. Sometimes it is useful to have a smallish, central, pseudo-altar—a side table or portable altar which can be stood anywhere. Appurtenances are brought as needed by attendants.

THE SANGREAL NOMINATION SERVICE

PRECEPTOR:

> In the name of the **Wisdom**,
>   and of the **Love**,
>   and of the **Justice**,
>   and of the Infinite **Mercy**,
>   of the One Eternal **Spirit**,
>   **Amen.**

Companions, we are here to welcome the awakening of another soul who hopes to share the Sangreal with all that bless the Holy Blood between them, and have sworn to serve its cause in this our Cosmos.

RESPONSOR: Blessed be an old relationship renewed in spirit through the Sangreal.

[knocks at portal]

PRECEPTOR: Who seeks?

CANDIDATE: A fellow soul in faith.

PRECEPTOR: What claim you?

CANDIDATE: Companionship.

PRECEPTOR: By what right?

CANDIDATE: By blood, birth, and belief.

PRECEPTOR: What will you?

CANDIDATE: I would help to bear the burden of belonging with the Holy Blood.

PRECEPTOR: Welcome is the will within your words. Enter with entitlement our circle of companionship.

ALL: [on entry give hailing sign, saying:] Glad greetings unto whom would gain the Greal.

[Hymn sung while Candidate and participants take their places.]

[Tune: "O God Our Help In Ages Past"]

1. What name to give a God have we,
   As mortals of this Earth?
   We dare not name Divinity
   Which brought us all to birth.

2. Yet should we find the slightest sign
   Of God in fellow-man
   We may describe this trace divine,
   As best a mortal can.

3. Inspire us Lord of Life we pray,
   For that is what we ask.
   Such is the work we face this day
   As our appointed task.

4. O help us now with this our aim,
   And make it crystal-clear
   What we should give as our God-name
   To our Companion here.
   Amen.

PRECEPTOR: Before we bring ourselves unto the Blessed Blood for fullest fellowship, we should first free ourselves from debts due unto Cosmos by inheritance of inborn wrongs which must be rectified before mankind may be redeemed and so set free from falling into flesh again.

All that anyone can do is to admit these with a willingness to work until we are delivered from them through the trials of time and enough experience of earth existence. What is important is that all enlightened individuals should understand the universal burden that we bear because our ancestors went wrong through thought and action. Realizing this, we should at least attempt to compensate for it in our own conscious lives by altering ourselves according to a simple spiritual vow entirely by our own volition. [To Candidate] Will you hear and hope to honor this?

CANDIDATE: I will.

PRECEPTOR: Then hear not merely words alone, but hold their meaning dearly in your deepest heart. [Preceptor recites the following oath:]

1. From the past, I willingly accept a proper portion of my forebears' faults which caused the worst of everything encountered on this earth and in my present person.

2. For this present I will work and pray with my whole heart and soul for the perfection of my self and species as I do believe the Will Divine in me directs by our most Blessed Blood.

3. For the future I will strive to serve the Sangreal Spirit faithfully so that we will become the best of beings possible to people on this planet, and eventually pass beyond embodiment of earth to *Perfect Peace Profound*.

Can you accept this as a code of conduct and a general guide for all your thoughts and actions in our world?

CANDIDATE: I can and will.

PRECEPTOR: Then promise so before all present, that your words of will be witnessed also by the Blessed Ones amongst us.

> [Here the Preceptor repeats the oath sentence by sentence, and the candidate, in turn, repeats each sentence after the Preceptor.]

PRECEPTOR: Henceforth forgive your ancestors for all their faults you have inherited, but also bless them for the benefits they have bestowed for blood to honor. Be a Blessing further bidden here upon the waters of forgiveness themselves.

> [Here the Priest blesses the water element.]

PRIEST: Let there be a firmament in the midst of the waters, so that sea and sky may separate into themselves. That which is above is like to that which is below, and that which is below is like to that which is above for the appearance of a single wonder. The sun is its father, the moon its mother, and the wind has carried it into conception. It ascends from earth to Heaven, and again it descendeth from Heaven to earth. We bear Thee in mind O Mighty Mother from whose wondrous womb our bodies walked upon this world. With thy salt comes wit and wisdom.

> [Here Priest salts the water.]

PRIEST: May we savor all that we experience with a grain of good sound sense, so that we are never wrecked with wickedness, but always borne to safety by the conscious currents in our sea of spirit.

Be Thou blessed, faithful friend of water, with the power, and in the service of that universal sea whose special scattered drops we surely are.

> In the name of the **Wisdom**,
>   and of the **Love**,
>   and of the **Justice**,
>   and of the Infinite **Mercy**,
>   of the One Eternal **Spirit**,
>   **Amen**.

PRECEPTOR: Let us pray the power of purity be present to protect us.

RESPONSOR: Cleansing us from filth and all corruption.

PRIEST: O Thou Supreme Source of Spirit, from whom flows a single stream of force which runs into the rivers that regenerate all life, Thee we adore and Thee we invoke. Thou dost ordain moisture which is like the blood of earth becoming sap in plants and sustenance in people. Speak unto us, thine inconstant and unstable creatures in the great tumults of the sea and we shall tremble before thee, speak unto us also in the murmur of limpid waters, and we shall yearn for thy Love. O Immensity into which flow all the rivers of life to be continually reborn in Thee. Ocean of infinite perfections. Height which reflects Thee in the depths, depth which exalts Thee to the heights, lead us into true life by intelligence and Love. Lead us into immortality by sacrifice that we may be found worthy one day to offer Thee water, blood and tears for the remission of our sins. Amen.

PRECEPTOR: [to Candidate] Hold forth now your hands to take the outer symbol of this action, but safely save its inner meaning silently in your most secret heart.

[Candidate holds hands over basin, while Priest pours the water over them, saying:]

PRIEST: Be you blessed, cleansed and consecrated, purified of purpose, cleared in conscience, and so made acceptable unto our Sangreal Spirit, from this moment forth and thus forevermore.

> In the name of **Wisdom**,
>   and of the **Love**,
>   and of the **Justice**,
>   and of the Infinite **Mercy**,
>   of the One Eternal **Spirit**,
>   **Amen**.

PRECEPTOR: [While Candidate is drying hands on offered towel] Even as you felt the wetness of that water yet might never mold it to make any form or solid shape, so will you sense the Sangreal in closest contact with your consciousness, yet be unable to compel it into any course of fixed foundation. It freely flows like liquid Love through all that touch it truly, so let it enter and enliven you as you explore existence. How now will you be known to we who are your close Companions for the Sangreal's sake?

CANDIDATE: I choose to call myself ____[Name]____.

PRECEPTOR: Be that so, but please accept another patronymic from us as your family of faith. We have chosen as your cognomen amongst our company the name of ____[Name]____ since such is our perception of the way which you appear. So let a seal be set upon you as a sign of light among us for the future and a mark of all you mean this moment in your service of the Sangreal.

ALL: *So mote it be. Amen.*

[Priest takes up anointing oil.]

PRIEST: Blessed be this sacred sign of light illuminating life. By its agency all darkness is dispelled, troubled waters tranquillized, injuries and illness healed, opposition overcome and universal benefits bestowed on us. Providence and power always abides in oil, and it reflects to us the radiance of an authority which is Almighty.

   The mark of majesty on Sacred Kings, and seal of sanctity on priests presiding at the Holy Mysteries is set with consecrated oil. May we honor here and now this offering of oil we need to grace the newly given name of our most gladly welcome member of this family of faith. Let light and Love be present for this hallowed purpose, permeating and prevailing everywhere, especially in this their active agent.

> In the name of the **Wisdom**,
> and of the **Love**,
> and of the **Justice**,
> and of the Infinite **Mercy**,
> of the One Eternal **Spirit**,
>   **Amen.**

[Priest says to Candidate, addressing by full new name:]

PRIEST: ___[Name]___, accept this altered name by which we know you now. Bear it with honor as an obligation to the Holy Blood. Let it serve you always as a special symbol of the Sangreal you serve, and also may it bring you every blessing while you work and wait within this world.

> In the name of the **Wisdom**,
> and of the **Love**,
> and of the **Justice**,
> and of the Infinite **Mercy**,
> of the One Eternal **Spirit**,
> **Amen.**

> [Priest anoints Candidate with right thumb on forehead, breast, right and left hands, then last under nose.]

ALL: ____[Name]____[Name]____[Name]____ *We welcome you within our Sangreal Circle.*

PRECEPTOR: You have heard how we accept you as another soul belonging with the blood. Let us listen to your Sponsor speaking in support.

> [All sit except Sponsor. Here Sponsor speaks briefly; at conclusion Preceptor says:]

PRECEPTOR: Thank you for that friendly testimony. [To others] Are there any adverse comments to consider?

> [If there are, Preceptor deals with them as seems fit, but if not, says to Candidate:]

PRECEPTOR: Is there something you would say as an acknowledgement?

> [Here Candidate is entitled to speak very briefly on his/her own behalf.]

PRECEPTOR: We have heard all that is applicable at this time. How shall we respond as a reply?

ALL: *We would share our Sangreal with loyalty and Love.*

PRECEPTOR: [to Candidate] What signifies the Sangreal to you that seek to serve it?

CANDIDATE: It is a special strain of spiritual blood mankind may bear relating us to the reality of life through Love, which is our own directive Deity and ultimate identity in *Perfect Peace Profound*.

PRECEPTOR: Is it held among all humans?

CANDIDATE: It is available by birthright and belief, or it is earnable by effort and devoted dedication.

PRECEPTOR: Are you a bearer of the Blessed Blood?

CANDIDATE: If I am may I discern it, if I am not may I deserve it.

PRECEPTOR: How is the Sangreal best served?

CANDIDATE: By sacrifice of self.

PRECEPTOR: What is the price we pay for partnership with it?

CANDIDATE: It is always bought by blood alone.

PRECEPTOR: As a sign of your sincerity and willing sacrifice, we ask of you a single drop of blood donated freely from your body that the Sangreal be truly served by you and shared by all of us with understanding.

CANDIDATE: [holds out left hand] Take it as a token of my trust and truth.

PRECEPTOR: [to all] Close now the Circle round our new Companion ____[New Name]____.

> [At this point, the Circle is closed by a long red cord being attached to the right hand altar horn, or equivalent, then passed from one to another sunwise around, being secured as convenient, or laid on floor. The other end attaches to the left horn of altar so that all action is enclosed. The drop of blood from Candidate is taken by whoever is best able to do this from the Candidate's left thumb with a sterilized needle. Some of the blood is used to paint in the Sangreal symbol for the Candidate, who also signs his name on it normally. This is best done with a fine brush for the blood, and an ordinary pen for the signature. A further drop of the blood is added to the wine, which should ideally have a drop from each Companion present already added in advance. All this action is covered by the singing of The Sangreal Hymn—which can be found in the Sangreal Blessing Service. At conclusion when all should be ready, the Preceptor says to the Candidate:]

PRECEPTOR: Consent to the completion of this Circle by becoming the last drop of blood to link us unto Deity.

> [Candidate places personal symbol, stained with his own blood, on altar or in tabernacle.]

CANDIDATE: I deliver this my bond of blood unto the Deity deciding **what is willed** within my being.

ALL: *So mote this be indeed. Amen.*

PRIEST: Blood is the life, and by it we are born, pass it onto progeny, then die and are delivered into immortality. Hallowed be the emblems we employ to mark these Holy Mysteries among mankind.

[Priest elevates bread.]

PRIEST: Behold this bread. Be it unto us our blessed body of belief by which we work with one another in this world.

[Priest elevates wine.]

Behold this wine, be it unto us the Blessed Blood that binds us to each other as a unity of spiritual strength.

Forasmuch as we have gathered into one accord with firmest faith that we shall find and gain the Sangreal which is the focus for our forces, may the Merciful and Mighty One preserve us for this purpose.

Anciently we sacrificed our Sacred Kings and sent them forth to seek the Spirit of Creation as ambassadors and mediators for their fellow mortals. Subsequently we invited them back into incarnation by the royal road returning them as our redeemers and regenerators through the inner truths their souls had touched and handed on to the awaiting ones within this world. Blessed be those beings and all they stand for unto us upholding their Tradition in our times.

Nowadays we know that the true sacrifice of life is made by men and women working out the will of the Divine direction in themselves, and offering their egos in obedience to Omniscient Deity.

Willingly do we submit unto the Universal One in us, and seek that Sangreal which is the special Spirit leading us to life through Love. Wherefore we invoke it at this instant, praying:

O Holy Spirit, best of all we bear within our human blood, illuminate, inspire, and integrate us with the Blessed Blood of Being which is the spiritual source of life, fount of our faith, and mainstream of our immortality.

Concentrate in us those qualities that we believe belong with royal blood, which are the finest found in human beings who rule themselves with rightness, honor, and according to the laws we learn that govern generosity and goodness as a practice among people.

Bring out the best in us, and change our worst into convenient waste we can reclaim as assets with advantage.

To all these ends, and every other ordinance connected or concerned therewith, may these elements be blest and consecrated at this moving moment.

[Over bread] Sacred to us as the Sangreal be this bread. With it may we become the mystic body by which soul and spirit manifest with mind in this our mortal world for the salvation of mankind. Amen.

[Over wine] Sacred to us as the Sangreal be this wine. With it may we become that Blessed Blood by which our beings are borne throughout the stream of life and Love in immortality. Amen.

[To all] **Take, eat, and drink this everyone for the eternal sake of our Companion soul who serves and shares the Sangreal among us all.**

> In the name of the **Wisdom**,
> and of the **Love**,
> and of the **Justice**,
> and of the Infinite **Mercy**,
> of the One Eternal **Spirit**,
> **Amen.**

[Gong. 4 strokes]

[The Communion is served by the Candidate, assisted by the Preceptor, bread first, followed by wine. There may be choral or musical background. The Priest is served first, and the Candidate and Preceptor last. When all is complete, the Priest says quietly:]

PRIEST: Let us share the Sacrament of Silence for the Sangreal's sake.

[All sit silently for a few moments. The Priest terminates the period by a knock. All rise.]

PRECEPTOR: Let us be enlightened by the light we bear within us.

RESPONSOR: Enlightening the lives of everyone we may encounter.

PRECEPTOR: For it is commanded that we dwell no more in darkness, but live consciously in light reflecting it forever to our fellow souls. Thus the symbol of our Sangreal is a light behind the blood, inspiring an illumination of our souls through life that knows not limits, but extends beyond existence. [to Candidate] Accept therefore a light that shall be yours to bear alone among us. Become a beacon and a watchfire we will wait and work with. Give good guidance unto those relying upon your radiance for discernment of their difficulties. Make all courses of the muddled clear ahead for them. Find and follow faithfully your pathway of progression. May you accomplish all of this and more with the assistance of our Sangreal Spirit sent you by the Lord of Life. Be a blessing bidden on this work of will.

[Here the Priest blesses the light or lamp intended for Candidate, saying:]

PRIEST: Let there be light no darkness may ever extinguish. Burn evermore O Fire of Love that ripens every spiritual seed. In the separation of thine essence from thy substance lies the work of wisdom. Thou art strongest of the strong, overcoming subtlety and interpenetrating all solidity. In thine adaption is the arcane art and secret of the sacred sciences.

We call upon Thee, O Father of All, radiant with thine illuminating rays. O Unseen Parent of the Sun, pour forth thy life-giving power and energize thy Divine Spark. Enter into this flame, and let it be agitated by the breath of thy Most Holy Spirit. [Here flame is lit.] Manifest thy power, and open for us the hidden temple which is concealed within this flame. May we become regenerated by thy light, and the breadth, fullness and crown of the solar radiance appear, so that the God within shines forth.

Be Thou consecrated faithful creature of the fire, through the power and in the service of that Supreme Light whose single sparks we surely are. Amen.

Immortal, eternal, ineffable, and uncreated Father of all things, who art borne upon the ever-rolling chariot of worlds which revolve unceasingly. Lord of ethereal immensities where the throne of thy power is exalted, from which height thy terrible eyes discern all things and thy holy and beautiful ears unto all things hearken, hear Thou thy children whom Thou didst Love before the ages began. For thy golden, thy grand, thine eternal majesty shines above the world and the Heaven of stars. Thou art exalted over them, O Glittering Fire. There dost Thou shine, there dost Thou commune with thyself in thine own splendor, and inexhaustible streams of light pour forth from thine essence for the nourishment of thine Infinite Spirit which of itself doth nourish all things and forms that treasure of substance ever ready for the generation which adapts it and appropriates the forms Thou hast impressed upon it from the very beginning.

Our unceasing exercise is to praise Thee and await thy good pleasure. We burn continually in or aspiration to possess Thee, O Father, O Mother, O Admirable Archetype of Maternity and of True Love. O Son, Flower of Sons, O Form of all Forms. Soul, Spirit, Harmony, and Index of Infinity. Amen.

[Here the Priest presents light to Candidate saying:]

PRIEST: Hold this with Honor.
Carry it with conscience.
Defend it with discretion.
Bear it for our blood.

In the name of the **Wisdom**,
and of the **Love**,
and of the **Justice**,
and of the Infinite **Mercy**,
of the One Eternal **Spirit**,
Amen.

[Here as quickly as possible all lights except the Candidate's are extinguished.]

ALL: *Alas! Alas! We dread the Darkness. Woe to whom the Light is lost!*

PRECEPTOR: Peace! Fear nothing while one flame is living to relight extinct ones upon earth. [to Candidate] Now you hold the only torch of truth that is the hope for every human here. Bear it as your life-blood, and relume us **as you will.**

[Here the candles are re-lit by the Candidate as everyone holds them out. This is done to music, choral, or any accompaniment. When completed Perceptor continues:]

PRECEPTOR: Realize from this your ultimate responsibility unto the light of lives, and learn to live so you may bear it in your blood until the end of everything.

PRIEST: Let us go forth with faith and fortitude to face the world awaiting us.

RESPONSOR: Bearing inwardly the light behind our blood that other souls may share in spirit.

PRECEPTOR: While widening our Circle so that we embrace the world.

RESPONSOR: With all our hearts and highest hopes.

> [While the Exeat Lux, which follows, is being chanted, the red cord symbolizing the blood links between everyone is wound up from one to another like a ball and eventually should be placed on the altar.]

The Exeat Lux

1. As I emerge from light and blood in my beginning; so shall I enter it again in life that has no ending.
2. O light, Thou hast directed me within thy ways of truth and goodness; by the blood am I delivered from the darkness and from error.
3. Thou revealest unto me the secret of all things; Thou directest me to the Divine One.
4. While I walk the way of light I shall not falter; Thou protectest me from pitfalls and from perils.
5. Thou lightenest my living soul; intelligence Thou givest to my mind, and in my heart Thou makest happiness.
6. Shining is my soul among thy brightness; radiant am I because of thine effulgence.

7. Thou hast fulfilled for me thy promise of redemption; blood has redeemed me in thy holy realms forever.
8. Glory be to Thee O Power; Thou alone art the Indwelling Spirit leading me toward perfection.
9. Therefore in thy Name will I go forth among mankind; joyfully will I reflect Thee to thy people.
10. Shine as thou wilt through me on earth, O Sangreal; so that all aware of Thee may find their certain ways to Heaven.

I. A. O. AMEN.

PRECEPTOR: As we commenced, let us complete.

RESPONSOR: In living light and Love forevermore.

PRIEST: O Sovereign Spirit we are serving through our Sangreal, bless Thou the blood we bear between us for the sake of fellow humankind. May every other single soul be led to light by their beliefs, and blessed unto everyone be life in thine eternal Love, shared through the silent sacrament of *Perfect Peace Profound*.

> In the name of the **Wisdom**,
> and of the **Love**,
> and of the **Justice**,
> and of the Infinite **Mercy**,
> of the One Eternal **Spirit**,
> **Amen.**

[Recessional accompanied by music. New Companion should lead bearing light.]

· 5 ·

The Wedding Service of the Sangreal

Introduction

It may be a surprise to modern Western youngsters, but religious wedding services were once not all that common in Europe. The customary thing to do was to become betrothed to one's proposed partner, which was only supposed to last for a limited period, normally a year and a day. This condition, however, was regarded as a legal and binding marriage for that short term, and any children born or conceived during it would be fully legitimate. Ordinary people were plighted to each other by "handfasting," or holding hands in the presence of reputable witnesses while declaring each other betrothed. Country folk would often do this at fairs: the lad would say "I'll take she," and the giggling girl would avow "and I'll have 'e." It was as simple as that. This was legal in Scotland up until very recent times. If, after a year and a day, they decided to stay on a more permanent footing, they then would go to the church and have their marriage solemnized with the blessing of God pronounced over them, and that would be binding for life. Hence, the English Church called the service the Solemnisation of Matrimony. It was frequently held in the church porch where it could be publicly witnessed.

Wealthy people regarded this as socially unsatisfactory since it seemed rather brief and offhand. So after the blessing in the porch, the party would enter the church where a more elaborate nuptial mass was celebrated with considerable pomp and splendor. The couple were considered as married already perforce of the betrothal, but from henceforth would be bound by indissoluble vows to each other taken in the presence of God and his faithful followers. It was these vows which were considered important because they were solemn promises made to each other which only death could cancel. A wedding was really a *welding* together, and the now disused forge at Gretna Green in Scotland, where the blacksmith welded a couple together over his anvil, is about the last relic of this surviving into our times.

Here we consider the Sangreal type of wedding which has all the old meanings in it in a modernized way. It is suitable for a temple or the open air, and needs very few appurtenances. An altar is set up on which are arranged a lamp or candle with a red glass for the flame to represent the Blessed Blood, a cup or chalice with wine in it, a long red cord often attached to the altar horns at the beginning which will reach the wrists of the bride and groom, and a knife in a sheath. The picture is completed with two wedding rings on a platter, one from the man to the woman, and the other from her to him. Great care should be taken not to confuse them. Either on the altar or on a stand by itself is a bowl of "bloodwater," which is holy water mixed with a drop or two of blood from the couple themselves and any friend or relative intending a special blessing on them. There is a brush or aspergillum having red bristles for scattering this at the appropriate moment. This water should be blessed previously to the Rite.

When the couple enter the area side by side they will find their way to the altar barred three times by rods held across their path by friends or attendants. The first rod (a black one) should be immediately inside the door; the second (a white rod), about halfway along; and the last rod (a gold one) just in front of the altar. These may in fact be held by the same two people who change rods as they go along. Since the rods are very light, they could, in a pinch, be held by only one person. It is a good idea to have adequate rehearsals for all those concerned before the ceremony.

The usual officiant is a Preceptor who may also be a Priest. Any other servers may be designated by him for whatever specific service that is required. Choral and musical arrangements are optional and to be stationed wherever convenient. It is a good idea to mark placements with different colored mats. Since the couple will take the memorial Sangreal lamp or candle away with them to keep and possibly relight on each anniversary, it could be a good idea if they supply it in the first place. The Preceptor is responsible for advising them on these points during prenuptial interviews and counseling.

Both will need an individual sponsor who must be prepared to speak briefly on behalf of each. It is customary for the woman to have a female friend and the man a male one, but this is not absolutely essential. It is also normal for those who are already legally married to request a Sangreal service additionally or even annually. Attention should be specially drawn to the clause which allows for separation if necessary, while still regarding the relationship as a blood-binding one for far longer than a mortal lifetime. It does not preclude remarriage to another person yet, without breaking the spiritual bond this Sangreal couple have accepted with one another.

The Sangreal wedding service embodies the ancient custom of mingling blood and sharing it in a modern symbolic form, and it also emphasizes the weight of responsibility borne by two souls who may be inviting others to share their lives and fortunes on this problematic planet. It could be described as a socio-spiritual affair which combines esoteric enjoyment with the most solemn and serious intentions. May it bring benefits to all who take any part in it, especially the principals concerned.

THE WEDDING SERVICE OF THE SANGREAL

PRECEPTOR:

In the name of the **Wisdom**,
and of the **Love**,
and of the **Justice**,
and of the Infinite **Mercy**,
of the One Eternal **Spirit**,
Amen.

Companions we are here in company together for the celebration of conjugal Rites between two souls who seek each other by our Western Spiritual Way of Light and Love. We come to wish them well, witness their agreements with each other, and invoke the greatest Blessing on them both from every aspect of Divinity in which we may believe. Let us bid them welcome in our olden way.

[Horn blast, fanfare, or other signal. Bride and groom approach supported by Sponsors, Attendants. The Bride is left, the Groom right. They meet the first barrier, a black one, at the back. Halt.]

PRECEPTOR: **Learn from this the first law of life together. Avoid all that you should not do if happiness and harmony are to prevail in married living. Know what is worst in you and shun it all you can. Do you so agree?**

ANSWER: We do.

PRECEPTOR: Pass and prosper.

> [The second barrier is met about halfway to the altar area. It is white. There may be music during actual processing. Halt.]

PRECEPTOR: **Learn from this the second law of married harmony and happiness. Accomplish all that you can do to make this possible. Know what is best in you and seek it always. Do you so agree?**

ANSWER: We do.

PRECEPTOR: Pass on and prosper.

> [The third and last barrier is gold, and met just before the altar area where Bride and Groom should remain.]

PRECEPTOR: **Learn from this the third and most important lesson of the golden mean in married life, that is the forgiveness of each other's faults and genuine appreciation of good qualities wherever found. Know what is best and worst in you. Then live within your means of either. Do you so agree?**

ANSWER: We do.

PRECEPTOR: Then lift the barrier between you and upraise it rightly.

> [This is done with guidance if needed, the rod barrier being held upright by its center between them, groom's hand uppermost.]

PRECEPTOR: **Learn last from this that obstacles you grasp together by the middle way can be converted into strong supports you may rely on to maintain your balance steadily through life. Do you so agree?**

ANSWER: We do.

PRECEPTOR: Then pivot on your point and face the people.

> [Using the upright staff as a pivot, the Bride goes forward and the Groom back half a circle each so that they face gathering still gripping staff.]

PRECEPTOR: True marriage is a social and a spiritual state of mutual responsibility between both human sexes. Not only these two people are involved, but also everyone with which they are connected. Most of all their children are affected if this couple choose to bear them. These will influence the future of our world and our beliefs in life according to the capabilities within their souls, and the genetic possibilities they have inherited through both their parents. This may be minimal, or very much indeed as destiny decrees. Have such important matters been considered carefully? Are these, our fellow souls and friends, now ready to assume responsible behavior to each other and the rest of us by such commitment? Do they fully realize their obligations everywhere concerned? Who is prepared to sponsor them as worthy to be wedded in our Western Way of Light within this world? Who vouches for this woman?

SPONSOR: I do.

PRECEPTOR: Tell us what you believe to be the truth, yet let your words be briefly gentle and compassionate. Say why you think the marriage would be beneficial for this woman and for all of us concerned.

> [Sponsor speaks her piece.]

PRECEPTOR: Thanks be to you from all of us.

ALL: *Amen.*

PRECEPTOR: Who vouches likewise for this man?

SPONSOR: I do.

PRECEPTOR: Tell us what you believe to be the truth, yet let your words be briefly gentle and compassionate. Say why you think the marriage would be beneficial for this man and all of us concerned.

[Sponsor speaks his piece.]

PRECEPTOR: Thanks be to you from all of us.

ALL: *Amen.*

PRECEPTOR: If anyone knows any valid reason why the wedding should not here proceed, this is the only opportunity for a proclaiming so in public now, or otherwise observe a private silence on the subject evermore.

[Pause.]

PRECEPTOR: Then are we all agreed together that this marriage-mating is indeed a worthwhile act of Love and trust between these fellow souls who ask our blessing on their nuptials?

ALL: *So mote it be. Amen.*

PRECEPTOR: Therefore let us lift our hearts and souls towards the Supreme Spirit of all life on earth and everywhere throughout existence, asking Its attention to our present prayers and practice, saying:

O Thou Lord of Life, consider these the children of thy consciousness who mean to marry for the sake of spiritual union in and by the Blessed Blood of our belonging with the Western Inner Way of light. Witness here their words of will toward Thee in each other. Help them to keep their promises and find fulfillment of their heartfelt hopes. Defend them in their difficulties and preserve them in all perils. Grant them good health and every happiness permissible within thy plan for human people. Accept them as an agency of thine awareness in this world, and make them worthy of this vital work among mankind. Live Thou through them, that they may ultimately live in Thee as everlasting life and Love. Amen.

[Here is sung the first hymn, either one as requested, or the following tune of "O God Our Help In Ages Past."]

1. Come Holy Spirit of all lives,
   Be with us here this day.
   For by thy blessings Nature thrives
   Within our Western Way.

Chorus: *O Blessed Love, O Blessed Light,*
Pour forth Thy Power Divine.
Extend Thy mercy and Thy might,
By making these hearts Thine.

2. By Blood didst Thou redeem our race
   And sent us forth to quest,
   For all that has the slightest trace
   Of what must be our best.

Chorus: *O Blessed Love, O Blessed Light,*
   Pour forth Thy Power Divine.
   Extend Thy mercy and Thy might,
   By making these hearts Thine.

3. By Blood Thy lines of life descend
   Throughout our human chain
   Of ancestry that never ends
   Till we reach Thee again.

Chorus: *O Blessed Love, O Blessed Light,*
   Pour forth Thy Power Divine.
   Extend Thy mercy and Thy might,
   By making these hearts Thine.

4. Bestow Thy blessings on those now
   That pledge themselves by Thee
   To one another by a vow
   Of life-fidelity.

Chorus: *O Blessed Love, O Blessed Light,*
   Pour forth Thy Power Divine.
   Extend Thy mercy and Thy might,
   By making these hearts Thine.

Amen.

PRECEPTOR: [to couple] Turn now full circle and await the action. Rely no more on your symbolic Staff, but only on your resolution which it represented.

[Staff removed]

PRECEPTOR: Spiritual matrimony is a mutual sacrifice of soul to soul, by bonding blood with blood because of our beliefs in Deity as our deliverer from final death into immortal living light. In ancient times, this was symbolically shown by mingling both bloods then sharing this from the same cup. Today the externalities are altered, but their inner sense remains the same. Attend this action.

[Blessing red cord]

PRECEPTOR: Be this accepted as an emblem of that blood which freely flows between you both and binds you unto one another by the bonds of outpoured Love alone.

[Blessing cup of wine]

PRECEPTOR: Be this wine accepted as a worthy symbol of the spiritual blood which must be shed by God so that humans may eventually earn it on this earth. Energize this emblem, O Eternal One, that it may truly serve thy Spirit for its present purpose. [To couple] Hold forth your nearest hands above the cup.

[Preceptor binds Bride's right wrist and signs with knife.]

In this sign sacrifice yourself. Give that you may be given, empty yourself that you may be filled, end mortality that you may be eternal, and blessed be your blood forevermore.

[Preceptor drapes cord to cup, and repeats action on Groom's left wrist.]

Peace be with you both at present, though married life is seldom without struggles.

[Preceptor gives knife to Groom and sheath to Bride.]

PRECEPTOR: If ever you become at daggers drawn with one another as any wedded humans may be, here is the formula for your forgiveness and reconciliation. First bury your blade within the grave of every grudge.

[Groom puts knife in sheath held by Bride and they continue holding it.]

PRECEPTOR: Now lay the whole upon the altar of your firmest faith in life and say together: **We give our quarrels unto God that they may be converted into loving peace.**

[This is done.]

PRECEPTOR: Furthermore, if ever you should both agree to separate as selves upon this earth according to the laws of man, remember that the bonds of blood can never break in spiritual spheres of life where we are all connected indissolubly together. Separation is a social gesture only, made as an acknowledgement of individual will which should be made with understanding Love and must be mutual. This is the way. [To Bride] Untie him, saying: **Because I love you I absolve you from your obligations to me as a human being alone. Beyond that we are one by blood forever.**

> [She does so; then Preceptor to Groom:]

Do likewise, then give me that cord.

> [This done, Preceptor lays cord round cup sunwise, then says:]

PRECEPTOR:

> All life begins and ends by blood
> In one long time through space and time
> Eventuating as existence everywhere,
> Involving everyone within its cosmic coils.
> Each one of us are cells in its eternal stream,
> Linked all together by the energy of Love
> Hence God and Good, are truly Love indeed.
> So let us live in Love with life forevermore.
>
> Amen.

> [Preceptor presents lamp to couple.]

PRECEPTOR: Behold this symbol of the light within the blood. Let it become your certain guide through life and its obscurities. Take it together.

> [They do so]

May the Light Divine illuminate your ways within this doubtful world, inspiring you at every step you take upon its problematic paths. Let it lead you surely from a state of mere mortality to everlasting entity in light beyond all limits from whence no return is ever made by man.

> [Replaces Lamp on altar. To Bride:]

Now with Enlightenment bestow the blessing of this cup upon your chosen one with these old words: **Take this my blood, be with it as Thou wilt.**

> [Groom accepts cup and drinks. Words and action repeated from man to woman. Preceptor takes back cup and empties it, returning it to altar with the words:]

PRECEPTOR: **Life. Be Thou one. Created and consumed by thine own consummation of the Love Thou art.**

As every one of us is but a single link within the endless chain of life, so let the jointure of these living links before us be well represented by the customary rings with which they pledge each other.

> [Blessing rings]

Blessed be these ancient symbols honored as a sign of faith between two souls whose bodies wear them constantly as tokens of the spirit they aspire to share together. It has been said that Deity is like a Circle whose circumference is everywhere and center nowhere. Therefore in this sign be God acknowledged and approached.

May these earthly emblems bear the heavenly blessing of an inner influence which will incline their holders' hearts to mutual Love and trust throughout incarnate life, and later lead them indissolubly into unison with *Perfect Peace Profound*.

> In the Name of the **Wisdom**,
> and of the **Love**,
> and of the **Justice**,
> and of the Infinite **Mercy**,
> of the One Eternal **Spirit**,
> **Amen.**

The Admonitions

[Bride first, Groom second]

Do you ____[Name]____ before us all assembled bodily or otherwise accept ____[Name]____ as your freely chosen partner for this life within our world? Will you endeavor to be loyal and loving through the best or worst of circumstances you may meet as human beings? Will you strive to seek and contact consciously the God within yourself and also in your marriage mate? Will you treat him/her honestly and honorably for the sake of all you hold most holy and respect or reverence as true spiritual standards of behavior in our Western world? Do you believe in your ability to uphold these worthily, and do you intend to make your marriage work as best you may by every conscious means at your command?

ANSWER: I do.

[After both affirmations have been made]

PRECEPTOR: Then let your pledges to each other and the power behind you both be made and heard by Heaven and your faithful friends on earth here present for that purpose. Take each the proper ring, and then repeat after me while regarding each other.

[Both Bride and Groom say and do the following. The Bride always recites first.]

I____[Name]____accept you____[Name]____ as my husband/wife according to the laws of Heaven and earth in which we both believe. As I am to you, so may you be with me, and as we are to one another, so may Deity itself dispose of us. In witness of my words and will, receive and wear this ring from me from this time forth.

In the name of the Wisdom

> [touch ring to thumb]

and of the Love,

> [first finger]

and of the Justice,

> [second finger]

and of the Infinite Mercy,

> [ring pushed home—third finger]

of the One Eternal Spirit,

> [kiss ring on finger]

Amen.

[After Groom completes pledge, Preceptor turns to people and proclaims:]

PRECEPTOR: All here have heard and witnessed these essential words and acts of will between two souls among our company on earth. Therefore through our human ears and eyes these things have reached the consciousness of God who is Omniscient and Omnipresent. As an imperfect earthly agent of that perfect power which is eternal Love, I proclaim and bless your partnership in life as man and wife together. Wherefore live henceforth that you may truly

Be. Of. One. Blood.

[They embrace.]

In the name of the **Wisdom**,
and of the **Love**,
and of the **Justice**,
and of the Infinite **Mercy**,
of the One Eternal **Spirit**,
Amen.

[While they embrace, the Preceptor sprinkles them with lustral "blood water" during the benediction.]

It is Done
They are one.

[Here a second hymn is sung. Any hymn of choice or the following sung to the tune of "Praise My Soul The King Of Heaven."]

1. Thou that made both Man and Woman
Bless our bridal pair this day.
Help them while they are yet human,
Guide them on their Inner Way.

Chorus: *Bless them truly,*
Guard them duly,
King of Life and Lord of Love.

2. We who are their fellow mortals
Wish them well this Earthly life.

May they progress through its portals
   Free from ills and serious strife.

*Chorus: Bless them truly,
         Guard them duly,
         King of Life and Lord of Love.*

3. Let them live in such a fashion
   That each one brings out the best
   In the other by compassion,
   So that both are always blest.

*Chorus: Bless them truly,
         Guard them duly,
         King of Love and Lord of Love.*

4. Loving laughter, joy and gladness,
   Be with these throughout their lives
   With a minimum of sadness
   While their faith in Life survives.

*Chorus: Bless them truly,
         Guard them duly,
         King of Life and Lord of Love.*

Amen.

PRECEPTOR: Thanks be to Thee, O Constant King of Cosmos, in whom alone originates the royal blood of our redemption, and that sacred sacrifice ennobling our human race above all other forms of life upon this planet.

   Blessed be the deed which we have done amongst us here this day, and may it benefit not only those it honored specially, but everyone throughout its chain of consequences evermore.

ALL: *So mote it be. Amen.*

> [At this point are included any particular songs, music, customs, or items specially requested by the bridal pair. This must be decided in advance of the ceremony. If there are none, or at the end of them, the Preceptor calls everyone to order, by saying:]

PRECEPTOR: As with a wedding ring, there is no end that is not also a beginning. Now is always the end of our entire past and commencement of our whole future. Here we have come to the end of a beginning, and commencement of a conjoint line of life we hope and pray will be successful as a social and spiritual partnership among our people. May it bless us all as we bless it. Therefore there is only this to say in farewell to our friends now newly wedded before we greet them gladly otherwise:

> **Fare forth from here in peace and live.**
> **Fare forth from here in peace and learn.**
> **Fare forth from here in peace and Love.**

And blessed forever be the blood with which you both belong.

> In the name of the **Wisdom**,
> and of the **Love**,
> and of the **Justice**,
> and of the Infinite **Mercy**,
> of the One Eternal **Spirit**,
> **Amen.**

> [The Bride and Groom leave the area beneath a triumphal arch of whatever seems appropriate to suitable music. The Preceptor and anyone so inclined stay by the altar for brief private prayers on their behalf.]

· 6 ·

The Act of Last Anointment

Introduction

The intention of this Rite is to help adjust the mind to the fact and finality of death as a single personality. The timing and circumstances of it are therefore a function of the individual situation. It should obviously be given as near death as possible, yet while some consciousness remains in the person who is dying. If possible, the Rite may be followed by administration of the Sacrament, (the Rite of Release), though this could occur on another occasion. Everything really depends on the judgment and capability of the administrator. Friends of the dying may be present, providing emotional control can be assured.

It is also possible to include additional prayers as may seem necessary (at the discretion of the administrator), or a hymn sung or special music played, but any additions should be made *after* the complete anointment has been made. The Rite should be conducted without undue interruptions. If the condition of the Anointee seems moribund, it should be assumed that residual consciousness may yet be present, and the Rite proceeded with accordingly.

If the initiatory name of the Anointee is not known, the personal name will serve, or the familiar name if possible.

Since the chances are that the Anointee will be in bed, an Attendant should be prepared to uncover the feet, bare the breast, or arrange the hands as needed. The prevailing attitude should be quiet confidence, but the disposition of the Anointee should be of primary consideration.

THE ACT OF LAST ANOINTMENT

PRECEPTOR:

> In the name of the **Wisdom**,
> and of the **Love**,
> and of the **Justice**,
> and of the Infinite **Mercy**,
> of the One Eternal **Spirit**,
> **Amen.**

By birth do we begin our active beings in this world and through the doors of death depart again. What matters most between these end events is how we make ourselves as humans, and contact each other in a common consciousness that grows to Godhood.

[to Anointee]

PRECEPTOR: Therefore, close Companion sharing this experience of existence with us through the Sangreal, since you seem intending to quit incarnation on the next stage of our necessary spiritual Quest, we will ask you to attend and heed these helpful thoughts which are intended to remind you rather than instruct you of their import.

As a servant of the Sangreal you should know that you are not about to die and disappear entirely in extinction of your entity. Instead you will identify with wider worlds and change your consciousness completely. This can be adjusted with as it occurs, for it is a normal, natural process of progression to be undergone by everyone on earth who has a body. You are not alone, but are accompanied by all who ever died since spirit borrowed bodies to become the people of this planet. Some of these are also servants of the Sangreal who will always hear and help another soul who calls with confidence on their assistance. First, however, you should free yourself from fetters you have made yourself which may yet bind you unto this material world because you either cannot bear to break them nor completely clear them by a definite dismissal.

What is born by Love into this world should also die in Love with life itself, so that a further birth in higher form and spiritual spheres can be the consequence. Therefore you should never harbor hates nor anything at all that keeps you captive to this world with wrong and useless urges causing endless chain effects committing you and others to a troubled future fate. So straightway free yourself from these as fully as you may be making a firm act of faith in your ability to do so, saying and meaning most sincerely in your mind and soul:

O Supreme Spirit of Eternal Energy and Love whom I see through the Sangreal, I implore forgiveness for the debts I duly owe to life through my own faults and failings. I admit responsibility for all my wrongful acts and pledge my present promise to redeem them as I am afforded opportunities. Balance Thou between what I owe life and it owes me, then cancel out conditions that affect us all adversely. I am sincerely sorry for my share in the misdeeds of our mankind, and I will truly try to make myself a better sort of spiritual being for whatever future I must face with fortitude. Amen.

> [This is repeated by the Anointee, if possible aloud, or otherwise mentally. In either case the Preceptor goes through it slowly, line by line.]

PRECEPTOR: With the Living Spirit in me I am witness of your words and will. It has heard as I have heard, and It can comprehend all human consciousness much clearer and more truly than a merely mortal mind. Divinity is not deceived, nor can the conduct of a human being be hidden or obscure to its omniscience. Yet fear not for your own forgiveness by your merciful and mighty Maker, but receive and recognize your reconciliation through this mark of meaning fixed upon your forehead with anointing oil as agent of that living light behind the Blessed Blood uniting us in faithful fellowship. Take this token as a sign of sure salvation and assured acceptance of your soul by a compassionate Creator.

[Here the Preceptor signs forehead with oil while praying:]

PRECEPTOR: Accept O Lord of Life, the spirit, soul and self of this thy human here incarnate as ____[Proper Name]____ who belongs by blood belief within our Western family of faith which serves Thee through the Sangreal.

> In the name of the **Wisdom**,
> and of the **Love**,
> and of the **Justice**,

and of the Infinite **Mercy**,
of the One Eternal **Spirit**,
Amen.

PRECEPTOR: Let us pray. [All present join in.] O Lord of Life be kind to our companion in extremity of earth existence. Be it with him/her however thy Divine Decision may direct. If back into embodiment, then heal him/her of infirmities and help him/her work whatever will of thine inspired the reason for that respite. Likewise if he/she should depart for service in a disembodied state of being, we would beg that every Blessing be bestowed upon him/her in fulfillment of our faith. In particular we pray that all attachments to this world will prove no problem nor prevent his/her passage to the highest spheres of spirit. May only links of altruistic love alone oblige him/her for the Sangreal's sake to keep in contact with our most extended mortal consciousness on earth. Thy will be worked in every world. Ours to ask and thine to answer. Blessed be thy Being forevermore. Amen.

PRECEPTOR: [to Anointee] As a sign of your intent to serve the Supreme Spirit through the Sangreal, you are invited here to hold forth both your hands.

> [This is done by Preceptor or Assistant if impossible for Anointee. Preceptor then anoints palms of left and right hand saying:]

PRECEPTOR: Blessed be the hands of help and hope extended everywhere with faith and friendship. As you have helped your fellow humans in this world so may others aid you in the afterlife.

> [Preceptor gives special grip.]

PRECEPTOR: Farewell good friend. God greet you with a kindly clasp and welcome you with holiest hospitality. May all the Mighty Ones receive you royally.

> In the name of the **Wisdom**,
>   and of the **Love**,
>   and of the **Justice**,
>   and of the Infinite **Mercy**,
>   of the One Eternal **Spirit**,
>   **Amen**.

PRECEPTOR: Now set straight your feet to signify a willingness to walk within the needful narrow way that leads to light along the pathway to perfection.

> [Feet uncovered, Preceptor anoints dorsal surface left and right saying:]

PRECEPTOR: Blessed be the feet so firmly set upon our faith way to an ultimate of total truth that they will never deviate from following the natural design which forms our central course through Cosmos. Continue on your Quest by single steps upon the royal road until our ultimate is reached and recognized as *Perfect Peace Profound*.

> In the name of the **Wisdom**,
>   and of the **Love**,
>   and of the **Justice**,
>   and of the Infinite **Mercy**,
>   of the One Eternal **Spirit**,
>   **Amen**.

PRECEPTOR: [To Anointee] Stay still and hold our Sangreal Spirit in your heart where it will animate and energize you everlastingly.

[Preceptor anoints breast over heart saying:]

PRECEPTOR: As a human heart makes blood flow round a mortal frame so does our Sangreal circulate the Cosmic Blood of Being Itself, Whose single cells we surely are as individuals. Exchange therefore your human heart for an eternal one that neither fails nor falters through the many changes you must make and modify within your character in each and every incarnation. Centralize yourself around the Sangreal as a seed spark of Divinity to whom you dedicate your being because you bear it in your blood. May this Holy Mystery at the heart of your beliefs sustain your soul to life in light beyond embodiment.

>In the name of the **Wisdom**,
>   and of the **Love**,
>   and of the **Justice**,
>   and of the Infinite **Mercy**,
>   of the One Eternal **Spirit**,
>   **Amen**.

[Pause. To Anointee]

When you will, and as your soul is summoned, send it forth with perfect faith that you will surely find your proper place and from that point continue with your spiritual work of self-construction. Concentrate with care upon eternal and essential spiritual subjects. Integrity, identity, and immortality. Reject all retrospection, neither ponder upon personalities nor anything pertaining to your past ephemeral existence. Regrets are useless though resolves have value, and intentions of the utmost all importance. Point yourself at *Perfect Peace Profound* and aim at its attainment. Hold to the highest hopes. Have confidence in the compassion that creates and then consumes you ceaselessly. Look to life as a deliverance from death. Learn its lessons and advance yourself to live in light through Love. Be it with you **as you will**, and grow to Godhood evermore.

PRECEPTOR: Let us pray. [All present join in.] O Thou Lord of every life and Divine Disposer of our destinies, we acknowledge thine authority above us. Care for our companion ____[Initiatory Name]____ coming to an earthly end. Save his/her soul and spirit by the Blessed Blood of our belonging with the Sangreal. Bring him/her to future birth within its wonder for the sake of all that serve it also. Send here and now those holy needed spirits and appointed angels who will guard and guide him/her through transition to superior states of being beyond a body. Be with us, O Blessed Ones, and help a human at the end of earth existence. Hear and help us also as we seek to serve as faithful friends and close Companions to the very last of life spent on this sphere. Now there is no more that we may do as mortals. Therefore to thy tender loving care will we commend the soul of our Companion whom we Love on this our side of life and will continue to pursue with prayers so long as we survive. We will remember our relationship with him/her as firmest friends forever. Be all Blessings bidden on him/her, In the Name of the Wisdom, and of the Love, and of the Justice, and of the Infinite Mercy of the One Eternal Spirit. Amen.

PRECEPTOR: So may all mankind be saved and brought to blessedness by their beliefs in better ways of living than this world seems likely to supply with any certainty. Blessed indeed are they that so escape embodied incarnation into fuller freedom of the spiritual spheres. Thanks be for this deliverance from bondage to a body, and all gratitude be given to the Grand Designer of this plan for our perfection in the universal ultimate of *Peace Profound*.

> In the name of the **Wisdom**,
> and of the **Love**,
> and of the **Justice**,
> and of the Infinite **Mercy**,
> of the One Eternal **Spirit**,
> **Amen**.

[Here ends The Rite of Last Anointment.]

· 7 ·

The Rite of Release

Introduction

This Rite corresponds with the "Holy Viaticum," or "Last Sacrament," and is to be administered when the participant is considered to be approaching the end of incarnate life. Its beauty lies in the fact that it may be repeated if the patient lingers and requests it. If circumstances permit, it may be given following the Annointment, but should not be given twice on the same day. The Annointment may be given only once.

The fundamental idea of this Rite is that although physical death may deprive the Sangreal Sodality of a member on one life level, it adds to the membership on the most important inner level. Therefore, the external bodily loss is also an internal spiritual gain, and this Rite is properly a celebration and recognition of this actuality.

It is very important that the right type of Officiant administer the Rite. He or she must have complete confidence in its efficacy and total sincerity in conducting it. Nothing less will do.

Almost everything in this Rite depends on the Officiant's personal ability to handle unusual situations should they arise. If the dying person is totally moribund, the Officiant himself will consume the elements in the name of the dying one. The various situations should be anticipated and the answers worked out in advance. The most important factor is *intention*, and plans must be made as to how that intention may be ritually signified.

It is easy to recognize in this Rite the idea that the *dead* simply enter the *living* of another form of expression. In the old rituals it was expressed as "We are each other," or as Christianity enjoins each to "Love one's neighbors as oneself." The Sangreal is in reality no more than "pre-Christian Christianity" through symbolizing its belief in "Blood as a binding element of Life between specific people, and the spiritual equivalent of blood relating us with a Father-Mother Deity as an origin of life itself." This was quite clear to initiated people years ago but now the meaning has been lost through time and diversity of dogmatic arguments.

If others are present, they may partake of the Communion. They may also remain and continue their extemporaneous prayer, devotion or rosary until the end. Those present should be kept to a minimum.

Requirements for the Rite are preconsecrated bread and wine, lustral fluid in a bowl, a symbol of the Sangreal, and at least two candles set up on a nearby table. The elements are first covered and then uncovered in the presence of the sick soul.

THE RITE OF RELEASE

PRECEPTOR:

    In the name of the **Wisdom**,
       and of the **Love**,
       and of the **Justice**,

and of the Infinite **Mercy**,
of the One Eternal **Spirit**,
Amen.

Sacred is the Sangreal amongst its servants.

RESPONSOR: Blessed be the blood with which we all belong.

PRECEPTOR: [and all including the sick soul, if possible] I believe in One Supreme and Sovereign Spirit as our universal Lord of life and light of which we are integral units in its cosmic corpus.

Likewise I believe we should become as blood within that blessed body, sharing its immortal spiritual structure and communing with its consciousness until our complete unison with it in *Perfect Peace Profound*.

Also I believe in all that indicates this primal purpose of our individual selves, and I accept the Sangreal as the symbol of a true relationship with its reality. Amen.

PRECEPTOR: For by the Sangreal we do not definitely die, but live in light from life to life. It is the savior of our souls and our deliverance from darkness and destruction. Wherefore do we praise its power and presence saying:

[All present join in.]

PRECEPTOR: O Sangreal of our Western Inner Way, be with us always as our other self in spirit, leading us to larger life, enhancement of experiences, purposeful progression on our paths, and extension of existence into Everlasting Entity. May every one of us be blessed in and by that blood we all belong with in the the spirit of the Sangreal and the touch of its tremendous truth.

[scatters lustral fluid]

In the name of the **Wisdom**,
and of the **Love**,
and of the **Justice**,
and of the Infinite **Mercy**,
of the One Eternal **Spirit**,
Amen.

[Priest or Preceptor uncovers the Elements and presents them to the departing soul, afterwards replacing them temporarily on the table.]

Behold the blessed symbols of our flesh and blood. Bread for the body, wine for the blood whereby we are related in a common bond of consciousness as an especial family of faith within the West. This is the identity we share and serve together so that we may enter the Eternal Entity we neither know by name or nature, but whom we believe is Sovereign Spirit of our universe and therefore call our King of Cosmos. Blessed be its Being evermore. Amen.

Keeping contact with each other through our symbol of the Sangreal means that we will mediate the spirit that it represents as a reality among ourselves. As an existing entity we will become one blessed whole together as a total truth, sharing the same soul which is the Sangreal itself. Death does not diminish nor divide our Sangreal soul. It only offers wider spiritual space for us to unify ourselves, and also it affords an opportunity for an improvement of our characters.

[to the departing soul directly]

Continue then through us O Close Companion. Share our souls if you intend existing as an entity. We welcome you within us and we Love you as another life enlarging our existence everywhere. Besides, it is your birthright if you care to claim it by belonging with the Blessed Blood in unison with us who live the Western Way of Light. In token of this truth, take this the bread that signifies our body and the sign of your salvation by its Spirit.

[communicates bread]

Also accept with will this wine which is the everlasting emblem of our blood. It brings you immortality because of your belonging with it intimately.

[communicates wine. Preceptor finishes elements himself.]

PRECEPTOR; O Merciful and Mighty Maker of mankind on whose Divinity alone we all depend as mortals, hear and help us as we ask assistance and the bounty of thy blessing on our thoughts and actions. Help to close a human life with complete confidence in thy compassion and the certainty of its continuation in the Love that binds us all together by the blood of our beliefs.

Lord let now the living soul of this thy servant leave its feeble flesh and so depart with dignity into the light of our origination. Hold forth thy holy hands to take it from this woeful world to spheres of spiritual splendor. Bring it to beauty in thy bright beneficence, and may it meet with mercy in thy magnanimity. Thou are the only One to trust entirely through extremities of our existence. Therefore let thy Will be worked in every world while we accept it as an absolute authority.

Praised be thy presence by the people it illuminates with inspiration, and all glory be unto thy greatness that embraces everyone eternally. Amen.

PRECEPTOR: Lord of Life we also will expect eventual release when we resign our bondage to our bodies.

RESPONSOR: While we will always strive to serve that body of belief which we belong with by our blood.

PRECEPTOR: So may we continue as a constant company of souls both in and out of bodies seeking our objective of the Sangreal with fervent faith.

>   In the name of the **Wisdom**,
>   and of the **Love**,
>   and of the **Justice**,
>   and of the Infinite **Mercy**,
>   of the One Eternal **Spirit**,
>   **Amen**.

· 8 ·

The Sangreal Funeral Rite

Introduction

The basics of this ceremony are very old, comprising three main incidents. First, the absolving of the deceased from all obligation to the congregation and a hope that this would reach to wider areas. Second, the kindling of a memorial light from which others might kindle theirs, and last, a Communion among special Companions, extended to those wishing to participate. Preferably the chalice and paten should be placed on the coffin at least momentarily; so should the light.

It was considered that the progress of a soul was impeded by any debts or obligations owed to living people. Therefore, if they cancelled these voluntarily, the soul would be free to proceed "Godward." Lighting a candle or lamp has always been a sign of remembering the dead by inviting them to join the fires of friendship in a Circle of companionship. The "Communion of the Flesh and Blood" was once the actual consumption of selected portions of the corpse, so that everyone shared something of the departed one: a sacred act of special intimate significance, implying absorbtion by incorporation of a loved one. All these ancient customs are symbolized by their present emblems in a modern manner, yet the inner meanings still remain intact.

The light is kept burning, so that everyone who wishes may kindle one of their own from it later. None of these should be kept

114 • SANGREAL CEREMONIES AND RITUALS

in front of a photograph of the deceased, since they should be remembered as a "presence" rather than a personality. They are always to be thought of as beings of *light*, radiantly and warmly *alive*—never as a silent, motionless corpse. Every thought should be directed at helping the departed *away* from this world towards higher and better levels of living.

Every possible element included in this ceremony has been calculated to help the deceased rather than reassure the relatives, and it is in accordance with the finest esoteric Traditions of Western practice. The surviving spirit is constantly held in mind, and the corpse relegated to its proper place as a mere remnant. We are not so much regretting death as celebrating the continuity of a liberated soul through symbology commemorating this event.

There is nothing to prevent additional prayers or hymns at the discretion of Directors (those who have organized the funeral), though the timing has been carefully calculated to suit the average use of a modern crematorium chapel. At the committal, sounding a horn as a hopeful sign of awakening should not present serious problems, but it is best to have a real, rather than a recorded horn, if possible. Some suitable wind instrument is symbolically needed, for it represents the "call to life" and the "resurrection of the dead."

The rather beautiful prayer at the commencement is taken from Eliphas Levi's "Ritual of Transcendental Magic,"[7] and is the prayer of the air, but seems particularly apposite for the invocation of the Life Spirit in relation to the transcience of human mortals. Any reasonable requests from the departed as regards hymns, special prayers, etc., should be given priority by the Director.

---

[7]Eliphas Levi, *Transcendental Magic, Its Doctrine and Ritual* (Samuel Weiser, Inc., York Beach, Maine), page 229.

THE SANGREAL FUNERAL RITE

[Introductory music as coffin is borne in. When all is ready:]

PRECEPTOR: Companions, we have come to celebrate the mystery of death, which is the common end of every creature made of mortal matter on this earth. All that is born must duly die. That is the law of life within our world, and every single one of us is subject to its sovereignty. Let us accept this as a certainty with confidence that we shall learn to live beyond the limits of our bodies and become much more than merely mortals.

ALL: *So mote it be. Amen.*

PRECEPTOR: For the essence of existence is eternal in itself, animating all of us who seek identity with it forever. Whosoever truly wills to **live** need never perish, save as a human personality inhabiting this planet. In and as our spiritual selves, we are indeed immortal. Therefore let us pray unto the power which breathes the breath of life into our beings.

Spirit of Light, Spirit of Wisdom, whose breath gives and takes away the form of all things. Thou before whom the life of every being is but a shadow which transforms and a vapor which passes away. Thou who breathest forth and the limitless immensities are peopled. Thou who drawest in, and all which came forth from Thee unto Thee returneth. Endless movement in the eternal stability, be Thou blessed forever. We praise Thee, we bless Thee in the fleeting empire of created light, of shadows, reflections, and images, and we aspire without ceasing towards thine immutable and thine imperishable splendor. May the ray of thine intelligence and the warmth of thy Love descend upon us. That which is volatile shall become fixed, that which is shadow shall become body, the spirit of the air shall receive a soul and dream be thought. We shall be swept away no more before the tempests, but shall bridle the winged steeds of the morning and guide the course of the evening winds that we may fly into thy presence O Spirit of Spirits, O Eternal Soul of Souls! O Imperishable Breath of Life! O Creative Sigh! O Mouth which dost breathe forth the life of everyone within the ebb and flow of thine eternal speech, which is the divine ocean of movement and of truth. Amen.

PRECEPTOR: All born of human blood alone must duly die, but whoso shares the spiritual bloodstream of the Sangreal will surely live beyond a mortal body as an entity incorporated by the blessed body of immortal life itself.

While we are bound upon the Cosmic Cross of birth and death, we must endure an earth existence until we have earned and learned enough to liberate ourselves into that everlasting **light** from whence there need be no return, and so we shall thenceforth remain in *Perfect Peace Profound*.

Therefore we would ask of Deity for our deceased Companion, only those entitlements that we expect ourselves when we depart this world.

1. May he/she be safely guided through the Doors of Death, and helped to higher living levels than we have among us here.

ALL: *Grant, O Good and Gracious One, this may be so indeed.*

2. May he/she be afforded every opportunity for altering him/her Self according to the Holy Will within his/her special Spirit.

ALL: *Grant, O Good and Gracious One, this may be so indeed.*

3. May he/she never suffer without spiritual need, nor experience adversity without advantage in it.

ALL: *Grant, O Good and Gracious One, this may be so indeed.*

4. May every happiness and harmony be his/hers to share with every other soul in the same state of Heaven.

ALL: *Grant, O Good and Gracious One, this may be so indeed.*

5. May his/her living Spirit be allowed to link with ours in close companionship and loyal Love.

ALL: *Grant, O Good and Gracious One, this may be so indeed.*

6. May he/she truly gain the Greal that holds the highest hopes for our humanity, and pass from thence to *Perfect Peace.*

ALL: *Grant, O Good and Gracious One, this may be so indeed.*

All this and whatsoever more that may contribute to the well-being of our late Companion is our present prayer on his/her behalf. May it also be the Will of the Most High and Holy One, Who is the single Source of Blessedness forevermore.

ALL: *So mote it be. Amen.*

PRECEPTOR: Who will bear witness in this world for our most silent member here among us?

SPONSOR: I will.

PRECEPTOR: Then speak with sympathy while we will pray the Lord of Life to listen through our ears.

> [Here the Eulogy is delivered. Ten to fifteen minutes are sufficient.]

PRECEPTOR: We have heard a human estimation of our fellow entity. We do not know, nor may we question what may be the ultimate Divine decision. What we can do here and now, is set him/her free from any obligations to ourselves as we would hope to be forgiven in our future. Therefore be magnanimous and merciful. Forego what might be forfeited. Claim no compensation from our late Companion but the Blessings of a single soul sent forth to seek its immortality and true identity in living light. All in agreement with this action—signify your sympathy.

> [Signify by raising hand. When signs are received from those present, Preceptor lays a hand on coffin.]

PRECEPTOR: On behalf of those who acquiesce, and in the hope that every other human would agree, we hereby set you free, O ____[Name]____ from every sense of obligation unto us on earth. We renounce our rightful claims upon you, and release you from your debts that you may seek your spiritual destiny unencumbered by them. We shall not deter you nor detain you from your Holy Quest. Now do we commit you to the care of our compassionate Creator. May you be absolved from every fault and failing, for if we can find it in our human hearts to free you, how much more may be expected of our Maker the All Merciful? You are bound to us by nothing now except the Blessed Blood and links of Love alone. Henceforth may life be with you **as you will**.

> In the name of the **Wisdom**,
> and of the **Love**,
> and of the **Justice**,
> and of the Infinite **Mercy**,
> of the One Eternal **Spirit**,
> **Amen.**

PRECEPTOR: Blessed be the light of our origination.

RESPONSOR: Into which we shall again return. Amen.

PRECEPTOR: Our Spirits have been likened unto single sparks from one essential energy of **Light and Life.** As an earthly emblem of this spiritual truth, we will consecrate and kindle a memorial light which will become a covenant of consciousness between us and the especial soul whom we would hold in kind remembrance. Let us never call it back to mind in mortal form, but always as a shining one of spirit linking us with living light.

Be this illumination consecrated to the memory of the individual soul whose earthly incarnation was presented to us in the personality of ____[Name]____ Blessed be it both for us and all who seek the Sangreal together for the sake of truth.

> In the name of the **Wisdom**,
> and of the **Love**,
> and of the **Justice**,
> and of the Infinite **Mercy**,
> of the One Eternal **Spirit**,
> **Amen.**

[A close relative kindles flame and places light on coffin.]

PRECEPTOR: Who will be forthcoming as the guardian of this flame?

GODWARD: I will.

[Preceptor presents light.]

PRECEPTOR: Henceforward, bear it, share it, and revere it as instructed.

GODWARD: Let life preserve me for this purpose.

PRECEPTOR: Here we shall share the Sangreal with each other, acknowledging our kinship in the kingdom of creation.

RESPONSOR: For we are indeed each other, sharing selfhood in the entity without an end.

PRECEPTOR: Behold the ancient honored elements of bread and wine, with which we symbolize Communion of the Holy Spirit in our souls. May these mean for us the body of belief we hold in common as Companions of the Blessed Blood. Let us look upon them also as a corporate symbol of our late Companion, so that in partaking of them we proclaim our willingness to offer him/her a welcome in our hearts as long as we may live together in harmonious and wholesome Love. Amen.

[Over the bread:]

Sacred to us as the Sangreal be this bread. With it may we become the mystic body by which soul and spirit manifest with mind in this our mortal world for the salvation of mankind. Amen.

[Over the wine:]

Sacred to us as the Sangreal be this wine. With it may we become the Blessed Blood by which our beings are borne throughout the stream of life and Love in immortality. Amen.

Take, eat and drink this for the sake of the surviving soul and spirit whose abandoned body lies among us here and now.

[Quiet gong]

[Communion is only shared by chosen Companions normally, but no request for inclusion should be rejected without very adequate reasons. Music meanwhile. The last few drops are scattered on the coffin with these words:]

PRECEPTOR: Blessed be the Holy Blood we bear between us as a single soul beyond all bodies, enlivened and enlightened by the Spirit of our Sangreal forevermore. Amen.

As we memorize you with our minds, so may we harbor you within our hearts. Let Love lead us through life to **light** that has no limits, and thenceforth to *Perfect Peace Profound*. Amen.

Hymn

[Tune: "O God Our Help In Ages Past"]

1. O Peace Profound, the Perfect end
   Of whoso lives by birth.
   Be thou the firmest final friend
   Of those who leave this Earth.

2. May every lesson we have learned
   Point out our Paths to Peace.
   And mean our freedom fully earned
   When mortal life must cease.

3. Short of this greatest goal ahead,
   Let all of us be sure
   That souls whose mortal frames are dead
   Must other life endure

4. Through births and deaths let us live on
   Until we have outgrown
   All need to live, and be as One
   In *Perfect Peace* alone.

                                       Amen.

The Committal

PRECEPTOR:

> In the name of the **Wisdom,**
> and of the **Love,**
> and of the **Justice,**
> and of the Infinite **Mercy,**
> of the One Eternal **Spirit,**
>   **Amen.**

    Here will we relinquish these remains unto the elements which then return them for reuse by fellow forms of life upon this earth. This is nothing but an empty envelope which we shall leave behind us. Our memories of the surviving soul must cherish it with constant care within this world until we may encounter it more closely in the spheres of spirit.

    Therefore do not mourn the passing of a merely mortal body which disintegrates to dust, nor of a personality which perishes to fragments of forgotten earth existence. These are but transient, and easily rebuilt at every birth. Think of those things which are eternal, and extend us to an ultimate attainment of an infinite identity in *Peace Profound*. We give goodbye to flesh and form alone. Now we would say unto the living spirit that has left them:

1. Pass from us and make more progress on your pathway to perfection.

ALL: *May peace and power be with you all your way.*

2. Find and follow faithfully the light that leads you into life through Love.

ALL: *May peace and power be with you all your way.*

3. Seek the sort of spiritual self that should be yours as Deity decrees.

ALL: *May peace and power be with you all your way.*

4. Blend with the Blessed Blood which is the mainstream of our immortality.

ALL: *May peace and power be with you all your way.*

[Here the coffin is disposed of.]

[If in the earth:]

Accept then earth our offering of a human husk. Change it from corruption to continuance of earth life otherwise, and so complete the cycle of creation in our cosmos.

[If by fire:]

Accept then fire our contribution of a corrupt carcass. Change it for us into a revealing radiance that will disperse our darkness by the burning torch of truth.

[If in the sea:]

Accept then water our deposit of the dead within your depths. Change this for us into forces flowing around our world to nourish nature everywhere.

[As coffin disappears:]

**Farewell fading flesh.
Salutations, strong surviving spirit!!**

[Horn fanfare]

In the name of the **Wisdom**,
    and of the **Love**,
    and of the **Justice**,
    and of the Infinite **Mercy**,
of the One Eternal **Spirit**,
                Amen.

Closing

Companions, we have witnessed but the passing of a body and a personality back to the Source of Power from whence they came. Everything they represented will eventually return renewed into existence. Nothing has been lost but only altered. Now it remains for us to realize our own responsibilities unto the soul and spirit still existing as an entity. May we fulfill these faithfully, as we would want them obligated to ourselves by others in our turn.

Debts due from the living to the dead can only be discharged by dedication and devotion to a common cause, every aid available afforded to their nearest ones in need of care and consolation, and lastly by a right remembrance of them as they truly are in preference to their past peculiarities.

So much and more should surely be expected of those souls that serve our Supreme Lord of Light and Living through the Sangreal. Let us therefore pray the power be sent to us that we may put this into present practice.

> In the name of the **Wisdom**,
>   and of the **Love**,
>   and of the **Justice**,
>   and of the Infinite **Mercy**,
>   of the One Eternal **Spirit**,
>   **Amen**.

· Part III ·

Calling Upon Deity

· 9 ·

The Healing Service of the Sangreal

Introduction

All spiritual healers have their special individual techniques. Therefore, whoever acts as agent for the Inner Forces with this Sangreal Service of Healing has to decide for him or herself how to treat each case. However, the preliminary prayers, annointment, and actual contact with the hands are mandatory. Other items are at the healer's discretion, who must decide what to include or omit. Chants or hymns may be changed so long as any substituted do not contravene the Sangreal code of consciousness. The healer can be any member of a Sangreal Circle having such a charismatic gift, or from any other organization providing they are in agreement with Sangreal principles. This healer usually sits on the left hand of the altar and the Priest or Preceptor on its right. When in action however, the healer moves wherever necessary and is in control of the happenings.

Those to be healed should sit in the central seats while the healthy members of the congregation sit around them. Should the distance between seats be too great for holding hands, people may grasp the ends of each other's girdles. Sexes should be alternated as much as possible to make an even mix. Those to be treated ought to be kept to convenient minimal numbers. Management of stretchers or wheel-chairs calls for practiced handling, and if professional attendants are needed, the attitude of those outsiders should be ascertained in advance so that the presence of any contra-consciousness may be prevented. Provided that people are no more than open minded or entirely neutral, there is no objection to their attendance, but if they happen to be hostile or quite unsympathetic they are best excluded.

The rythmic chant is something very special, calling for some practice and coordination. Physical movements are slight and reminiscent of "dovening" while there is an element of spontaneity about them though the sonics are carefully synchronized. The idea is that of "pushing power" towards the individual being treated through the healer. The chant suggested, though wordless, is suited for general purposes. Specific sonics for treatment of definite diseases are a study in themselves and depend absolutely on exact experience by accomplished healers. This suggested chant consists of soothing sounds made by most mothers to injured, ill, or upset infants. By tonic Sol-Fa notation, the sonics are:

Do Ti La So
Do Ti La So
Do Ti La So
Fa Mi Re Doh

The special Sangreal symbols are those normally kept in the aumbries on the altar standards of individual temples having the blood and signature of the Sodalitarian included with them. If felt necessary, a photo of the person and specimen of hair may also be added. Here they are placed in a separate container, usually with a clear lid so that they can be seen, and placed somewhere prominent in the temple, often on the southern wall in a small shrine marked: "Pray for the progress of ____[Name]____ ." This is the wall dedicated to Michael the Solar Archangel of Healing, and the place of "Greatest Light." If and as healing comes, of course, they are returned to their proper place, or in the contrary case of death to the Shrine of Remembrance in the north.

The list of names is displayed outside the temple itself in an adjoining room with the usual notices. It is incumbent on members to read these and include them in prayers either individually or collectively. Names may be announced as either temple names or normal ones, or even both. It is proper practice for visitors to temples to perambulate the precincts and touch both Shrines of the Sick and the Dead, saying appropriate brief prayers for each. Those wishing to send helpful thoughts at the absent, should visualize the special shrines as a focal point for such projections.

The symbol of the most needy person for prayer intercession is normally placed on top of the others so it can be seen immediately. Otherwise their names may be written clearly on a card in front of the shrine.

In the case of an absent person, their symbol may be presented by proxy before the healer, and the proxy recite the prayers on their behalf, receiving also the annointment and treatment while holding the symbol and putting him/herself in place of the sufferer. Should a symbol not be available, a substitute may be made providing some linkage with the absent one, such as a photo or signature, is obtainable and attached to the symbol.

It should be noted that no definite directions have been made for offerings of incense. This may be at any convenient point if required, done in advance, or omitted altogether. It is absolutely optional, and it should first be ascertained if asthmatic or bronchial people are likely to be present, when consideration of these comes first.

What is of greatest importance is that every applicant for healing should be properly prepared in advance so that they understand the implications of everything, and realize what is happening the whole time. None should be allowed to participate in a Healing Service who are unaware of the principles involved. It should be particularly stressed that normal medical practice is included in the Sangreal system of healing. The Sangreal can use anything as an agent, or influence anyone, including doctors and surgeons. Healing may depend on a single thought being inwardly suggested to a doctor's mind, or some skilled techniques fitted to a surgeon's fingers. Whatever medium of healing that comes handiest is utilized by the Sangreal. "Miracles" come in all shapes and sizes and most of them are rarely recognized as such. Preceptors of temples are mainly responsible for seeing that candidates for healing are as properly prepared as if for initiation. Attitude is of the utmost importance, and if that seems incorrect, then no Healing Service should ever be permitted. Habitual attendance at Healing Services should be strongly discouraged, since they tend to devalue the practice.

Preferably a Healer should come from another group so that candidates are not known personally to him/her. This prevents the personal factor interfering with the process.

A record of results should be kept, but may be available only to the Officials of the temple concerned. Case histories should include any unusual happenings or unlikely events connected with the case being studied. It could be a good idea to appoint a specialist-student for this purpose, preferably a medically trained person prepared to consider alternative methods, specific chants, and the entire field of supernormal healing in general.

It is pointed out that death is the most complete bodily healing of all diseases, and is in no circumstances to be considered a total failure in the event of this happening with an extremely diseased person. Entire circumstances must always be taken into account, such as age, general condition, etc. Degrees of amelioration following a healing Service are also of importance.

Another thing to look for is the ability of the healer. Some are more successful in specific cases than others. For instance, a Healer might be successful with eyes, but not much else. It is well to know who is best at what, but it must be remembered that a healer only *mediates* or acts as an agent for the entire inner energy of the Sangreal itself. Actual healing depends entirely on the subjects' ability to absorb and apply this. None are ever healed against their wills. These possibilities should always be considered.

THE RITE OF HEALING

PRECEPTOR: Let us seek out the Sangreal with hope of healing.

> In the name of the **Wisdom**,
> and of the **Love**,
> and of the **Justice**,
> and of the Infinite **Mercy**,
> of the One Eternal **Spirit**,
> **Amen**.

RESPONSOR: So will we all with fervent faith. Amen.

PRECEPTOR: Blessed be the blood of our believing and becoming.

RESPONSOR: And sacred is our service in it since its being began.

ALL CHANT [usually in Gregorian style]: In distant days our Sangreal began with royal blood of Sacred Kings who shed it freely for their kinsfolk's sakes, from whom we have inherited its traits and traces in our times.

Our teaching tells us that this came at first from contact with a higher line of life than our humanity, and that such interbreeding caused a special strain of spiritual consciousness to influence the structure of our inmost souls from that time forth.

It has been said we are the children of our Father-Mother God, and if this be true indeed we are related by a common bond of blood with Deity and one another as an especial family of faith upon this earth.

Again tradition tells us there are many other families of faith upon this earth, each with its own inheritance and obligations to be honored and observed as we will uphold ours on this occasion.

For we are of the Western Inner Way, being bound together by the blessed Bond of Blood which is the Sangreal itself whose whole identity we share and serve as we invoke it here and now among us all through signs and symbolism proper for that purpose.

PRECEPTOR: Blessed be the blood behind our beings.

RESPONSOR: Which is our holiest heritage and purest pledge of Perfect Peace.

ALL CHANT: Because the Sangreal is that within our blood which makes us kings to rule ourselves with rightness, while we are also priests who sanctify and sacrifice our human lives in service to the Highest Holy One of Life and Light.

This is the mystery of Melchizadek the priest-king prototype of our Tradition who descended from Divinity directly bearing bread-wine symbols of the Blessed Blood. Hence he is our one Grand Master Figure to be followed in the gaining of our Greal.

Since unto us the Sangreal means maximum nobility and honor possible in human nature dedicated unto Deity for the perfection of our species as a people on this planet.

So will we also seek the Sangreal for the sake of health brought back to those that have it neither in their bodies nor their minds and souls among our mortal membership. For what we want with faith, we ask in action.

PRECEPTOR: There is no sickness in the Sangreal Spirit.

RESPONSOR: But only in the bodies or beliefs of they that serve it.

PRECEPTOR: Let us identify the influence that can combat calamities among our company, dismissing all diseases and averting accidents or other incidental illness.

ALL CHANT: The Sangreal is an entity composed of conscious energy supplied by everyone who serves its spirit. We of the West have built it by belief in our own destiny decreed by Deity because of blood relationship with its reality.

For many centuries we have constructed this most mystical intelligence which has attained an almost independent state of spiritual identity and an authority of action as our special archetype.

We cannot claim to have accomplished this without assistance from advanced and higher agents of awareness than our fellow humans have alone afforded. Thankfully do we acknowledge this, admitting our indebtedness to such superior authorities of inner action.

So we acclaim the Sangreal as our faithful Folk Soul, blood of our blood, life of our lives, consciousness of our creative concentration, epitome of all our esoteric energies, champion of our companionship, formator of our fate and worthwhile future in this world. Hail Thou true holder of our trustful hopes, and leader on our Western Way to light.

PRECEPTOR: O Blessed Being we think of as the Sangreal because of ancient origins, be conscious we are calling your attention to us.

Respond to this our recognition of the spirit which we share together, and communicate among us an awareness of your power and presence in our people.

Here we set your special symbol on our altar as a focus for our forces. Make this a means of making contact with our consciousness while we will pray for future health to be bestowed upon those people who present themselves with hopes of healing.

[Unveils and lights lamp in symbol.]

Behold the light behind the blood: become inspired by its illumination. Blessed be the bright beneficence that binds us all into a single soul which is the Sangreal itself.

ALL: *Hail that in us which is ourselves in it. We that are a fraction of this fullness, welcome here our wholeness everywhere.*

Sangreal Healing Hymn

1. Love Divine that didst begin us
   Hopefully thy Sign we hail
   By the Blood of Life within us,
   Be in truth our Sang Real.

Chorus: Sign of faith and fellow-feeling,
  Send us strength in times of need.
  Grant us now the gift of healing,
  Hold out hopes of health indeed.

2. Keep us in a state of fitness.
   Since we ask to aid thy cause.
   Let us live to work and witness
   All the wonder of thy laws.

Chorus: Sign of faith and fellow-feeling,
  Send us strength in times of need.
  Grant us now the gift of healing,
  Hold out hopes of health indeed.

3. Show us how we are related
   To each other as one soul
   Which is made and mediated
   By thine own essential Whole.

*Chorus: Sign of faith and fellow-feeling,
        Send us strength in times of need.
        Grant us now the gift of healing,
        Hold out hopes of health indeed.*

4. Thus if one of us is ailing
   In the very least degree,
   By so much the rest are failing
   To achieve full unity.

*Chorus: Sign of faith and fellow-feeling,
        Send us strength in times of need.
        Grant us now the gift of healing,
        Hold out hopes of health indeed.*

5. Therefore we that have sufficient
   Health ourselves will gladly share
   What we have with those deficient,
   Or in need of special care.

*Chorus: Sign of faith and fellow-feeling,
        Send us strength in times of need.
        Grant us now the gift of healing,
        Hold out hopes of health indeed.*

6. We thy single cells are praying
   For correction of disease.
   Set us straight without delaying
   Send at least some signs of ease.

*Chorus: Sign of faith and fellow-feeling,
        Send us strength in times of need.
        Grant us now the gift of healing,
        Hold out hopes of health indeed.*

7. Thou the Blessed Blood that bore us,
   Set us free from every pain.
   Cleanse us, cure us, and restore us
   So that we may serve again.

Chorus: *Sign of faith and fellow-feeling,*
   Send us strength in times of need.
   Grant us now the gift of healing,
   Hold out hopes of health indeed.

8. Let thy healing power suffuse us
   With its curative effect.
   Fail us never, nor refuse us,
   Lest we perish through neglect.

Chorus: *Sign of faith and fellow-feeling,*
   Send us strength in times of need.
   Grant us now the gift of healing,
   Hold out hopes of health indeed.

9. We who seek the Supreme Union,
   Merge our essence into Thine.
   Share with us the Great Communion,
   Mix our water with thy Wine.

Chorus: *Sign of faith and fellow-feeling,*
   Send us strength in times of need.
   Grant us now the gift of healing,
   Hold out hopes of health indeed.

10. Hear us, help us, send thy healing,
    To these needy in distress.
    Here we ask thee while appealing,
    For thy Power to come and bless.

Chorus: *Sign of faith and fellow-feeling,*
Send us strength in times of need.
Grant us now the gift of healing,
Hold out hopes of health indeed.

PRECEPTOR: O Sangreal, send us health that we may serve, since how can ailing people possibly assist with anything that aids our Western Way? We implore your intervention in our illnesses, so that infirmities may modify, improve, or even be averted altogether by the blessed healing of the Holy Blood.

Show us at least some reason for our sickness and supply a remedy or send us strength to bear them bravely. Direct our doctors and send surgeons skill to act as agents setting us in order once again that we may serve our future purpose on our paths of faith.

Best of all, restore us rapidly to a condition where we can continue with that work which is the Highest Holy Will behind our beings. We do not dare have hope of healing for a purely personal purpose, but only for the sake of fitness to fulfill our functions as appointed by the Being that began us.

So if it is your will that we should work with you O Sangreal Spirit, hear and heal us of our individual infirmities as far as faith allows this action. Dismiss diseases and send forth the sickness from our systems. Be the bloodstream causing energies of curative effects to circulate through everyone. Keep us in contact with whatever brings us benefits and will ameliorate our worst afflictions. Set us free from suffering and sadness. We are only sad because we are prevented by our pains from giving good and faithful service to our common cause within the West. Remove therefore this reason, and allow us to resume our work with gratitude for grace received.

Failing this, then show us how to serve while we are hampered and discouraged by our disabilities. Teach us to turn them into some advantage from a spiritual standpoint. Should humans have to suffer, let this not be lost, but somehow bring a Blessing as a bonus. Grant us good from every evil we endure with enterprising effort.

Such are the attitudes of our approach O Sangreal Spirit. Now we shall need much closer mutual contact. Who offers for this office?

HEALER: O Sangreal of Succor, may I make myself available as agent for the forces of your inner influence to act on individuals who ask for healing of infirmities and help with their affairs of health.

Even if I am unworthy of this work I ask permission to proceed because I so sincerely seek to bring your benefits and Blessings to those souls that suffer and request relief. So for their sakes far more than mine, accept me as a willing mediator, and work through me **What is willed by blessed and Divine direction.**

Come Companions and assist with every effort to restore these otherwves of ours to rightness for the sake of stronger faith among us all.

> [Here the Companions link hands around the temple looking inward at the ones awaiting healing in the center. The Healer stands before the altar on which the anointing oil is placed. The two nearest Companions on either side, each take an end of the Healer's girdle which they secure firmly enough to cause tautness. The sick advance, or are brought one by one before the Healer who anoints the forehead saying:]

HEALER: **Now may your need be satisfied by our most blessed Sangreal.**

In the name of **Wisdom**,
    and of the **Love**,
    and of the **Justice**,
    and of the Infinite **Mercy**,
    of the One Eternal **Spirit**,
        Amen.

[Now the Healer "lays on hands" as guided by inner inspiration, usually on the head alone, while the Companions sing or chant.]

AH	HA	HM	MM
AH	HA	HM	MM
AH	HA	HM	MM
MM	MM	MM	MM

[This is repeated rhythmically, accompanied with body movements which do *not* involve breaking of hand grips for the duration of the treatment for each individual. The Healer is in control here and is responsible for regulating action. The Preceptor and Responsor are usually the ones holding the ends of the girdle. The oil is taken from and replaced on the altar by the Healer separately for each individual. The sick return to their central seats after treatment.]

HEALER: With hearts conjoined, let hands be loosed among this company.

[Hand grips loosened, Healer turns to altar.]

HEALER: Thanks be unto the Highest Holy One that I have served the Sangreal in this Sodality. For any failures be my mortal fallibilities to blame, while every gratitude be given to that Blessed Power behind my person which so employed it as an agency of spiritual action. Praised be that power alone for anything accomplished.

> In the name of the **Wisdom**,
> and of the **Love**,
> and of the **Justice**,
> and of the Infinite **Mercy**,
> of the One Eternal **Spirit**,
> **Amen**.

[Healer retires or sits beside the altar.]

PRECEPTOR: But still our thanks be sent to those that make themselves a means of mediation.

ALL: *We all agree. Amen.*

[All make slight acknowledging bow to Healer.]

RESPONSOR: Let the Sangreal symbols of those souls which we will pray for be presented.

[Here the Sangreal symbols of the sick which have been preselected are offered up by the Preceptor at the altar. Those who can kneel do so.]

PRECEPTOR: O Spirit of the Sangreal hear and heed us. These are the special signs of those that have attended here in hopes of healing at our hands.
    Even as we classify them all together for consideration and inclusion in particular prayers for their improvement insofar as possible, so also do the same in spirit and select them specially for treatment by the only blood that holds our hopes of health and harmony among us all. Amen.

RESPONSOR: May our remembrance of suffering souls speed their recovery.

[Preceptor places symbols in special container which stays in permanent view of people.]

PRECEPTOR: Whoso would win the Holy Quest should question first his fitness to achieve this aim. As we are one, who shall attain while some of us are sick and are not able to continue on our Quest with confidence?

If the sick hold back the healthy surely it is best to help them win their way, because we will not truly gain the Grail while they are left behind.

Therefore, we should always say some special prayers for the afflicted, since this helps alleviate the burden borne by all that share a common spiritual cause.

This is the special symbol to be thought of as a focal point for prayer. [indicates it.] Mark and make a mental image of it for projecting inner potencies. Associate it always with these names now newly added to the numbers of afflicted needing prayers within these precincts.

[Here a list of the people treated is read out.]

Unto these and all that ask for aid from Sangreal sources, may a Blessing be most gladly given.

> In the name of the **Wisdom**,
> and of the **Love**,
> and of the **Justice**,
> and of the Infinite **Mercy**,
> of the One Eternal **Spirit**,
> **Amen.**

RESPONSOR: And also thanks that we have worked with honor.

PRECEPTOR: Be it borne in mind that miracles may not be known as such by those expecting some extraordinary circumstances. They might manifest quite quietly and secretly, having slow yet certain end events of healing.

Often this occurs through ordinary happenings which would never have occurred had not some spiritual agency been brought to bear with active will.

So do not demand a sudden answer from the Sangreal. Wait with faith a while to see what it will send, and afterwards request a reason if replies appear ambiguous or else evasive. Normal healing is a proper process, not a hasty happening of nature. Offer it a timely opportunity to operate according to the claims of each and every case.

Only at the end of everything accept whatever is the ordered will of the Almighty and adjust with that, for Deity alone decides the final fate of mortal man. Amen.

ALL: *So will we all. Amen.*

RESPONSOR: Nevertheless have hopes of necessary healing.

ALL: *With all our hearts we will.*

> [Here is included a brief optional period during which any particular prayers, addresses, or requested items may be inserted, or a thanksgiving hymn may be sung instead. This period should not be unduly extended and may be omitted altogether. At the end, or continuing from previous place:]

PRECEPTOR: Support and strengthen us O Sangreal.

RESPONSOR: So that belonging with the blood will bring us Blessings.

PRECEPTOR: The best of Blessings is harmonious health without which we shall scarcely serve the Sangreal effectively or energetically. Holding health remains our own responsibility to this extent. We dare not deny the laws of life deliberately and then demand some intervention of our Sangreal for freeing us instantly from what we well deserve by disregarding reasonable rules for keeping in condition. Therefore those who are unwell or otherwise unable to fulfill their functions properly, should frame petitions something in this style: O Sangreal Spirit, I am sorry that I cannot contribute my share of service due to disabilities and physical infirmities. For whatever willful conduct could account for this I ask forgiveness and request remission. Restore me back to rights by whatsoever remedy may seem most suitable, and set me straight to work that I may do my dedicated duty in this world with faith fulfilled.

So I sincerely ask your aid in this my present plight, not for my needs alone but mostly that I may become of benefit to others. Hence I hope to have sufficient health for future service sent to sustain me through this time of trouble and assure me of assistance afterwards in all adversity. Amen.

RESPONSOR: Remark those words and then remember them.

ALL: *So will we all. Amen.*

[Preceptor takes up lustral bowl and scattering brush.]

PRECEPTOR: Now be our blood a Blessing on the needy and a benefit to everybody else that seeks the Sangreal.

[Preceptor lustrates gathering, saying:]

In the name of the **Wisdom**,
      and of the **Love**,
      and of the **Justice**,
      and of the Infinite **Mercy**,
      of the One Eternal **Spirit**,
            Amen.

RESPONSOR: Shall we share the Sacrament of Silence that the Sangreal may manifest within our minds and souls.

[All adopt meditational postures. Preceptor says after short interval:]

PRECEPTOR: May we that work our mystic way of Western light in life become more worthy of the blood we bear, observe its ordinances in ourselves, and always honor it in other humans. Since we have been privileged to serve its purpose in alleviating our afflicted, let us here disperse with hope and due devotion, giving gratitude for any good that will accrue from all our actions.

> In the name of the **Wisdom**,
>   and of the **Love**,
>   and of the **Justice**,
>   and of the Infinite **Mercy**,
>   of the One Eternal **Spirit**,
>   **Amen**.

[Recessional of Officiants to music or in silence. Remainder may stay as long as they require and leave the temple either individually or in file later.]

· 10 ·

Sangreal Exorcism of Evil

Introduction

A Service of Exorcism is about the most serious affair which can be undertaken by any religious practitioner, and should *never* be tackled lightly, or without extreme necessity. In most Christian Churches, a written authorization from a bishop is required first, and this is a sensible precaution which should commend itself to alternative disciplines.

An Exorcism is usually called for because it is believed that a person or place has been afflicted by energies hostile to humans, derived from inner sources once termed "demonic" or directed by some distinct intelligence with malicious intentions toward mankind. Unless this presumption can be proved, or at least very sound and reasonable suspicions of its veracity, no Exorcism is called for, but a "Banishing Blessing" might possibly be in order. Some direct link between the subject of an Exorcism (person or place) and an entitized intentional evil must be traced before Exorcism could be of the slightest use. In other words, there must be intelligent or conscious evil involved somewhere. Occasionally, it must be admitted, the psychological effect of an Exorcism Service by itself can be extremely useful. Every single case must be judged on its own merits entirely, and full and ample justification for the Service provided before a single move is made towards its performance.

Most cases where personal exorcism is concerned come under two headings:

1. *Po*ssession, or a complete "takeover" of a personality by an invading "demon" or malicious entity. This "being" literally lives in the body of a victim and is fully conscious through it, behaving in many objectionable ways, displaying abnormal abilities, and acts in a manner which is totally alien to the rightful owner of the personality and its body. Such a case is more than extremely rare, and exceptionally difficult to deal with. Strictly speaking it is a task which only experts (and they are almost equally scarce) should attempt.

2. *Ob*session, or the annoying intrusion and persistent suggestiveness of an unwanted evil entity. This may happen occasionally or with varying degrees of frequency. This is not entirely uncommon, but can easily be counterfeited, for instance, when someone is trying to hide guilt feelings and so has invented a convenient demon to blame rather than assume responsibility for their own intentional actions. It is often more than difficult to decide whether a claim of obsession may be genuine or not, yet the authenticity of any case is the very first thing to establish. It should never be assumed that personalized powers like "devils" are responsible directly for unusual happenings without strong supporting evidence. Such evidence must be carefully weighed and considered before any decision is taken regarding a formal Exorcism.

To exorcise a person is no easy matter. Their conscious consent must be obtained first, and preferably that of close relatives. If violence is likely, restraining Attendants must certainly be present with means of sedation if needed. No advance sedation should be given, however, because full consciousness is necessary. It is advisable to check personal insurance first and make sure about all liability clauses. A disclaimer should be signed in advance by the subject and/or their nearest relatives. This last is a very sensible precaution, because a contrived lawsuit could be the motivation for requesting an Exorcism, and the issues might be very involved and complicated for those concerned. So it is strongly advised that a prior meeting be convened of those closest to the problem, and a final decision only reached after a majority vote.

For similar reasons, records or tape recordings of Exorcisms are at the discretion of Officiants, but could have legal implications. Nothing should be done without the full (and written) consent of the parties concerned. On the whole it is best that no Exorcism should ever be done except at the repeated request of the subject or his/her closest relatives. No Exorcism should ever be "pushed" or "sold" as an ideal solution to a spiritual problem. Needless to say, there should *never* be any fees demanded or specific charges suggested. No encouragement should be given to those who might desire the Service for the wrong reasons. If, for example, the subject is suspected of being an exhibitionist demanding attention, no Exorcism will be necessary. The guiding rule is that no Exorcism should be attempted until the usual remedies of medicine, psychiatry, etc., have been tried without effect.

There are all kinds of abnormal behavior possible during an Exorcism, and should be expected or at least prepared for in advance: violent behavior, abuse, screaming, attacks on the Exorcist, absolutely anything of an unusual nature. It may even be necessary for a sedative injection to be given and the Exorcism discontinued—in which case it should be abandoned with the final prayers, and resumed on another occasion. The subjects may spit, vomit, excrete explosively, or wet themselves. Alternatively they may only drool while dull and unresponsively withdrawn. All these possibilities should be considered, and if need be allowed for.

Most cases of possible invasion by "Dark Forces" are no more than dramatized expressions of purely personal idiosyncrasies. It is true that in some cases the sheer psychodramatics of an Exorcism alone will work wonders with those who need some excuse for being persuaded to deal with their own problems, and it could be permissible under those circumstances. Its gravity and importance should then be stressed up to the limit, and a tremendous play made of its production. Even so, it should only be an absolutely last resort.

Immediately after an Exorcism, the subject should be taken care of by those sympathetic and understanding enough to rally round and give comfort and counsel. No one should ever feel abandoned with no support. Aftercare is of extreme importance and the subject should always feel able to call for help. At the same time they ought to be strongly encouraged to resist re-invasion and only ask such support when they have come to the end of their own resources. On no account whatever should they ever be made to feel either an outcast or in the least unwanted because of an Exorcism. The whole operation should be regarded in the light of a remedial exercise applied as a customary manner of dealing with an emergency or necessity which could happen to anyone. Correct psychological handling is absolutely essential.

It is not necessary for a subject to be in a temple. Any ordinary room will do, preferably one which is least liable to damage (for obvious reasons). Usually the subject is sitting and is faced by the Priest and Preceptor (who are out of arms' reach). The other operatives are behind them, while any needed Attendants for restraining or sedating the subject are immediately behind him/her, or at least conveniently close. These arrangements will depend entirely on circumstances, and all such details must be fully arranged beforehand.

If a place rather than a person is the subject of Exorcism, the feeling of evil may be very strong indeed and a considerable number of people will be needed to perform the Exorcism (as many as are needed) before it feels "clear." The place should be treated as if it were a person, and the Sangreal seals (which can be of paper or plastic) affixed to its walls or wherever convenient. At the earliest moment afterwards, some religious Rite (preferably the Sangreal Sacrament) should be performed there, again preferably during the day, at first.

Both the Priest and the Preceptor ought to be experienced, of commanding presence, and very fit physically. No diseased person (apart from the subject) should ever attend an exorcism, and certainly no pregnant woman, or a menstruating one. Everyone present should have very sound ideas of what is going on, and all should certainly be fully adult and of good intelligence; no nervous or unstable person ought to be allowed, and positively none that want to take part "just for the thrill of the thing." Motivations need to be most carefully checked by those organizing the ceremony. The idea of "staging a show" must be avoided at all costs. An Exorcism is *not* an enjoyable exercise, but an onerous responsibility which should only be entrusted to those able to appreciate this properly.

It must always be kept in mind that the efficacy of any Exorcism depends entirely on the degree of Divine Energy that can be mediated by the mortals who offer themselves for the task. There are some evils far too powerful to be dealt with by any mere handful of well-meaning yet inadequate humans. Therefore it would be no use whatever for a very few people to try exorcising all the evil in the world. Possibly a place might hold more evil than a person, and could not be coped with by a small group of enthusiastic, but insufficiently potent people. God may be All Powerful, but the humans It must work through on these occasions have very definite limits indeed. All God can do is work up to the full extent of those limits, which may not be realized by the people concerned. Therefore it is always wise to decide beforehand whether a proposed Exorcism is likely to come within the competence of those attempting it. It may, however, be safely said that no one single human being is capable of holding enough evil in themselves which could not be countered by a concerted effort on the part of others.

It can scarcely be emphasized enough that the Exorcism depends for its efficacy on the strong application of intention which acts as a "carrier wave" for superior spiritual energies invited to use this means as a medium of action. All humans concerned are acting as agencies for the real "Inner Powers" which operate the workings. Let none suppose they could do it unaided or of their own volition only. All that humans are supplying is the needed leverage for the "Forces of Light" to act with. None supposing otherwise should be allowed to take part in the ceremony.

The Preceptor is responsible for taking charge of the conduct throughout, and making sure that everything is in a state of readiness. Checklists are advisable. It is important that all is conducted with calmness and quiet authority. No shouting or bullying is permissible, and it may be noted that oldtime curses and objurgations are absent. A voice may be strong and powerful, yet must never be raised beyond the point of complete control.

The idea of "getting a name" for the invading "presence" is quite important, because it focusses the forces down to personal levels where it is easier for human comprehension and confrontation. Persuading a person to "give a name" to their "pet demon" may be extremely difficult, and need not be pressed beyond a certain point. What is important is that the exorcising parties have something definite to name it. Inventing a name is often a matter of inspiration, and may be done in the case of a place in advance of the ceremony, but should only be written (preferably in big letters with a felt tip pen) on a stiff slip which has to be held visibly by one present until the moment of burning and "name deprival" comes. The ashes, when dead cold, may be ceremonially heaped on the hand of the subject or scattered anywhere if a place is concerned. A plate of some kind is useful for collecting ashes.

Under no circumstances whatever should an Exorcism be attempted by one individual alone. It takes a least four people to present an Exorcism of this type, which is strictly of a "General Purpose" nature, but may be modified or altered by the addition of prayers wherever considered necessary. The chorus of the hymn may be repeated wherever needed to cover a gap or emergency, or sections repeated by themselves as often as seems necessary. All Exorcisms are very individual matters, and have to be "played by ear" in every case. It is impossible to lay down hard and fast procedures which must be adhered to unvaryingly; flexibility is often required. At the same time, there are general priniciples which have to be observed, however the format may alter, and these have been followed in our example.

The idea of "leading the presence away where it can die down in peace" is not a new one, but is sound in theory. The Swordbearer takes the lamp (which is not the only light) entirely out of the place or room and sets it on a floor or low position, where it is slowly extinguished by turning it down, or pinched out with fingers, never blown out with breath. In a house the obvious place is a bathroom or lavatory where there are drains which connect with earth. Water is left runnng or toilet flushed symbolically. Outdoors, bare earth will do, preferably close to running water. The Swordbearer returns to the main party when function is complete. He has to imagine the diminishing entity following behind him all the way.

Incense is certainly permissible, and is the responsibility of the Thurifer to maintain at reasonable intensity. It should be of the "astringest" kind, sharp smelling, or reminiscent of hospitals. Robes throughout will be quite plain, though the Priest may wear an apron and cuffs. Any pectorals should be pinned to the clothing, and girdle knots securely tied in a "reef knot" that will not come undone. Great care must be taken that a subject cannot grab loose ends of clothing, or at least will have difficulty doing so.

At the application of the elements during the Expulsion, everyone should very strongly imagine the dissolution of the intruder back to its basics. The name should be dismissed from the mind as the paper burns. All present should point directly at the person being exorcised, and gesture accordingly. They too may breathe out expulsively at the appropriate time. The person need not be unduly wetted with the water element, but if some salt can be introduced into the mouth, that is always to the good. The possibility of being bitten might be borne in mind, and need not be risked unnecessarily. Salt may be then scattered on the person or applied however practical.

Everyone should know exactly what they are supposed to do in the case of an emergency, and every possible contingency imagined and allowed for in advance. It is a good plan to hold a "briefing session" prior to the Service with all likely to be present, and discuss everything with extreme thoroughness and detail. All present must be full participators in the ceremony, and no "observers" or "onlookers" allowed (any more than untrained people are allowed inside operating theaters). In fact, it might be a good idea to make a comparison between an Exorcism and a surgical operation, one being a physical cutting out of disease and the other much the same thing on a spiritual scale.

Minor forms of self-exorcism may certainly be practiced alone and positively encouraged among people, but full scale ones *never*. Also, the preparation for an Exorcism Service is important. Officiants at least should spend a preliminary period of up to three days of "prayer and fasting." A moderate vegetarian diet is usually sufficient, and smoking and alcohol are prohibited as well. Cleanliness of clothing and at least a bath or shower a day is called for, while some stricter practitioners consider a colonic irrigation may be helpful, and due attention to nails, hair, etc., is necessary. The room or place should be "tidied up" in preparation, too.

It is advisable to "brief" the subject in advance of the ceremony if this is practical. Sometimes it helps, and sometimes not, but no harm can be done in explaining what should or should not be done or might eventuate. Great care must be taken not to force suggestions on people which they might act on to simulate expected behavior. An open, hopeful mind is best, though unlikely in an Exorcism candidate.

Extreme care is needed in deciding whether an Exorcism is called for or not, and all psychological factors most carefully taken into account. Again and again it must be emphasized that only extreme cases call for an Exorcism. In the case of poltergeists, for example, Exorcisms have little or no effect as a rule, because intelligent entities are not involved. Such may prove the rule, again, in the event of supernormal happenings without definite intelligent direction. Exorcisms are *specific* procedures for use against evilly motivated energies, and if such conditions do not apply, then they are automatically ineffective.

Sometimes nothing obvious happens at all, apart from everyone feeling rather tired and drained, yet there is a shared sense that whatever was there of evil has withdrawn quietly without any fuss. So much the better, yet there may be a feeling of disappointment among some present in being "deprived of a show." Let everyone understand that "giving a show" is *not* the object of Exorcism, and removal of evil *is*. It is also important not to "relax your guard" after a ceremony of this nature, and a communal meal (without alcohol) as soon afterwards as possible is a good idea. Satisfaction without surfeit is the key here.

Exorcisms have been much abused practices in former times, and devalued and often ludicrous ones in more recent periods. Correctly used in proper circumstances, they can be of the greatest service, but otherwise they are no more than pathetic performances of absurd antics. They should be a demonstration of human solidarity against the worst which is able to enter us, and treated in that light are of considerable value, but never otherwise. Services should be undertaken with a serious and solemn air, read very deliberately and slowly with considerable emphasis on significant wording. Nothing should be hurried (except perhaps emergency procedures), and commonsense in everything is the greatest asset of all.

It may be remembered that Exorcisms per se are of very ancient origins, and every rational system of belief has them in some form or other, however they differ in practice. This present Sangreal adaption is typified by both faith and rationality, but is no more proof against misuse and deliberate misinterpretation than the rest. It is to be regarded as a format for an act of faith, and by no means as an infallible antidote to evil.

SANGREAL EXORCISM OF EVIL

[This is a general form of Exorcism for application to a person or place. If a person, then they will be sitting as directed with Preceptor and Priest facing out of reach, while others are placed appropriately or as convenient. If a place, distribution of participants will be as seems best according to circumstances. The Preceptor opens proceedings.]

PRECEPTOR: Companions, we have come to exclude evil from this person/place, at present known to us as ____[Name]____. Firstly we will free ourselves, for fear of offering it an alternative accommodation in us. Let us admit we have no personal power to do this deed, and so we seek the aid of our Omnipotent and Sovereign Spirit, who is Lord of Light, Protector of the Powerless, Ruler of the Righteous, Intender of Integrity, and Banisher of every baneful influence that harms humanity or acts against mankind with malice for malignant motivations. Hear and help us, Highest Holy One.

PRIEST: Thou that causeth Cosmos out of chaos, life and light from death and darkness, grant that good will grow while evil is extinguished so that holy harmony prevails in this particular person/place. Cleanser of corruption from the face of all creation, we are offering ourselves as agents of thine energy on earth which actively opposes everything and every entity devoted to destroying thy work of will which has been hallowed and set up for our salvation. If indeed we may be worthy to assist this mighty work, we here hold ourselves in readiness for what will be required of us.

PRECEPTOR: Companions, we ourselves must be made clean from such corruptive inner factors which affect our souls and acts of intent with an adverse influence. While we are acquiescent of the works of evil in ourselves how can we ever hope to push it far from other people? Therefore let us say sincerely and affirm with all our faith:

[All repeat after the Preceptor, clause by clause.]

I will truly try to work the holy will within me as a mortal human.
I am a champion of our spiritual cause beneath the banner of the Sangreal.

I am pledged to fight the powers of darkness as a duty of my faith in loyalty to the Living Lord of Light.

I intend negating every evil from my fallible and faulty nature.

Since I have not the sufficient strength in my own self for all this action, I here humbly ask assistance at the hands of Heaven and the hosts thereof.

PRIEST: Send us speedy strength O Thou the Source of every spiritual energy. May the power and presence of Archangel Michael be apparent and protect our purpose and ourselves from all the fearsome forces of the Dark Destroying Ones. O Prince of Peace, and Likeness of the Living Lord. Commander of the Heavenly Hosts and Overcomer of the Opposition. Drive your lance of light into the Dragon of Distressing Darkness, and defeat those demons which would drag us down into the depths of Hell with its infernal horrors. Vanquish every vice and evil. Support us as we struggle with you for supremacy against our universal adversary. Be with us Blessed Michael at this moving moment. Hear us as we call for help O Shining One of the celestial company. We need your knowledge and experience in evicting evil. Pour forth your power to free us from this pestilence. **Now! Now! Now!** We will mediate you Michael. Motivate and move us mightily.

> In the name of the **Wisdom**,
> and of the **Love**,
> and of the **Justice**,
> and of the Infinite **Mercy**,
> of the One Eternal **Spirit**,
>   **Amen.**

PRECEPTOR: Let us invoke the individual elements of life traditionally trusted as our liberators from the influence of evil. Flame and fluid. Light and liquid. Here will we hallow them and seek the service of their ancient symbolism.

[Priest lights lamp.]

PRIEST: As all darkness cannot quench the least of light, so may evil evermore be banished as the true illumination of our infinite intelligence increases in us. Blessed be this flame which marks the battle of mankind against brutality and beastliness from our first striving with a flaming stick until our last eventual liberation into living and eternal light.

> In the name of the **Wisdom,**
> and of the **Love**,
> and of the **Justice**,
> and of the Infinite **Mercy,**
> of the One Eternal **Spirit,**
> **Amen.**

PRIEST:[holding salt] Creature of salt that saves our bodies from corruption, symbolize for us the Sangreal factor in our blood wherewith our souls are saved forever by the faith we hold in our most holy heritage.

[casts salt into water in Circle Cross pattern]

With this water sanctified by blessed salt, so will we work to purify this person/place from filth of evil entities or forces. As ordinary water washes all our dirt away by dissolution, so may this special emblematic element help us to exorcise the malice and misfortune we must encounter and confront with needed courage and the knowledge that we are obeying our obligations to the Holy One whose own redemptive blood this symbol seems to represent.

> In the name of the **Wisdom**,
> and of the **Love**,
> and of the **Justice**,
> and of the Infinite **Mercy**,
> of the One Eternal **Spirit**,
> **Amen.**

PRECEPTOR: Whoso would quit our company from any fear or lack of resolution, you are here reminded of your last and final opportunity to leave us. Otherwise remain and do your duty by the Deity whom we have sworn to serve with honor.

> [bells]

PRECEPTOR: Cleanse and confirm yourselves according to our custom.

> [All here, starting with Preceptor and ending with Priest, pass their hands across the flame and wash their hands with a few drops of lustral, affirming:]

ALL: [individually] *Forgive my faults most Gracious God. With all my will do I reject the rule of wickedness. Witness my words and help me Highest Heaven.*

> [When all complete, Preceptor continues.]

PRECEPTOR: Assume your armor and proclaim your personal protection.

[Led by Preceptor, everyone says phrase with appropriate gestures. Gestures are in keeping with the words, such as touching head for helmet, chest for armor, etc.]

I assume the armor of my firmest faith in our Almighty One who promises protection for us on our Paths of Peril undertaken in a spiritual service. Hope is my helmet, and belief my breastplate. I am sheltered by a Shield that bears the Cosmic Cross of Light and Life. The penetrating power of my sharp Sword is point of purpose, while its edge is eagerness to sever spiritual evils from whatever they infect within this world. Upon my upheld breast I bear the mystic symbol of the Sangreal, that most Blessed Blood we share and serve. With my consciousness I will construct a circle of protection round my person which I pray will keep me in the constant care of my Creator through this time of trial and forbid the forces of the Wicked One to break its boundaries. See it symbolized with this good girdle which is worn around my waist and will remain as a reminder of the larger limits that encompass us with universal energies of loving light.

> In the name of the **Wisdom,**
>   and of the **Love,**
>   and of the **Justice,**
>   and of the Infinite **Mercy,**
>   of the One Eternal **Spirit,**
>   **Amen.**

PRIEST: Bless, O Lord of Life and Light, these boundaries we have chosen for this coming conflict. Let them be impregnable to every evil influence that might oppose the outcome of this issue as another truimph for the forces of thy total truth.

In the name of the **Wisdom**,
    and of the **Love**,
    and of the **Justice**,
    and of the Infinite **Mercy**,
   of the One Eternal **Spirit**,
         Amen.

[asperses and signifies limits of Cosmos by spreading arms wide.]

PRECEPTOR: Here begins our battle on behalf of holiness against the adversary whom we hope to answer and avert with all the strength of spirit and the Sangreal on our side. So strive—and sing:

[horn blown]

ALL: [Tune: "Onward Christian Soldiers"]

1. Move us mighty Michael, striving on our side,
   With the Cross of Cosmos, going as our guide,
   Darkness is defeated, evil put to flight,
   With the Sword of Spirit and the Lance of living Light.

Chorus: Out, out, out, all Evil, Out, out, out, all Ill,
    Go, depart, and vanish, with our words of will.
    Elsewhere in existence, find some place to stay,
    Here is no more harbor, therefore fade away.

2. Help us holy angels, grant us every grace,
   Drive out every devil, purify this place.
   We will act as agents, so provide the power,
   Pour it through what we will do, and help us at this hour.

Chorus: Out, out, out, all Evil, Out, out, out, all Ill,
Go, depart, and vanish, with our words of will.
Elsewhere in existence, find some place to stay,
Here is no more harbor, therefore fade away.

3. God of all our goodness, work with us a while,
Exorcise all evils, vanquish what is vile,
Be our benefactor, Lead us into Light,
Save us surely and securely, changing wrong to right.

Chorus: Out, out, out, all Evil, Out, out, out, all Ill,
Go, depart, and vanish, with our words of will.
Elsewhere in existence, find some place to stay,
Here is no more harbor, therefore fade away.

4. By the Blessed Bloodstream, we will go with God,
Ruling resolutions with a righteous Rod,
Doing every duty working every way,
At any plan perfecting man, providing we all pray.

Chorus: Out, out, out, all Evil, Out, out, out, all Ill,
Go, depart, and vanish, with our words of will.
Elsewhere in existence, find some place to stay,
Here is no more harbor, therefore fade away.

PRECEPTOR: Since in the first place mankind made it possible for evil to exist within this world at all and is the reason it remains here, the responsibility is also ours for its remission and eventual complete cessation in our course of evolution. This means that we must modify and alter nature all the time, not only in ourselves, but all around our beings. We can only do this with our consciousness directed by Divinity or otherwise inspired by evil influences from elsewhere. In other words, our best beliefs or worst impulses. What we do decides our destinies. Ours is the option. Out of the Eternal Energy we have conceived the concept of a good and gracious God Who is the benefactor of the best intentions in us. Now let us personify as nearly as we may, the malignant ill-intention present, and addressing it directly for its information say:

O Evil One, it is the will of the eternal in us that you should give up your grasp and go from this particular person/place peacefully without doing any willful damage on your way. If you are intelligent, you will perceive there is no profit in persisting with your presence. If you are witless then you will instinctively feel force expelling and ejecting you as we advance our Exorcism. All we ask is your continued absence from our company. Here, your habitation is unwelcome and unwanted. There is a proper place for everything until its universal ending. Even evil. Ask Abaddon, patron of the pit, for an admission. Go where you will be granted an appropriate accommodation. Here is not your natural home, so leave your lodgement and depart to darkness. Quit these quarters quietly and quickly. We will bless your banishment, or curse deliberate disregard of these commands. They do not come from us alone, but they originate with the Omnipotent Eternal One, whose word must surely be obeyed by every separate spirit manifested in existence. Wherefore you are given leave to go and live elsewhere.

PRIEST: By the Living One of Love and Light,
By the Blessed Blood of our belief,
By every Holy One of Heaven,
By every Liberator that has lived on earth,

[All respond after each line with **Get out and go!**, gesturing as they do so.]

> In the name of the **Wisdom**,
>   and of the **Love**,
>   and of the **Justice**,
>   and of the Infinite **Mercy**,
>   of the One Eternal **Spirit**,
>   **Amen.**

[Priest lustrates.]

PRECEPTOR: Now we would know you better by your name. How shall we hear it? Can we call you anything at all?

> [If the subject is a person, the name is demanded repeatedly in different ways and tones. If an answer is given, that is accepted and the entity addressed by that name until later in the Rite. If no satisfactory name is given, or it is a place in question, an invented name, which must be appropriate, is given with the formula:]

Since you will not name yourself, we choose to call you ____[Name]____ for our present purpose, and will write and give it to a Guardian.

> [This is done on convenient slip of paper, which must be held visibly for the rest of the Rite.]

PRIEST: ____[Name]____ be known to us as this which we have named you for convenience of our consciousness.

> In the name of the **Wisdom**,
>   and of the **Love**,
>   and of the **Justice**,

and of the Infinite **Mercy**,
of the One Eternal **Spirit**,
Amen.

PRECEPTOR: ____[Name]____ there is no point to your persistence, since we are determined to dislodge and drive you from possession of this person/place. We are persistent people also, and make no mistake that we will win, however hard our spiritual struggle proves. We will endeavor endlessly to rid our world of wrongs and wickedness including your intrusion at this instant. Delay not your departure, but desist and be dismissed without our further warnings or a frightful fuss.

PRIEST: By the Right of Raphael,
By the Might of Michael,
By the Grace of Gabriel,
By the Acquiescence of Auriel,

[All respond with gestures, **Get out and go!**]

In the name of the **Wisdom**,
and of the **Love**,
and of the **Justice**,
and of the Infinite **Mercy**,
of the One Eternal **Spirit**,
Amen.

[lustrates]

PRECEPTOR: Obtrusive evil entity ____[Name]____ are you after energies from our environment, and do you seek to steal the strength that should be ours by all the laws of life? What is it you want apart from our attention? Are you feeding on our forces and abstracting the resources which are ours by rights? Such is spiritual theft, that is prohibited by every law of life again. Be reminded that these laws are real and binding both on good and bad alike for government of a Divine Existence which extends in all directions. You are breaking these by being here at all, so we shall here invoke their intervention on our best behalf.

PRIEST:

By the Laws of Light, enjoining equilibrium of energies,
By the Laws of Life, enjoining every entity to earn its own existence,
By the Laws of Cosmic Compensation, that correct each critical unbalance in our universe,
By the Laws of Balanced Being, arranging all affairs with accuracy and authority,

> [All respond with gestures, **Get out and go!**]

> In the name of the **Wisdom**,
> and of the **Love**,
> and of the **Justice**,
> and of the Infinite **Mercy**,
> of the One Eternal **Spirit**,
> **Amen.**

> [Priest lustrates.]

PRECEPTOR: ____[Name]____, what appropriate penalties will be incurred for breaking or ignoring these injunctions? Inwardly, the spiritual sufferings inflicted automatically on any conscious creature contravening the commands of Cosmos. Outwardly, the break up of whatever type of body served the entity as an external shell for its formation. Distress, deterioration, then disintegration altogether. The inevitable end to every evil. Spiritual suicide. Such is the final fate of energies opposed to the Eternal One, whose will ordains the order of this world. You know there is no argument nor yet appeal against the natural forces that you face which will extinguish you entirely if you do not desist from present practices. Therefore—think—if you are able to assess alternatives. We will summon further spiritual aid for our support and succor.

PRIEST: Come celestial coadjutors and take control of this strange spiritual situation. Here is hovering an entity upon the edge of our expulsion. Afford it an alternative accommodation in some world where it and we may never meet again. Take it away and put it in its place we pray you. Restrain it, and remove it from this realm where we would work for peaceful progress. Prevent it from polluting our proximity, and segregate it from the spiritual structure of our human habitance. It is an invader and intruder which we do not want and will not welcome. Since you may communicate with it more clearly than we can, make manifest the meaning of this message to this alien, and advise it how it should depart with neither hesitation nor delay. Please enforce our Exorcism with your powerful presence, and prevail against our old antagonist with every energy available.

> In the name of the **Wisdom**,
> and of the **Love**,
> and of the **Justice**,
> and of the Infinite **Mercy**,
> of the One Eternal **Spirit**,
> **Amen.**

PRECEPTOR: Hear us again, O agency of ill-intention ____[Name]____. Have you considered changing your abode because it could be an advantage in your interests?

What have you to gain from hostile humans glorifying their God, provoking you with prayers, and activating anything they can conceive against you all the time? While you were unrecognized, you were unhindered or opposed in any way, so you might be malicious from the strength of secrecy. Now that you are known to us you are exposed to everything we have that helps us fight you from all angles. That is not a very pleasing proposition from your point of view, for it is profitless and gives no opportunity for gain but only leads to bitter loss of what you wanted. On the other hand, we have no plans to follow or pursue your flight to any distant destination. Once we are free from you, you will be free from us. We do not detain you, neither do we need you. Go!

PRIEST:

Because God bids you to begone ____[Name]____,
Because Archangels are against you ____[Name]____,
Because Reason rejects you ____[Name]____,
Because we will not have you here ____[Name]____.

[All respond with gestures, **Get out and go!**]

In the name of the **Wisdom**,
and of the **Love**,
and of the **Justice**,
and of the Infinite **Mercy**,
of the One Eternal **Spirit**,
Amen.

[Priest lustrates.]

PRECEPTOR: ____[Name]____ as our blood has antibodies which attack invading illness and bacteria, so has the holy cosmic bloodstream of the Living Lord of Light a counterpart. This is our Sangreal, a special spiritual strain with active antibodies which oppose all organisms threatening the health and harmony of our Eternal Entity. We are servers of that Sangreal, and also bear it in our blood. If you endanger our integrity, we also are the agents of your own extinction. Poison for poison in each other's presence, and in ours persists the potency of the Omnipotent. We are deadly if we do our duty by the Blessed One whose body we defend with all our will. Remain and you are duly doomed to ruin past any prospect of reintegration. You are the impurity it is our purpose to obstruct and then eventually eject from the Most Blessed Blood. Such is our spiritual obligation, and we shall fulfill it faithfully. We are at the end of warnings. Either exit at this instant, or be exorcised immediately. Part from us in peace, or persist in peril.

PRIEST: In the name of the Almighty,
In the names of all Archangels,
In the names of all the Archetypes,
In the name of normal Nature,

> [All respond with gestures, **Get out and go!**]

PRECEPTOR: ____[Name]____, you have here six seconds of our time to make your move. Strike them with the sword.

> [Swordbearer draws sword and strikes gong in second strokes, then stands with drawn sword in a position of readiness.]

PRIEST: ____[Name]____, **revert back to your basic being and retreat.**

> [Loud gong-crash. Priest lays hands on subject of Exorcism, usually head, or whatever is convenient. Others apply hands wherever possible.]

By the elements of life I banish and expel you from your fixity within this form.

> [Here elements are handed to Priest by the servers.]

Away with the Air.

> [blows sharply in face]

Flee from the Fire.

> [sets light to name-paper]

Wane with the Water.

> [lustrates]

End with the Earth.

> [applies salt]

Cease with the Spirit.

> [Makes sign and affixes Sangreal seal to wall, if place; around neck, handing on breast, if person.]

> [All respond with gestures, **Get out and go!**]

Now, ex-entity of evil, you are nameless and will drift towards your doom with absolute indifference. Be entirely banished, exorcised, and totally eradicated from this form forthwith prohibited to you since it is put beneath the sure protection of our Supreme Spirit and the God of Goodness, unto whom we give all gratitude.

In the name of the **Wisdom**,
    and of the **Love**,
    and of the **Justice**,
    and of the Infinite **Mercy**,
    of the One Eternal **Spirit**,
        Amen.

[Gong]

PRECEPTOR: If what is left of you feels lost, then look upon this light and follow it into finality. It will give you guidance as you go. Fix upon that light and follow where it leads until diminishment and darkness. Fare forth and finish. Fare forth and finish. Fare forth and finish.

[lowers voice until ending in whisper.]

[Here the chosen guide, usually the Swordbearer, takes up lamp and bears it slowly away to selected place, where it is set in position, then slowly extinguished. In the meantime, the Priest takes up the pace of the proceedings.]

PRIEST: Thanks be to all the Holy Ones that have assisted us until the end of this endeavor. So let evil ever be extinguished by the Blessed Light, being totally transmuted into innocent and active energy available to aid the ends of evolution. Since creation is the change of chaos into Cosmos, show us how to do the same on our small scale of destiny. Let our lives become an endless Exorcism, altering all beastliness to blessedness, faults and failings into faithfulness, weakness into worthiness, and everything of evil in our natures, into what we need that makes us better, so that we may bear it in our blood and serve the Sangreal in a finer fashion.

ALL: *So mote it be. Amen.*

PRECEPTOR: Let us also bear in mind that many evils are not easily extinguished, and while we may believe that we have beaten them, they smoulder secretly and can break out again into another conflagration. Vigilance alone will vanquish evil in the end. Wherefore be watchful and alert. Do not be disheartened if more efforts are demanded in eliminating evils that we have encountered. Consistent courage is the call of Cosmos in the face of fear and forces of the opposition. Do not doubt that we will ultimately win, but until then be cautious and continue with the work of wisdom. Let no laxity nor overconfidence obscure what we have done this day, and if we are requested to repeat the incident, then let all be ready to attend the action. Be a Blessing bidden as we ask it on us.

PRIEST: O God of Goodness in us, grant us grace and spiritual strength to struggle always against every evil we encounter on this earth. Enlighten us upon its early origins, and teach us often how we should distinguish what derives from mankind only, from the far more dangerous malice of what in former days was termed the Devil. Above all, teach us to transform the worst within us so that it becomes our best. Help us to harness every energy to serve this spiritual end. We believe this is the work our blood instinctively impels us to perform while living in this perilous and puzzling world. Now we need a special Blessing so that we may bear the burdens sent to us because we are alive and active in the service of the Sangreal.

> Blessed be the blood that lets us live and serve the light until the end of everything

in *Perfect Peace Profound*. May the might and mercy of the Perfect Power sustain us from this moment forth, forevermore.

In the name of the **Wisdom**,
       and of the **Love**,
       and of the **Justice**,
       and of the Infinite **Mercy**,
       of the One Eternal **Spirit**,
                  Amen.

[Priest scatters lustral.]

[All exit to triumphant music or singing of a suitable hymn. Subject of Exorcism usually between Preceptor and Priest, but always according to circumstances.]

· 11 ·

The Rite of Rejection

Introduction

This Rite is the formal excommunication of a member from any Sangreal Sodality Group. It must be stressed that this is *not* in any way a "trial," but a definite execution of an agreed sentence previously pronounced among a tribunal of inquiry into the conduct of an offending member. It is essentially a formal and final demonstration of decision, and that is all. There are four grades or levels leading to excommunication: 1) Suspension, 2) Sequestration, 3) Exclusion, and 4) Excommunication. Members suspended in level 1 are usually forbidden Temple services alone. Sequestration means Temple and social contacts are broken off. Exclusion means only the most formal associations are allowed and no personal names are used except ordinary surnames. Excommunication means no contacts of any kind are allowed, nor is the person to be mentioned further except as one who is dead and dishonored. Breaches of this code are to be reported, and offenders disciplined as soon as possible. Up to the last three exclusions, membership may be re-established after appropriate reconciliations, but the last extinguishing of the Flame means literally for the rest of a human lifetime.

The member in question must know the details of proceedings taking place against him/her, and be given every chance to attend any tribunals and explain or defend him or herself from accusations or assumptions. All questions are entitled to an answer, and normal procedures for courts of inquiry apply.

When a decision is finally reached, this must be communicated to the defendant, by letter if necessary, but is best done in the presence of witnesses. It could be done by presentation of a colored counter[8]: brown for Suspension, light grey for Sequestration, dark grey for Exclusion, and of course, black for Excommunication.

If the defendant wants to appeal the above decision, he/she has every right to do so, but there is a limited time allowed, usually one month, after which, if no appeal is received in writing, sentence is automatically carried out. Defendant is not allowed to attend this ceremony.

Normally, the whole proceedings are carried out by the Circle to which the defendant belongs, but they are responsible through the Secretary or other Officer for notifying all concerned as to what is happening. If they run a group magazine or other such organ, or subscribe to a joint publication, notice of the expulsion or suspension of a member must be inserted as clearly and briefly as possible. No specific reasons need be given. Full details must be recorded in the minutes of the meeting.

The strictest possible precautions are to be carefully observed so that absolute impartiality is practiced throughout the whole proceedings. Tape recordings are to be made of oral examinations and may be produced in evidence. Any evidence of purely personal dislikes or suspicions alone will invalidate proceedings. Conduct of defendant or criticism on moral or behavioral grounds alone is not admissible, unless it is criminal in a severe[9] sense. The sole criterion is attitude or declared outlook of the defendant in relation to the Sangreal Itself, which could include unreasonable treatment of appointed officers, depending on circumstances.

As many members as possible are to be convened in order to obtain a consensus of opinion, and the statement read out at the

---

[8]The Cord Herald Messenger of the operative group is responsible for delivery of this.
[9]"Severe" means murder, rape, arson, larceny, sodomy, gross fraud, etc.

beginning of this Rite is to be as brief and concise as possible, signed and witnessed by at least two senior Officers of the Sodality Circle involved. All proceedings are to be in conformity with normal judicial practice, yet condensed to absolute essentials. The dialogue takes place between the Pontifex and Preceptor with attendants as needed. This action may take place in a Temple with the Sanctuary veiled and seating arranged as convenient.

The fact that this Rite has duly been performed must be communicated in writing to the member concerned as soon as possible following the Rite, preferably by certified mail.

It is of course hoped that this Rite will never be needed in practice. The only way to ensure this is to make obligatory a sufficient period of probation prior to an individual's admission to the Sodality. Pre-admission tests and trials should be sufficient to promise fidelity and loyalty to the Sangreal concept.

THE RITE OF REJECTION

PONTIFEX:

> In the name of the **Wisdom**,
> and of the **Love**,
> and of the **Justice**,
> and of the Infinite **Mercy**,
> of the One Eternal **Spirit**,
> **Amen.**

Companions we are deeply in distress because the Blood is being denied and called into contempt by one who has a birthright claim to it and moreover is a member of our Sangreal Sodality. This is the termination of that trust misplaced, and we have met to finalize it formally. These are the circumstances and the situation.

> [Here a complete statement is read out by the Preceptor who concludes:]

PRECEPTOR: Here must we all admit responsibility for this regrettable rejection. Someone was the Sponsor of this soul, while others were Officiants at ceremonies which confirmed its status in the company of our Companions. Everyone encouraged it to work within our Western Way of Light, and since our special system is that of the Sangreal, this can be controversial if it is not comprehended absolutely as intrinsic to an individual.
    Here we have an instance of such incompatibility. Someone that has come to treat our concept of the Sangreal with indifference and incivility, and we believe by forfeiture of faith is utterly unfit for further service with us in this world. So here we have to take appropriate action for expulsion from our mortal membership.

PONTIFEX: Set up the symbol of this soul to act as focus for our forces and let the light be lit that represents our true relationship with one another.

> [Here the Sangreal symbol of the member concerned is produced in a prominent position. If possible his/her own initiation lamp is used, but if not available, a candle with a name attached to it will serve. When this is done, the Pontifex continues.]

The Rite of Rejection

Commence the Questions.

> [Preceptor addresses the symbol by the Sangreal name of the subject.]

PRECEPTOR: 1. ____[Name]____ do you believe the blood we bear is blessed?

ALL: *Not to our knowledge.*

PRECEPTOR: 2. ____[Name]____ are you spiritually satisifed with our Sodality?

ALL: *Not to our knowledge.*

PRECEPTOR: 3. ____[Name]____ have you held your obligation oath in honor?

ALL: *Not to our knowledge.*

PRECEPTOR: 4. ____[Name]____ have you done the duties which you pledged you would perform with either loyalty or love?

ALL: *Not to our knowledge.*

PRECEPTOR: 5. ____[Name]____ would you be willing to renew relationship with us?

ALL: *Not to our knowledge.*

PRECEPTOR: 6. ____[Name]____ do you sincerely seek to share our spiritual standpoint?

ALL: *Not to our knowledge.*

PRECEPTOR: 7. ____[Name]____ do you intend to work with us the Western Way in which you were initiated?

ALL: *Not to our knowledge.*

PRECEPTOR: 8. ____[Name]____ then is there any reason why we should continue to regard you as a welcome one within our company?

ALL: *Not to our knowledge.*

PRECEPTOR: Let us put this problem into prayer.

ALL: *So will we all. Amen.*

PONTIFEX: O Sangreal Spirit, witness well our words, since they are said in sorrow for their circumstances.
    We have found a fault within our fellowship and are attempting to correct this through the solemn severance of its cause within our company. If there be any blame to bear because of this, we take it on ourselves more than the member we shall sever. Why did we never know beyond all bounds of doubt his/her suitability for service in our faith? Is this failure really ours for faulty recognition of the facts or disregard of our obvious duties? Whatever may be at the bottom of this breach, we shall be critical of our behavior and correct it as we can when we are certain what went wrong.
    So far as we have failed we seek forgiveness. We sought to serve, but only made a bad mistake for which we suffer on this sad occasion. We are sincerely sorry this has happened and we hope to change our conduct for the future.
    Support us then, O Sangreal Spirit in this truly tragic task, and authorize our actions as we come to the inevitable end of our conclusions.

In the name of the **Wisdom**,
and of the **Love**,
and of the **Justice**,
and of the Infinite **Mercy**,
of the One Eternal **Spirit**,
Amen.

PRECEPTOR: While we must always be observant of the Blessed Blood in others and respect it for that reason, we are not obliged to need the presence of their persons in the confines of our sacred Circles. Especially those entrants who refuse to recognize or honor obligations they have undertaken to observe in our unique Sodality.
 Therefore in extremity we may exclude them from our mortal membership, and bid a ban on their attendance at our meetings. At worst, we can conclude companionship completely and entirely excommunicate them from our fellowship within this world. Such expulsion shall extend unto the limits of incarnate lifetime.
 Be it clearly comprehended by Companions that this severance is for the sake of spiritual health and harmony among us all, and no more than may befall our bodies if disease dictates the need. Moreover since we must learn how to live without whichever member should be sacrificed, so shall we have to learn the same without that soul we need to sever now from our Sodality. Are we completely confident we shall survive our operation with success?

ALL: *Such is so according to the best of our beliefs.*

PRECEPTOR: As need be known by all, dismissal is accomplished by degrees. The first by cutting of a cord and signifies a short suspension. The second by a solemn burning of the special symbol, lasting a lot longer. The third by blotting out the Sangreal name from books of membership which means it is indefinite. The final fourth expels entirely by extinguishing the flame to signify relationships may never be resumed so long as life exists. Here we shall be working to the (number)th degree of our dismissal. Are we ready to begin that banishment?

ALL: *Such is so according to the best of our beliefs.*

PRECEPTOR: First, have the facts been fully and completely cleared by due discussion among all concerned in this calamity?

ALL: *Such is so according to the best of our beliefs.*

PRECEPTOR: Has the subject of our present session had a proper opportunity to purge him/her self of opposition to our purpose and return to rightful and accepted conduct in our company?

ALL: *Such is so according to the best of our beliefs.*

PRECEPTOR: Then should we be to blame if we did not decide to do this necessary duty?

ALL: *Such is so according to the best of our beliefs.*

PRECEPTOR: So we have no known option open to us save to see this through with sadness. Apply the action of the first degree.

PONTIFEX: ____[Name]____ as your cord is cut, so do we disconnect you from companionship. Separate yourself and stand apart.

[Pontifex cuts cord. Gong is struck.]

ALL: *Alas, alas, we cannot from this moment forth contact our old companion.*

> [Here the degrees are continued as necessary until an ultimate is reached, when the concluding section is followed out.]

PRECEPTOR: Apply the second action of more solemn sequestration.

PONTIFEX: ____[Name]____ as human hopes have flared and then dissolved to dust and ashes, so ends your work with us.

> [Pontifex lights and burns symbol. Gong.]

ALL: *Alas, alas, our heads are heaped with ashes as we mourn our missing member.*

PRECEPTOR: Apply the action of a necessary namelessness.

PONTIFEX: ____[Name]____ let the name we gave in gladness now be blotted from our book of fellowship.

> [Here the name is blotted out by Pontifex.]

PONTIFEX: Nameless one among us now, revert to the remembered patronymic of your person ____[Name] ____.

> [Here the proper personal name is used. Gong.]

ALL: *Alas, alas, we can no longer call our old Companion by the blood name we once knew.*

PRECEPTOR: Apply the final fatal action.

PONTIFEX: As this flame is evermore extinguished, so is the individual it stood for excommunicated and expelled from us in full finality. Amen.

[Pontifex extinguishes Flame. Gong sounds.]

ALL: *Alas, alas, how much we may have lost to light.*

[Short silence.]

PRECEPTOR: So may we always save the Sangreal from faithlessness and blood betrayal by exclusion of its enemies from fields that we have sworn to safeguard.

ALL: *So mote it be. Amen.*

PONTIFEX: O Sangreal Spirit be the welcome Warden of our Western Way by blood salvation. Strengthen our security by making us more watchful and alert so that we shall be well aware of anything that weakens, wastes, or wantonly erodes your energy to any definite degree.

As we have here most duly dealt with one occasion, so may others also come to cope with whatsoever they think constitutes a contravention of the laws protecting your pure light.

Be a benediction bidden upon all we undertake or may yet do in the defense of our most Blessed Blood.

In the name of the **Wisdom**,
and of the **Love**,
and of the **Justice**,
and of the Infinite **Mercy**,
of the One Eternal **Spirit**,
Amen.

[Four gavel knocks, and the session disperses.]

· 12 ·

The Service of Commination

Introduction

A "Commination" means a denunciation or threat. In the spiritual sense it indicates a specific denunciation of some definite evil, plus the threatening of evildoers with Divine retribution. This is justifiable when extremities of evil become too great for normal human beings to tolerate with equanimity because they would feel guilty of complicity if they did *not* invoke the Deity to intervene in certain cases of human barbarism or injustice. This Rite should **never** be used for personal, trivial reasons, though it may be used on individual accounts in extreme instances if sufficient warrant applies. There would have to be very good and grave reasons however for working this Rite on purely personal grounds. Though it conceivably could be carried out by a single operator, it would be unlikely to prove very successful as a one person performance.

It is assumed that the Rite will be carried out in response to some specific evil worked in this world at some definite time and place by identifiable or classifiable people involving moral or material injuries to other humans or serious detriment caused to spiritual principles directly concerned with the Sangreal. In other words there has to be a positive "target/aim" which is objectively discernible. It also takes for granted that there will have been enough prior notice of the Rite for all involved to have thoroughly thought out all its implications, possibly discussed it among themselves, and reached definite conclusions and decisions about it. Again, under *no* circumstances should this Rite be worked "just to see what happens" or for any reasons except the most serious. It should be regarded as an extremity to be used only when all human efforts by themselves have proved ineffective, and nothing except a direct Divine intervention seems likely to restore unbalanced conditions among humanity.

The purpose of this ritual is first to demonstrate entire disapproval of a specific evil, thus clarifying the position of its workers, and second to manufacture a mystical means of dealing with it by designing a "thought-form" or "telesmatic image" to combat the evil. This is a carrier of consciousness which is pre-set and tuned to specifications which could at least ameliorate whatever situation or circumstances have caused a deep enough reaction to call for its creation.

In oldtime theology, it was supposed that the Deity intervened in human affairs through the media of "angels," or agents which were special creations of the Divine Mind, and specifically charged to carry out commands according to classified categories. They would do precisely what they were designed for, and nothing else. They were particularized projections of Divine Power. To some extent we are doing this all the time with our modern electromechanical "messengers" made to carry out our intentions. With this Rite we are doing no more than making a "messenger" without physical mechanisms of any kind, and constructed of pure consciousness alone. If it is reminiscent of projecting a rocket, that is only in accord with our own century. Ancients would have mounted their equivalents on horses, formed them with wings, or anything suggesting speed and energy.

This is definitely not a ritual for the inexperienced. All participants should have at least minimum experience and practice at "thought-forming," and everyone present should be in enthusiastic agreement with the purpose of the Rite itself. Although it is almost self-explanatory, the following points should be noted:

1. The "working symbol" on the altar may be anything at all that evokes the Rite's purpose most completely in the minds of

beholders. This may be a photograph or composite, including maps, diagrams, figures, or any pictorial or symbolic representation of the reasons behind the Rite. It has to be prominent, not inconveniently large, neat, and above all effective. It may need a special stand or "monstrance" for its presentation.

2. When first forming the "angel," all should imagine an energy stream flowing from themselves at the solar plexus towards the space immediately in front of the altar. The Priest is on the right (black) pillar position and the Preceptor on the left (white). The energy flow should be visualized as an amorphous mass which the Priest stirs with the sword deosil. The general principle is to start from the center with small movements, and go on to larger ones making an upright ellipse outlining the area of the finished image. Style of gestures change with its development.

3. Note that the "inner essential nature" of the angel is made first, and the external appearance formed and fitted afterwards. The Priest indicates all points with the sword, working sometimes like a sculptor with a statue, and sometimes like an artist with a brush. For instance, the eyes could be two quick stabs with the point, and the mouth a short line—anything to give an impression of *formation*. In old times it was believed that supernatural beings could build their bodies out of suitable smoke, hence the incense association at this point. In fact, after the Thurifier has censed the spot where the angel is being made, he will leave the thurible at the edge of the altar where it will continue to send up smoke. Care must be taken here in arrangement, and the thurible may be left until the end of the Rite. Incense should be a "Mars/Jupiter" combination of sharp and sweet, but whatever is deemed suitable may serve well enough.

4. Everyone should visualize the angel appearance coincidentally with the script, which has to be read slowly and emphatically at this point and may be repeated at significant points in two tones of voice—tenor and baritone, if possible. As the points are made, the Priest will outline them with the Sword. A light flexible sword is advisable for that reason. The angel should be seen from whatever angle it is viewed, but as it is made to turn and move in a complete circle on its axis, it should be seen to do this as indicated by the point of the Priest's sword again. This movement too may be

repeated more than once with musical accompaniment. It is unnecessary to visualize wings on modern angels—they are jet-propelled. The clothing however may be the traditional gown and cloak.

5. The "target" is a fairly large Circle Cross like a gun sight, or maybe just a plain Circle two feet in diameter. It is either of metal, or painted with metallic paint. It may be about an inch wide or less. It will normally be on top of a stand at about six feet high, and stand close to the wall in an exact position so that it lines with the altar and the literal place on earth in question. Careful compass bearings have to be taken here, though an approximation will serve. A refinement here would be a destination card and mileage clearly readable, just below or above the Circle.

6. The name of the angel is most important, and the Priest is responsible for this item. It may be an acronym connected with the mission, or anything short, emphatic and suggestive of it. Alternatively or additionally the angel may be given a number corresponding with that identifying it in the "Bidding Book," which is a handwritten record of the mission, instructions, and anything connected such as date, time, persons present (Lodge names only), etc. Subsequent associated happenings may be added later. This book is normally kept in the Temple in some perpetual place, and the Secretary is normally responsible for it. It is *only* for use in ceremonies similar to this one in intention.

7. Just prior to "launching," everyone should apply all the inner pressure they can via the symbol on the altar behind the angel which may be imagined as being in a poised position. This pressure builds during the countdown, and when the moment comes, gongs bang, horns blow, and an explosion may be made with a starting pistol, then all follow the flight of the angel like a rocket through the target towards its destination. It may be noted that the general call of *Aaawayyy* is another rendering of IHVH.

8. After the "launch," there should be a feeling of accomplishment but still a realization that contact has to be kept up with the angel by sending thoughts and prayers after it from time to time, always being careful to think of it by name and/or number. There may be a brief interval for private meditation here if desired.

Music or sonic effects can be brought into this Rite at appropriate moments, but great care is needed for selection, because a wrong choice can ruin the psychodramatic effect completely. The dress is "working order:" Aprons, cuffs, and pectorals for Officers, habits and girdles for others.

It must be remembered that eventually when it is felt the angel can serve no possible further purpose on its specific mission, it must be recalled and returned to its source of origin by a "reabsorption" process, and a due record be made in the "Bidding Book." The working principles of "angel-making" can of course apply to other procedures and are worthy of attention and study for future use.

THE SERVICE OF COMMINATION

PRECEPTOR: Companions, there are things we cannot bear within this brutal world without revulsion and reproach. Nor are we required to be resigned or think that they could possibly conform with any will proceeding from a God of Goodness. what we have in mind this moment is an opposite occurrence, evidently evil, and the worst of what we can expect within this wicked world. It is [here the event is described succinctly].

Such is the way we see it, so we would invoke the compensation clause within our laws of life to deal with it directly and decisively according to the rules of retribution as defined by all our best beliefs because of our Beloved Blood. Put up a prayer of purpose.

PRIEST: Listen, O Thou Lord of Light unto our observations on this deed of darkness done within this wretched world. We are calling Thine attention to it through our consciousness and our abhorrence of it. Perceive this instance of an ill-intentioned action in particular, and punish whosoever perpetrated it with whatsoever is appropriate and if possible immediate. We are horrified that such a sinful thing could be connected with humanity, and we are also sorry and ashamed to share that same humanity with those that work such wickedness. Woe unto them upon whom will descend the wrath of thy Divinity. Deal with them as they deserve and smite them swiftly so that they will suffer some of what they have inflicted on the innocent and helpless victims of their viciousness. If vengeance is Thine own, then we invoke it now and need to know the truth of such a saying. Show us Thy Strength, Thy Justice, and Thy Judgment. As Thou art Almighty—**act.** We will witness the effects of Thine exerted energy upon the evil creatures we condemn to thy condign consideration. If we insist upon requesting retribution for their frightful actions and intentions, do Thou, O Divine One, send the special power for its performance through those mortal and material agencies that are made most available. Amen.

ALL: *So mote this be. Amen.*

PRECEPTOR: We will admit that evils on this earth are multifarious and more than any man can count. So why should we select this special specimen for focussing the forces of our Sangreal sword? All we may answer is that we have suffered a degree of shock which makes us move in the direction of Divinity and angers us into this action. We are driven to our depths almost in desperation, and demand that Deity itself should be involved in dealing with this wickedness. It is more than we may tackle on our own. Set out the symbol signifying our object so that we will see and sense it.

> [Here the symbol is set on the altar. It may be anything that serves to sum up the situation. Possibly a photograph, or any composite that evokes mental and spiritual energies from understanding viewers.]

PRIEST: May this make an adequate and factual focus for our forces. Let this act as a lens that concentrates our consciousness according to the laws of light. Further, may it form a means of making contact with the energy we must evoke effectively if we intend to raise it for retributary reasons.

> In the name of the **Wisdom**,
> and of the **Love**,
> and of the **Justice**,
> and of the Infinite **Mercy**,
> of the One Eternal **Spirit**,
> **Amen.**

PRECEPTOR: Retribution is an insufficient reason for this Rite. Full recompense must also bring rewards and benefits unto the innocents who may have suffered injuries and ills in this appalling instance of injustice. Punishment alone is purposeless unless clear compensation comes to every victim. Put this properly in prayer.

PRIEST: O Eternal Energy of Equilibrium for whom we have no name except our Blessed Lord of Life and

Balance of our Beings, answer this appeal to Thee as our Almighty Cosmic Cause. Thou art the requiter of our wrongs and the rewarder of our wronged ones by a reciprocally balanced action. Each event invokes thine intervention automatically according to thy law of level living. Here we have an instance in our world which we consider calls for such redress and recompense. Condemn and compensate with one awarding act, O Mighty Maker of Mankind. Set this situation straight and help the honest who are hurt as well as visiting thy vengeance on the wicked that have hurt them. Project thy power into this purpose therefore, and then act with all thy working will. Amen.

ALL: *So mote it be. Amen.*

PRECEPTOR: It has been said that nothing needs be just because God wills it, but it is willed by God because that thing is just. That is a fundamental of our faith, and justice is our general hope for the humanity we share with other souls. This is all we ask for, justice that will justify our invocation of it in this instance. Moreover it must also prove applicable to all that place themselves at its Divine disposal. Whoso judges will be judged and tried in turn, and if unjustified will bear the blame for a presumptuous prayer. What we invite on others we invoke upon ourselves with interest if it is unfairly asked and maybe motivated out of purely personal pique or other wrongful reasons. Has this been considered carefully, and will we risk the wrath of an unjustly goaded God?

ALL: *We are acting with an innocent intention out of righteous wrath ourselves. God grant us guiltlessness and give us grace.*

PRIEST: O Perfect Power, we would not trouble Thee with trivialities, but this to us is an important burden which we cannot bear without communicating our concern that Thou wilt deal with it as thy Divinity demands. We are acting in good faith and guided by the formulae which we have found and try to follow for the best that we believe of our Beloved Blood. All we ask Thee is to activate our innermost intentions on these outer living levels. Amen.

PRECEPTOR: It once was said with truth that God hates sin yet loves the sinner. Let this lesson give us grace to order this occasion honorably. Unsheath the upright Sword that symbolizes action and devoted duty to the Deity.

[Priest unsheaths sword and upholds it.]

PRIEST: May might and mercy be upheld and put in practice with united wills.

ALL: *So mote it be. Amen.*

PRECEPTOR: On all occasions when the Old One manifested anything to man, it was by means of blessed messengers or angels sent especially to execute its individual task. Let us here help our Creator to construct an angel with our combined consciousness. Concentrate upon the merits of both might and mercy which will build this being. Place it also under the protection of a Senior Spirit. So shall force and form be molded by our minds and souls into the image we intend to work our will. See this being built up before the altar which it faces as we make it mentally. Since all such conceptions come from archangelic archetypes at first, we surely should approach those that are most appropriate to aid this action.

PRIEST: Archangel **Khamael**, we ask you to supply the sword, and **Tzadkiel** the shield with which to arm the angel we create together with our combined consciousness. Guide it, Godlike **Mikal** with your mighty lance of light and let it work the will within us all. Be this temple a most willing womb which may indeed be impregnated through imagination by a spiritual seed imparting energy into the egg we offer as an ovule of concerted consciousness. **Khamael! Tzadkiel! Mikal!** Come to this conception and invest it with authority.

> In the name of the **Wisdom**,
> and of the **Love**,
> and of the **Justice**,
> and of the Infinite **Mercy**,
> of the One Eternal **Spirit**,
> **Amen.**

PRECEPTOR: Conceive, gestate, then bring to birth this gift of a creative God.

[Priest gestures with sword.]

PRIEST: Creature of consciousness first be conceived then born amongst us as an angel in appearance, bearing might and mercy as your mission. This is the generation and gestation of your inner nature. Later we will build your body by belief and our imagination acting in this incense of intention which we offer for your focus into form.

[Incense offered and allowed to arise before altar.]

Let the elements of life themselves empower you with their potency, providing you with energy as their effective agent. By the air, let loose a blast or breathe a blessing.

[Air offered by breath.]

From the fire be fearsome foe or welcome warmth.

[Censer shaken.]

With the water, overwhelm or cleanse caressingly.

[Water sprinkled.]

Entering on earth, eliminate its evil ones, or else enjoy its offerings.

[Salt sprinkled.]

Bring retribution to the bad and ruthless, but towards the good and gentle be most gracious and magnanimous, most of all to those that have been wronged or ruined where we will show you with our pointed prayers, then send you there as an avenger and an instrument of our intentions. Exist as energy. Live as law. Persist as power. By our blood you are becoming as a blessed angel or extinguisher of evil. Be both as we advise and Deity directs. Come to co-consciousness and know your nature.

> In the name of the **Wisdom**,
> and of the **Love**,
> and of the **Justice**,
> and of the Infinite **Mercy**,
> of the One Eternal **Spirit**,
> **Amen.**

PRECEPTOR: Fix now the necessary form and features that we may perceive and make them properly according to the ancient process. All should see these from appropriate angles of their present situations.

[This means that all present should visualize the appearing angels as facing the altar from their own viewpoint. Thus few will see the actual face, while others only see its back or side angles from their places. When the angel-concept turns and moves, they should then visualize according to following instructions.]

PRIEST: Behold a being that is truly awful and angelic in appearance. Coming clear as it condenses. Robed in red and blue. Bound with a waistbelt wrought of brass and silver steel, from which there hangs a wallet and a scabbard for the sword he holds aloft in his right hand. The wallet carries compensation for those righteous ones that have been wronged. The sword will smite the sinners in whatever way is suitable. On his left arm is bound a buckler or solid shield for the protection of all threatened people. This angel's face may be formidable or amiable according to the angle of observance. His hair is blondish brown and he has sunburned skin. He also has a golden circlet on his gallant head with certain symbols that describe his duty as appointed angel of our action. His eager eyes are piercing and peculiar, one being blue, the other amber. They are wide apart and wonderful. His lips are long and fully formed, with aquiline and noble nose above them. His chin is cleanly firm and forceful. Finally his feet are shod in sandals of the stoutest sort with wings to symbolize their swiftness. Altogether he is awe-inspiring and assuring. We will make him move and turn himself around towards all here assembled for an inspection through imagination. See him as he slowly turns upon his axis in a circle sunwise. Is he not magnificent and marvelous? Now note how he relaxes and returns his sword to scabbard, waiting for our orders with an open attitude while facing us from altar front.

Those orders are requested rapidly since he stands ready to receive them.

PRECEPTOR: Before this may be done, we must discern and know his duty-name. Inquire it or invent it.

> [Pause.]

PRIEST: The needed name is ___[Name]___. Give it good greeting.

ALL: *All hail ___[Name]___. Harbinger of hope and action.*

> [Hailing signs.]

PRECEPTOR: Now charge the creature competently and with necessary confidence.

PRIEST: [Gesturing]___[Name]___. You will keep in contact with our consciousness, and go to [location and description] on this earthly globe. There you will communicate with others of your kind and aid their action, or will work alone if no alternative is offered. Pursue and punish perpetrators and whoever is involved in instigating this swift summary of ill and evil.

> [Here the details are summarized briefly but clearly by the Priest.]

Also help all humans that are hurt or harmed in this affair and thus become their benefactor with our blessing. Take up this twofold task herewith and then accomplish it according to the will that we have placed within you and the power provided for that purpose. Prepare now to depart and do your duty. If in doubt, you may return and read your designated orders written in our Book of

Biddings here set out for you to see and mark the memory.

[Book displayed and placed prominently by the Priest.]

Otherwise your orders may be found from any of our minds. There you may read and afterwards remember them. Now take up your needed tension.

> In the name of the **Wisdom**,
> and of the **Love**,
> and of the **Justice**,
> and of the Infinite **Mercy**,
> of the One Eternal **Spirit**,
> **Amen.**

PRECEPTOR: Are we all in absolute agreement?

ALL: *We are one in will.*

PRECEPTOR: Then by the Blessed Blood begin, pray that power will be provided for propulsion. Put up a pointer target to project this angel into action and above all keep direction of departure free and clear from obstacles.

[Here a projector symbol, frequently a Circle Cross, is lined up with the directional aim of intention at the closed edge of the temple. When this is set up, the Priest prays:]

PRIEST: O Primal Power provide the pressure to project this angel ____[Name]____ on its appointed path of purpose. Send it success. At least let it contribute something to the spiritual cause of its construction. Whatever happens may it always work thy holy will and manifest thy might among mankind. Accept it also as an agent of our will we offer Thee in Sangreal service to thy Blessed Blood. Now let us launch it in the name of light. Amen.

PRECEPTOR: Compress all consciousness in readiness for the release. Aim from the altar through the target, following the flight with faith. Now commence the countdown with directions.

PRIEST: ____[Name]____ be alert and bring yourself to act according to instructions and intentions. Make yourself a missile with a mission. Though you have a human manmade motive, yet do nothing that is not decided by our Deity and sanctioned by our Sangreal. Accept alone the guidance given you by God. Obey our orders only insofar as they accord with absolute authority and infinite intelligence. That is your final factor to control your conduct. Follow then this countdown and fare forth on its conclusion. **Ten. Nine. Eight. Seven. Six. Five. Four. Three. Two. One.**

[knocks at each]

Go with God and Act!!!!

[Gong, horn, knock, explosion, noise.]

ALL: *Aaaaawayyyyyy.*

[Appropriate action and music.]

PRECEPTOR: All action is accomplished on our part, and now we need to pray that its performance will result in peace restored and hoped-for harmony established on this earth.

ALL: *With all our wills, Amen.*

> [Sit or kneel, Preceptor and Priest remain standing. Priest sheaths sword or leaves it pointing in direction of angel flight.]

PRIEST: Grant O gracious God, that only good may come from this our move of commination. Since neither Thou nor we can possibly condone events of evil in this perilous and wicked world, we hereby hope for thine approval of our act. Send thy full support for what we seek as the result of this concerted Rite with reasoned consciousness and fervent feelings. Work with our artificial angel **what Thou wilt**, condemning what is wrong, while yet consoling all the wronged and woeful ones. Bring everything to balance and equate erratic energies. Be Thou the Blessing of our blood and all that we believe in as we live and learn thy laws of Love. If Thou chastiseth those Thou lovest, we will Love our enemies when Thou wilt also chastise them in turn. Do this then O Divine One and deserve our deep devotion. Amen.

ALL: *So mote it be. Amen.*

PRECEPTOR: The need is now to send support and backing to our angel agent by believing in it and effecting its efficiency through thought and private prayer. Remember it must be recalled when its commission is completed and returned to where it came from in the first place. Let us be glad we have been given grace to serve our Sangreal with honor, and glory be unto the Blessed Blood.

PRIEST: With duty duly done, let us depart and learn to **live in light.**

In the name of the **Wisdom**,
    and of the **Love**,
    and of the **Justice**,
    and of the Infinite **Mercy**,
    of the One Eternal **Spirit**,
          Amen.

[Here the Exeat Lux may be sung by all, or departure made according to convenience.]

· 13 ·

The Rite of Reproach

Introduction

This unusual Rite is a modern reconstruction of a very ancient practice which is becoming almost a standard technique with many contemporary psychiatrists. It is generally known as "catharsis," literally purgation or "getting it out of one's system." It is necessary for good spiritual as well as ordinary physical health.

Throughout history humans have found that no matter how good, pious, or religious they try to be, life still goes wrong for them and disasters of all kinds continue to hit where it hurts most. Often the better they try to become, the worse Deity or fate seems to treat them. Adjusting themselves to this experience presents a most difficult problem.

Philosophically minded people may try to console themselves with theories about a Deity which continually tests them with trials to prove their characters, and the more they suffer on earth the greater will be their reward in a future Heaven. That may quiet the rational side of themselves but deep beneath the surface primitive feelings and natural resentments are bound to smolder in their souls and distill slow toxins which are more than liable to cause spiritual disease maybe years later.

In olden times folks knew exactly what to do. Go into their temples or wherever they met their Gods by appointment and kick up a cathartic commotion until they were exhausted and felt more capable of dealing with life on a fairer footing. Not for them the expensive psychiatrist of modern days with his "primal scream" and all the rest of his gobbledygook. They knew for a fact that if they made enough fuss with emotional outpourings before focal symbols representing their Deities, they would feel a lot better afterwards, and that was what really mattered.

Most official religions have abolished this old custom either because they think it is unseemly or wrong for various other reasons. Some may consider it only a waste of time and effort protesting to a God who seems to pay no more attention to people than a government. Whatever the argument, the solid fact remains that the average human benefits greatly by being enabled to "let off steam," or work frustrations and resentments out of themselves by some practical means. Here is one such means offered in a highly literate and comprehensible way, which at the same time gives full vent to suppressed feelings and emotions which it would be dangerous to retain in any human system.

Its advantage is that it may be worked alone or in company with others who are in agreement with its motivations. The important factor is that it ought never to be used for any but the most serious reasons. If worked for trivial or petty purposes it will soon lose all its efficacy and be useless in time of real need. Essentially the Rite of Reproach is a "fall-back." Like a safety valve or an electric fuse, it is there to fall back on when necessity invokes its function. Perhaps the best way to think of it is like an insurance policy which one would rather hold than cash in.

Therefore, a great deal of self-evaluation is called for before the Rite of Reproach is put into action, and full responsibility must be taken should that happen without entire justification, or at least the sincere conviction that such justification exists. Like the Commination, Exorcism, or Rejection Rites, the utmost caution must be exerted before using this Rite of Reproach. If there is any noticeable degree of doubt concerning its employment, then it is best not to work it. Often the knowledge of its availability in case of need is enough to avert the aggregation of inner tensions which might eventually cause such a need. That is the best possibility of all.

THE RITE OF REPROACH

In the name of the **Wisdom**,
    and of the **Love**,
    and of the **Justice**,
    and of the Infinite **Mercy**,
  of the One Eternal **Spirit**,
              Amen.

We are here because we have been hurt at heart
Yet suffer not our sorrows in sad silence,
But with bewildered anger and a smarting sense
Of some injustice and supposed ill-treatment
From those fatal forces that decree our destiny.
We are worried, vexed, and very sadly shaken
By a foreboding feeling we are being forsaken.
Most intensely may mankind be mainly injured
With what looks like lack of conscious care
Or indolent indifference by the only Being
Whom we would follow with the firmest faith
Providing we perceived the very slightest sign
Of whom or whatsoever we have deemed Divine.
So much may we withstand and willingly await,
Then comes a critically provoking pressure point
That shatters our serenity and stirs our souls
To troubled turmoil, making most disturbing doubts
Of Cosmic competence or will within our world.

Such is our situation. Now our strongest need
For inner intimation we are wrong indeed.

PRECEPTOR: Who is there to ask? What shall we say?
Is there an answer? Will we find our way?

RESPONSOR: To whom can we complain, or even call
Except the One Authority of all?

PRECEPTOR: Is it worth while? Will anyone attend?
Can we find cosmic consciousness our friend?

RESPONSOR: Why not? Would we be worse if we but
Try to raise some sort of spiritual reply?

PRECEPTOR: Then listen life—if anyone Thou art,
These are our troubles, heed us heart to heart.

Indictment

1. What sort of world supports such willful wickedness except our earth?
   Its most efficient evildoers and malicious members of mankind.
   Seem so successful, propersous, and potent. Is that ill inevitable?
   Here is a hateful empire of all evil. Cold, corrupt, and cruel.
   Disastrous and dangerous. Faithless, shameful, stupid, even futile.

See it with our sight, O Thou Eternal Eye! Behold its basic badness.
Feel it with our fingers O Thou Holy Hands. Touch it Thou truth.
Discover that deceit dictates and falsehood fairly flourishes.
Perceive how peculation pays, and evil earns prodigious profits.
Dishonest dealers always are recipients of the richest dividends.
Hypocrisy is highly honored; grasping greed most greatly glorified.
Above all, wealth is worshipped. Poor people principally punished.
Humans hold but one belief between them. "God is Golden."
Money is the major motivation and the mainstream of mankind.
Nature, man's more normal mate, is terribly ill-treated and so sadly shamed.
Humanity has hurt her badly and befouled her body. Pity her plight.
She is abused, abased, resources ravaged, purity polluted, utterly upset.
Man spreads his species recklessly, regardless of a ruinous result,
Plundering and poisoning his profiteering way in a weak world.
Waging war most mercilessly for the sake of some ambiguous advantage,
Or otherwise condoning out of cowardice all that ought to be abolished.
Such is the sorry state of souls for sale in mankind's supermarkets.

2. Now that humanity has knowledge how to end earth life effectively,
Increasing opportunities are offered for insidious invasion
Of whatever once was sacred, secret, or particularly private.
Probing people's souls pays well with money or in more peculiar ways.
Investigation is investment, if it aids an imposition of intent.
Seldom has our spiritual structure seemed so truly threatened,
Our beliefs betrayed, and highest hopes held in complete contempt.
Since scientific war is profitless if pushed past peak potential,
Instead of operating in a physically factual field of force,
Its terrible techniques are turned to inner areas of insane ambition.
Aimed at domination or destruction of the people on this planet.
Should this succeed, then we are straightway sold to spiritual slavery.
Our freedom forfeited for who knows what indefinite imprisonment
In cages of conditoned consciousness constructed by our captors.
Shall any soul so shackled ever rise again and reach its Individuality.
Above all else in its existence? Should that fail, our second Fall
Might make the first feel fairly faint and comforting by contrast.
This is the fate we fear! This is what altogether worries and alarms us.

How can we be happy or content in these calamitous conditions?
Given good guidance, we would gladly do whatever dedicated duty
Life itself may lead us to while we are looking for illumination.
Bereft of that, and blindly battling our way in this sad sphere,
We cannot say for certain we shall win against such strong adversity.
So what solution should we now apply? Answer, whosoever is most able!

PRECEPTOR: Have we been heard by any hidden ears?
How practical in fact are fervent prayers?
Suppose the Supreme Spirit near us now,
Said "Show me what you mean, and why, and how."

RESPONSOR: We willingly admit our guilt.
Do therefore with us **what Thou wilt.**
Yet pass no judgement from thy throne
Without acknowledging thine own!

[Heavy gavel knock]

Criticism

1. O Life of Lives, have humans failed to find
Or meet by best beliefs thine Overmind?
Will we obey thine orders, work thy ways?
Earn thine encouragement, deserve thy praise?
Those that find faith and altogether act
As if indeed Thou art our finest fact,
Too often also find, if asking aught,
They seldom see much more than merely—naught.

2. Creeds credit Thee our greatest total good.
   Who dares define or simply say what should
   Be taken in those terms by any here
   As actualities of consciousness made clear
   To mortal men, whose microcosmic minds
   Are forced to face what each enquirer finds.
   If no great good seems evident to see,
   What tells them then, to have great hopes of Thee?

3. We are familiar with philosophies that teach
   The powers of patience, or perhaps they preach
   Religious resignation to thy working will,
   Most grandly mentioning thy grinding mill.
   In spite of this, sad souls who seem abused
   Can have no comfort hearing Thee excused.
   Nor is an easy explanation any aid.
   To bearing living burdens on them laid.

4. It adds to this, that we are mortal men
   And women of this world, erupting when
   Our human hearts hurt hard enough to cause
   A lack of confidence in cosmic laws.
   We acted as thine influence inspired,
   Yet failed to find responses we required.
   What has life left to dream about or do?
   No precept takes the place of faith come true.

5. What sort of sense is there in trying to tell
   A homily, to souls that suffer Hell?
   It could be best, considering their cry,
   To render swift assistance in reply.
   As humans heed another creature's call,
   Hast Thou, their life, no hearing left at all?
   If those ignored who have invoked thy name
   Forsake their faith, should they be so to blame?

6. Since we are all alive as one affair,
   Thou too in human happenings should share.
   We being body, Thou the Supreme Soul
   Of what we hold to total as a whole.
   Divinity we never dare deny,
   As we now ask, refuse not to reply.
   O Maker of Mankind, work **what Thou wilt**.
   Be our best grace, for we are **Thy Worst Guilt!**

[Heavy double knock]

PRECEPTOR: How far with faith, and unto what degree
              Dare we rely upon Divinity?
              Can It be interested enough to care?
              Or are we wasting words on empty air?

RESPONSOR: Divinity may demonstrate its might
              In whatsoever way It reasons right.
              Can we conceive what conduct that
                could be
              At this earth end of its identity?

Argument

1. We will not argue any cosmic case,
   Nor hint (we hope) at a Divine disgrace.
   We say it seems to us this universe
   Might be much better if it were no worse.

2. If evil must eventuate in man.
   Perfection might be possible to plan
   If that which instigates the deed we do
   Altered its angles of approach anew.

3. Unless men's urging motives can be changed
   Or other alterations are arranged,
   On deepest driving depths of secret soul
   Shall we have hopes of gaining some good goal?

4. What agency alone may alter man?
   Enough to earn a conscience if he can
   And set him striving to achieve an aim
   Of more than mortal consciousness can claim?

5. Only one Overlife can cause that change,
   And in our view it seems so very strange
   We rarely recognize and seldom sense
   A trace of inner influence from thence.

6. Providing it were possible to pray
   Some secret, strange, or wonder-working way,
   Creating contact with the cosmic mind,
   What mention would we make of humankind?

7. And what again if we were truly told
   To tell the things we thought, and be as bold
   Or outright as an honest heart may be
   Before an equal Brother Entity?

8. Shall we suppose that this is surely so,
   And therefore let our thoughts and feelings flow,
   Everting energies of inner ill
   With openly opining **what we will**?

PRECEPTOR: Why not? If nothing lives past death,
   We lose but unimportant breath.
   But if indeed there truly should
   Be "Something"—we might gain some good.

RESPONSOR: Besides, it brings a real release
To pent-up souls in search of peace,
And so, we most sincerely say,
"Hear this then—whosoever may."

Adjuration

O Nameless One, whom all admit Eternal Entity,
If Thou art interested in us, or anything we are,
Then signify this somehow, so that we can clearly see
Even the smallest evidence thy spirit moves in man.
Moreover, make it known to us, thy people praying now,
That we would be particularly welcome partners
In thy special schemes that call for our cooperation.
Reject us not for reasons we will never realize.
If we are inadequate—arrange an alteration.
Counsel and correct us constantly, working **as Thou wilt**,
But be not distant and disinterested. Lead us in life!
Come closer, and awake a sense of spiritual sight.
Point out our paths perceptibly—then let us live them.
Partake of our perplexities. Feel our frustrations!
Especially those we endure on this occasion!!

[Specify if need be.]

**What if these were thine? Surely this is so indeed.
Then solve or suffer them with us, O Universal One.**

[Gong crash]

Whom or whatsoever are we?
Thine inherent imperfections!
Thy fallibility factors.
Erratics of existence,
Inaccuracies of intentions.

Complications of Cosmos.
And Divine dissatisfactions.
What should we not be, that we are?
Maybe thy maximum mistake,
Mad, muddling, misbehaving
  Man!!!

[Explosive crash—short silence.]

Admonition

So set us straight for thine own sake of cosmic comfort.
We do not dare expect escape from evil will be easy,
Nor are we anticipating miracles and marvels,
Incredible impossibilities and awesome acts
That utterly upset necessities of nature,
Or clearly contradict the character of Cosmos.
We ask not any such absurdities, and simply say:
"Be Thou thyself through us, but please be plainly
  potent.
Manifesting in our minds, or speaking in our souls,
Or anything at all to tell us that Thou art alive
And interested in our affairs as individuals.
We need no more than that to make our lives worth
  living."
Armed with such assurance in our spirits, we can
  challenge
The catastrophes of our conditions confidently.
While without it, we are worthless, each existence
  empty.
We waste our time and thine within a useless universe.
Which is more than we are willing to accept this
  moment.
Decide what we will duly do. Accept us as we are
And help us to attain some higher than a human state,
Or ignore us into an eventual extinction.

This is thy Cosmos, and we are thy creatures, therefore
   choose.
We would not hover hesitating were our roles reversed,
Nor act as a detached Divinity who looks at life
With utmost unconcern intentionally uninvolved.
What we would do, we do not know, but we would well
   believe
That were we Thee, as all authorities assume Thou art—
We would at least attempt to alter the most awful mess
Which mankind makes mismanaging this miserable
   world!

PRECEPTOR: Surely that is sufficient to be said?
            Why waste good words with any going
               ahead?

RESPONSOR: One last appeal to life, and we will end,
            Then later learn if we find it our friend.

PRECEPTOR: Be briefly succinct and sincere,
            Concise, and altogether clear.

Clamavi

**If Thou art there,
Then hear us here.
Answer by act.
If no one heeds,
We need new creeds
Facing that fact.
Are we one?
Is it done?
Yes or no
Be it so.
Amen.**

[Horn winds]

PRECEPTOR: Will it work good if we go on and on,
Will words link us with life in liaison?

RESPONSOR: Not necessarily, although we will admit
We want to say some things we think of it.

PRECEPTOR: Then let this be the last
Pronouncement to be passed.

Reflection

Have we actually helped ourselves or anyone at all?
Was this a total and a willful waste of talking time?
Were we some sadly stupid spiritual spectacle
Of hopeless humans, howling with humiliation
To nothing but non-being, and everlasting emptiness?
Or could we have contacted higher consciousness than ours
On other living levels of expressed existence
Capable of creditably changing our conditions?
May we believe that this might bring us welcome benefit
By ultimately banishing our own uncertainty.

PRECEPTOR: Our answers lie in life alone,
We share the harvest we have sown.
Since thoughts are seeds that seem alive,
Pray present plantings truly thrive.

In the name of the **Wisdom**,
and of the **Love**,
and of the **Justice**,
and of the Infinite **Mercy**,
of the One Eternal **Spirit**,
Amen.

[Recessional music.]

· 14 ·

The Sangreal Rosary

Introduction

Rosaries, or prayer-counting beads, are in use among most Faiths. Their purpose is only to ensure equability of rhythm with the repetition of ordered orisons. It also has the good psychological effect of engaging physical sense through touch with a soothing and calming motion, similar to stroking, as the fingertips feel polished beads slipping through them. This relieves a lot of stress and tension with average human organisms, and should therefore be valued on that account alone.

The Sangreal rosary is a collection of simple orisons which can be combined with the aid of an ordinary Christian rosary, obtainable almost everywhere. If really required, it would be an easy matter to substitute a Sangreal symbol for the conventional crucifix. There is no absolute need to do this however, since the sacrifice concept is identical with both Christian and Sangreal symbology, and man giving his life to God for the sake of fellow beings is indicated in each case. The regular "Formula Prayers" are:

1. At the Crucifix or Medallion at commencement:

I believe in one Supreme and Sovereign Spirit as our universal Lord of Life and Light, of Which we are integral units in Its Cosmic Corpus.

Likewise I believe we should become as blood within that Blessed Body, sharing Its immortal spiritual structure and communing with Its consciousness until our complete union with It in *Perfect Peace Profound*.

Also I believe in all that indicates this primal purpose of our individual selves and I accept the Sangreal as the symbol of a true relationship with its reality. **Amen.**

2. At every large bead:

O Maker of Mankind we bless thee with the blood we bear. Work Thou Thy will within us and assume authority above all actions.

Prosper and protect us with Thy Heavenly power as we attempt to help humanity on this our earth.

Let us not be lost to Light, but save us through the Sangreal Spirit. **Amen.**

3. At every small bead:

O Sangreal Spirit, binding us by blood unto our Western way of Inner Life, inspire and activate us always.

Lead us to Blessed Light by true self-sacrifice, until we reach and realize our ultimate Identity in *Perfect Peace Profound*. **Amen.**

Devotions consist of meditations on complete sets of any five connected topics associated with the Sangreal while also saying the above prayers automatically. Each meditation lasts for a single decket only, and in the case of community usage, the change of subject may be announced aloud by the prayer-leader. Here are some suggestions:

- The Five Hallows. Sword, Rod, Cup, Shield, and Cord.
- The Five Kingdoms related with Divine Awareness. God *Asleep* in Minerals, *Stirring* in Plants, *Dreaming* in Animals, *Awakening* in Humanity, and completely *Conscious* as Divinity in Cosmos.

- The Grail-Castle. External appearance. Entry. Courtyard and Gardens. Hospitality Hall. Grail-Chapel. (There are many variations on this theme.)
- The Five forms of Blood. The Blood of Begetting, Blood of Birth, Blood of Being, Blood of Dying, Blood of Discarnation.
- The Five Social Orders. Peasants, Artisans, Administratives, Nobility, Royalty.

It only needs to choose some special subject and divide it by five into a set of logical sequences from first to last, top to bottom, or minimum to maximum importance. It is important that there are rational connections throughout.

The first large, and subsequent three small beads after the Crucifix or Medallion, should be treated as a "run-in" and the prayers themselves concentrated on. Meditations commence with the second large bead.

· Part IV ·

Celebrating the Sangreal Year

· 15 ·

Sangreal New Year Service

Introduction

This Service should be self-explanatory, but briefly it consists of an annual spiritual stocktaking, a realignment of the self with its purpose, a rededication to one's path, and a Blessing bidden upon everything and everyone concerned. It is understood that members will disperse afterwards either to private celebrations with their families or a communal meal of companionship.

The only arrangement to be considered is a central table or stand, circular if possible, upon which the individual candles are placed to symbolize the sun. Each member is responsible for bringing his/her own candle in a holder which can remain under their seats until required. At that moment, all form a general circle close to the walls of the temple. First light is taken by the Preceptor at the left of the altar from the central symbol, passed across to the Priest on the right, who then passes it to the one closest to him and so on. (It is a good idea to have a hidden fire extinguisher handy.) This must be done in an orderly manner which is usually controlled by the Preceptor. Incense is optional.

Timing and coordination are very necessary and should be carefully calculated in advance. This means rehearsing to carefully timed tape-recordings of the rite. That is the reason for the indefinite period prior to midnight as an "elastic adjustment" to allow for an exact coinciding of the procedures. Periods for meditation between Commandments need not exceed five minutes at the most, but should not be briefer than about three on an average. An egg-timer in the shape of an hourglass may be helpful here, and makes for a nice "sands of time running out" symbolism.

It is also important that the "exclusion of the unreconciled" should be taken quite seriously, and any that cannot truly find it in their hearts to forgive other members of the temple for some past conduct for whatever reasons, should indeed quit the temple at that moment and pray privately in the anteroom until ready to ask readmission. In the rare event that they are unable to come to an understanding with themselves, it is their obligation to approach the Master of the Temple privately and sort out their problems at some later and more convenient date. It must be borne in mind that their conduct only applies in respect to fellow temple members. There is no need to exclude themselves for trivialities, such as disagreement with other people's idiosyncrasies of a purely personal nature. Only that which seriously prevents the passing of the Sangreal Spirit between different souls should be considered sufficient to call for self-seclusion during this Service. Should either the Priest or the Preceptor find it necessary to exclude themselves, they are responsible for delegating someone else to deputize forthwith. This applies to all Offices.

The New Year entrant should be a dark person traditionally, and the food and fuel they bear goes back to the old Stone Circle gatherings where the price of admission was a contribution to the central fire and something for the pot cooking on it. Right foot first is a very old custom. It meant an entrance in peace, because a left-footed approach was usually a military one with a weapon in right hand ready to strike.

There is nothing to prevent hymns or other items being introduced into the Service as may be thought fit. Robes are minimal or optional, though Preceptor and Priest should be robed suitably.

It is customary to keep the "New Year gifts" in a special box in the altar with the vessels, though they could be kept anywhere else suitable. They are consumed at the end of the year before their replacements are brought in. Preceptor or Priest is responsible. If possible a new person is found each year for the duty. Conventionally it is always the latest person to join the Circle, or apply for membership. Or it may be the youngest one.

The "kiss of peace" is given usually by placing hands on each other's upper arms or shoulders, the donor then lays right cheek first (or lips) to recipient's left cheek, then repeating on the right. The action begins with the Priest kissing the altar, continues with his passing it sunwards until everyone has participated, and concludes with the Preceptor kissing the altar. Each person must say the words audibly.

THE SANGREAL NEW YEAR SERVICE

PRECEPTOR: Companions, we have come to the conclusion of another year as calculated on our solar calendars. Therefore, we are seeking to take stock and estimate the expectations of our spiritual situation. Are we in accord with this intention?

ALL: *So mote it be. Amen.*

PRECEPTOR: Be a prayer pronounced on our behalf.

PRIEST: O Thou Creative Consciousness behind our beings, hear what is in our hearts and may our words become their truthful mirror in our minds.

We see ourselves as cells within Thy Blessed Blood and ask that we should do whatever duties are appointed by Thy Laws of Life so far as we can follow these according to our comprehension of them on our paths of progress. We see Thee also as the Supreme Spirit of that Sangreal we bear within our blood as humans who have recognized their high responsibility for spiritual service dedicated to Thy Deity as rightful ruler of our woeful world. Thine are its rights and ours its wrongs.

Here we hope to find forgiveness for our faults and failures, reconciliation with Thy Will intending our redemption, and enough enlightenment to take us yet a further year into the future with our faith confirmed by beneficial confidence in Thy companionship.

> In the name of the **Wisdom**,
> and of the **Love**,
> and of the **Justice**,
> and of the Infinite **Mercy**,
> of the One Eternal **Spirit**,
> **Amen.**

PRECEPTOR: To modern minds, what once was seen as sin or some offense against an angered God may now be designated differently, although its nature always stays the same. Essentially it is our conduct weighed against a code of ethics which we all agree should be our best and brightest standards for the spiritual behavior of such humans having any faith or hopes of higher life than that of lowly earth existence. The tale that our Tradition tells us of our origins on earth explains how our humanity began by our discernment of the difference between the primal principles of right and wrong. Out of that Knowledge came a need and the commencement of our Cosmic climb back by the branches of our Tree of Life toward the total Truth mankind may meet on top. In fact our fabled Fall supplied the spiritual reasons for our rising ever since through every stage of evolution and development towards Divinity. Let this Legend by recounted and respected as an allegory.

PRIEST: So God created man in His own image. Male and female created he them, and they were both naked and were not ashamed. And the Lord put man into the Garden of Eden to maintain and keep it, saying: "Of the Tree of Knowledge of good and evil thou shalt not eat, for in that day so shalt thou surely die." The serpent said unto the woman, "Ye shall not surely die, for God doth know that in the day ye eat therefrom your eyes shall then be opened and ye shall become as Gods yourselves by knowing both good and evil." So the woman then did eat and gave some to her husband who did also eat. Then they knew that they were naked, and sewing together fig leaves made them aprons. God called Adam, saying, "Who told thee thou wast naked? Thou hast eaten the fruit of the tree which I commandest thou should not." And Adam said, "The woman gave me of the tree and I did eat." The woman said, "The serpent beguiled me." So the Lord said to the serpent, "Upon thy belly shalt thou go and eat dust all the days of thy life, for I will put enmity between the woman's seed and thine." To the woman he said, "I will greatly multiply thy sorrow and conception." To Adam he said, "Cursed is the ground for thy sake. In the sweat of thy brow shalt thou eat bread until thou return into that ground, for dust thou art, and unto dust shalt thou return." Then the Lord said, "Behold the man is become as one of us, knowing good and evil, so now lest he put forth his hand and taking also of the Tree of Life may live forever..." Whereupon the Lord put him forth from the garden of Eden to till the ground from whence he was taken, and placed at the eastern entrance, cherubims and a flaming sword turning every way to guard the Tree of Life.

PRECEPTOR: So says the story of our start as an especial species on this earth. It traces to the time when we acquired a conscience, or capacity to realize responsibility for all our actions or our failures to fulfill our obligations to whatever faith we followed. The code of conscience covering our best behavior in the Western Inner Way is broadly based upon the Ten Commandments. Let us therefore deal with their decade in spiritual sequence and consider how we may have contravened their many meanings. Then we should seek some forgiveness from the God that gave them through inspired intelligence.

PRECEPTOR: Deliver and declare the First Commandment.

PRIEST: I am the Lord thy God who brought thee out of the land of Egypt and out of the house of bondage.

[Gong]

PRECEPTOR: Since these olden obligations must be understood by us according to a modern manner, we believe this means the way we see our Maker and our conscious concepts of Deity as it affects our individual and collective destiny. How have we honored the Divinity of our beliefs? Does our spiritual situation cause us credit or confusion? Do we need deliverance from any fate we fear? Are we in captivity of any kind or held as hostages to hurtful habits? Should we be set free from practices which are pernicious? Are we looking for a Liberator who will lead us into light? How grateful are we to the God that grants us grace and gives us life to Love with? Do we doubt ourselves or Deity? What is our position in regard to personal relationships with the eternal energy of our existence? Our collective concept of that primal power? Let us set up in imagination special scales with which to weigh our observation of this ordinance against the actuality it indicates. Begin this balance by a momentary meditation.

> [Silence during which all contemplate their relation to the First Commandment. The Preceptor terminates this with gavel knock.]

PRIEST: For whatsoever we have contravened in this Commandment, we sincerely seek forgiveness from the God who gave it, and would ask another opportunity of practicing it much more perfectly for yet a further year.

ALL: *With all our will, Amen.*

PRECEPTOR: Deliver and declare the Second Commandment.

PRIEST: Thou shalt have no other gods before me. Thou shalt not make unto thee a graven image, nor the form of anything that is in the heavens above or that which is in the earth beneath, or that is in the waters under the earth. Thou shalt not bow down to them nor serve them. For I the Lord thy God am a jealous God, visiting the iniquity of the fathers upon the children unto the third and fourth generation of them that hate me, yet showing loving kindness to the thousandth generation unto those that love me and keep my commandments.

[Gong]

PRECEPTOR: This tells us to be single-spirited and find no faith in fleeting forms, but only by beliefs based on the absolute authority of an Almighty Sovereign Spirit. It also indicates hereditary human inclinations in connection with such cosmic consciousness, or transmissible transgressions generated in our genes. Do we deliberately deceive ourselves in setting up inferior ideals instead of seeking out the spiritual truth? Invest convenient idols to conceal some awkward inner actualities? Blame some evil entity for our own badness? Put up pretenses in the hope of hiding what is wicked? Favor falsity in preference to pursuit of Truth? Refuse to recognize our own responsibility in dealing with Divinity the way it is instead of what we wish it was? Fail to follow up the lineal links of Love that should supply our guidance unto God? To discover such discrepancies let us set up the special scales with which to weigh our observation of this ordinance against the actuality it indicates. Begin this balance by a momentary meditation.

> [Silence during which all contemplate their relation to the Second Commandment. The Preceptor terminates this with gavel knock.]

PRIEST: For whatsoever we have contravened in this Commandment, we sincerely seek forgiveness from the God who gave it, and would ask another opportunity of practicing it much more perfectly for yet another year.

ALL: *With all our will, Amen.*

PRECEPTOR: Deliver and declare the Third Commandment.

PRIEST: Thou shalt not take the name of the Lord thy God in vain. For the Lord will not hold him guiltless that taketh his name in vain.

[Gong]

PRECEPTOR: With this there is a warning of devaluing Divinity to worthlessness. What good is any God that man misunderstands or treats with triviality? Here we have a commonsense Commandment that insists on the importance of our sacred Spirit concepts. Are we in agreement with it as an item of important implications? Do we deal with sacred subjects as they should deserve if we intend them to bring benefits and blessings? Are we wasting spiritual assets stupidly? What help are any holy names to humans who negate them? Regarding them with reverence will add to their efficiency in an emergency, while disrespectful use of them destroys their properties of power. Here we have to set up special scales with which to weigh our observation of this ordinance against the actuality it indicates. Begin the balance by a momentary meditation.

> [Silence during which all contemplate their relation to the Third Commandment. The Preceptor terminates this with gavel knock.]

PRIEST: For whatsoever we have contravened in this Commandment, we sincerely seek forgiveness from the God who gave it, and would ask another opportunity of practicing it much more perfectly for yet another year.

ALL: *With all our will, Amen.*

PRECEPTOR: Deliver and declare the Fourth Commandment.

PRIEST: Remember the Sabbath Day to keep it holy. Six days shalt thou labor and do all thy work, but the seventh day is a Sabbath unto the Lord thy God. In it thou shalt not do any work, thou, nor thy son, nor thy daughter, thy manservant nor thy maid, nor thy cattle, nor thy stranger that is within thy gates. For in six days the Lord made heaven and earth, the sea and all that is therein and rested on the seventh day, wherefore the Lord hath blessed the seventh day and hallowed it.

> [Gong]

PRECEPTOR: This simply means one seventh of a mortal life should be devoted to Divinity and given to the God of life in gratitude. Scarcely a colossal sum to consecrate for such a pleasant purpose. Will we grudge God our thinking time and refuse to recognize Him in our human recreations? Work and worship can be one if we combine our prayer with practice. Why should we expect a spiritual essence to keep careful consciousness of us continuously while we will not acknowledge It within ourselves? That is neither reasonable nor religious. Have we truly tried to keep communication channels clear between our Blessed Spiritual Source and this the human end of our experience? Machines will never work without good maintenance. How much maintenance is the minimum we need to get God going with our work? One day a week will do. So now set up those special scales with which to weigh our observation of this ordinance against the actuality it indicates. Begin the balance by a momentary meditation.

> [Silence during which all contemplate their relation to the Fourth Commandment. The Preceptor terminates this with gavel knock.]

PRIEST: For whatsoever we have contravened in this Commandment, we sincerely seek forgiveness from the God who gave it and would ask another opportunity of practicing it much more perfectly for yet another year.

ALL: *With all our will, Amen.*

PRECEPTOR: Deliver and declare the Fifth Commandment.

PRIEST: Honor thy father and thy mother that thy days may be long in the land which the Lord thy God hath given thee.

[Gong]

PRECEPTOR: This is the Commandment coming closest to the Sangreal and our spiritual bonds of blood. God may give us life in light, but it is our parents that pass life by blood on earth to us and therefore act as agents of our everlasting origin. So they stand as symbols of that Blessed Blood which we have sworn to honor and hold holy. How have we complied with this Commandment? Do we behave as our descendants could conceive the Blessed Blood should seem? Are we worthy representatives of its regality? This injunction is more subtle than may seem upon its surface. All its implications are to be considered carefully. What we are to parents, so are offspring to ourselves, and past and present put together must form the future of mankind. Let us set up the special scales with which to weigh our observation of this ordinance against the actuality it indicates. Begin the balance by a momentary meditation.

[Silence during which all contemplate their relation to the Fifth Commandment. The Preceptor terminates this with gavel knock.]

PRIEST: For whatsoever we have contravened in this Commandment, we sincerely seek forgiveness from the God who gave it, and would ask another opportunity of practicing it much more perfectly for yet another year.

ALL: *With all our will, Amen.*

PRECEPTOR: Deliver and declare the Sixth Commandment.

PRIEST: Thou shalt not murder.

[Gong]

PRECEPTOR: This clearly means the killing of another mortal for no reason that is ratifiable by any law of life. There are, however, many methods of committing murder humans could consider. Mankind may murder by neglect or nonsupport of the necessitous. Murder may be done by driving others to a state of desperation so that they destroy themselves. Contributions to the cause of wicked war may count as murder to some definite degree. Murder may be shared by many individuals according to involvement. All of us are probably participants to slight extents in the extermination of some human somewhere in this woeful world. Shall we here set up those special scales with which to weigh our observation of this ordinance against the actuality it indicates? Begin the balance by a momentary meditation.

[Silence during which all contemplate their relation to the Sixth Commandment. The Preceptor terminates this with gavel knock.]

PRIEST: For whatsoever we have contravened in this Commandment, we sincerely seek forgiveness from the God who gave it and would ask another opportunity of practicing it much more perfectly for yet another year.

ALL: *With all our will, Amen.*

PRECEPTOR: Deliver and declare the Seventh Commandment.

PRIEST: Thou shalt not commit adultery.

[Gong]

PRECEPTOR: Adultery is difficult in definition. Technically it signifies sex intercourse by people that belong with other partners. Infidelity in fact. Betrayal of belief. Treachery to trust. This Commandment can be broken by behavior of that sort apart from any sex. Deliberate deceit for personal profiteering pleasure. Falsity of faith. Connivance at concealing conduct that is treacherous. Deliberate desires directed at another person's partner. Rape in reality, or its requirement. Set up the special scales with which to weigh our observation of this ordinance against the actuality it indicates. Begin the balance by a momentary meditation.

[Silence during which all contemplate their relation to the Seventh Commandment. The Preceptor terminates this with gavel knock.]

PRIEST: For whatsoever we have contravened in this Commandment, we sincerely seek forgiveness from the God who gave it and would ask another opportunity of practicing it much more perfectly for yet another year.

ALL: *With all our will, Amen.*

PRECEPTOR: Deliver and declare the Eighth Commandment.

PRIEST: Thou shalt not steal.

[Gong]

PRECEPTOR: None need doubt the meaning of this maxim. To steal is to deprive another of an earned entitlement or property possessed for rightful reasons. Not only given goods, but anything at all of natural value, such as virtue or some spiritual attribute. Robbing anybody of a reputation is most reprehensible, and stealing has so many standards it is hard to find a formula inclusive of all incidents. In principle, the taking of a person's property without permission constitutes the crime of theft, but definition of degree is very variable. Decisions must depend more on the circumstances of each case than just an act itself for final individual judgement. Nevertheless we need to set up special scales with which to weigh our observation of this ordinance against the actuality it indicates. Begin the balance by a momentary meditation.

[Silence during which all contemplate their relation to the Eighth Commandment. The Preceptor terminates this with gavel knock.]

PRIEST: For whatsoever we have contravened in this Commandment, we sincerely seek forgiveness from the God who gave it, and would ask another opportunity of practicing it much more perfectly for yet another year.

ALL: *With all our will, Amen.*

PRECEPTOR: Deliver and declare the Ninth Commandment.

PRIEST: Thou shalt not bear false witness against thy neighbor.

[Gong]

PRECEPTOR: How much unhappiness is due to men's deliberate untruths about another mortal? Comments on character that ruin a reputation or are said for only spiteful reasons. But it can also be false witness if we say someone is wonderful, or good, or generous, when we know this is not true at all. None should be accused of anything without the strongest need and absolutely accurate authority for finding facts that dare not be denied. Speaking for the sake of starting scandal is a shameful thing to do. So is repeating rumors that are not reliable. It is said in speech are many pitfalls but in silence, none. This may be borne in mind when mouth stays shut. Silence sometimes makes a louder noise than many words we waste on lengthy arguments and ineffectual imprecations. Here we have to set up scales again to weigh our observations of this ordinance against the actuality it indicates. Begin the balance by a momentary meditation.

> [Silence during which all contemplate their relation to the Ninth Commandment. The Preceptor terminates this with gavel knock.]

PRIEST: For whatsoever we have contravened in this Commandment, we sincerely seek forgiveness from the God who gave it, and would ask another opportunity of practicing it much more perfectly for yet another year.

ALL: *With all our will, Amen.*

PRECEPTOR: Deliver and declare the Tenth Commandment.

PRIEST: Thou shalt not covet thy neighbor's house. Thou shalt not covet thy neighbor's wife nor his ox nor his ass, nor anything that is thy neighbor's.

[Gong]

PRECEPTOR: Greed and envy are the greatest enemies of human harmony, and here we are adjured to actively avoid them. Things and people are but temporary possessions. Death deprives us of them in an instant. Therefore, the self-tortures and all worries that we suffer on account of this Commandment are completely stupid, also utterly unnecessary. Why wear ourselves to wretchedness with pointless envy when the temporary owner of whatever property we covet is a perishable person and condemned to lose it anyway? Humans only hold their goods in trust from God. Why should we worry who has what since all must be abandoned in the end? Let us set up those scales again with which to weigh our observation of this ordinance against the actuality it indicates. Begin the balance by a momentary meditation.

[Silence during which all contemplate their relation to the Tenth Commandment. The Preceptor terminates this with gavel knock.]

PRIEST: For whatsoever we have contravened in this Commandment, we sincerely seek forgiveness of the God who gave it, and would ask another opportunity of practicing it much more perfectly for yet another year.

ALL: *With all our will, Amen.*

PRECEPTOR: Deliver and declare the last Commandment of our latest law.

PRIEST: Thou shalt love the Lord thy God with all thy heart and all thy mind and all thy soul, likewise thou shalt love thy neighbor as thyself. Little children, **love you one another**.

[Gong]

PRECEPTOR: This is indeed the greatest of Commandments given us. If it were kept consistently there never would be need for other ordinances. It is so sublime we are unable to appreciate its utterly supreme significance and sheer simplicity. Love is like a state of shared identity. The more that mingle mystically together with the oneness of a single spirit, then the larger grows the Godhood amongst all. Such is the Sangreal that binds by blood and blessedness those souls that share it with integrity because it is their true illumination. Love is linkage in the light. The condition of a common consciousness as One Beloved Being. An altogether unique unison. An actual experience of each other's entity as if it were one's own. That is the Love which we should seek within the Sangreal. A Love that cannot be expounded or explained but has to be experienced before it can be comprehended to the least extent. While we cannot be expected to completely keep this highest of Commandments while we have our human frameworks full of failures, let us at least put up a prayer that we will honor and attempt it to the best of our bemused abilities.

ALL: *With all our will, Amen.*

PRIEST: Beloved Sangreal Spirit of our Blessed Blood awake within us all. Let us live for but one moment in that state of spiritual mystic **Love** wherein we should hold one another holy. By and of that **Love** be all our former faults forgiven and absolved that we may face another coming year with confidence because we have a cleared conscience. Father—forgive us. Mother—make us clean. We are thy little children trying to love each other for thy sake.

> In the name of the **Wisdom**,
> and of the **Love**,
> and of the **Justice**,
> and of the Infinite **Mercy**,
> of the One Eternal **Spirit**,
> **Amen.**

[Gong. Silence.]

PRECEPTOR: Here is an important hiatus. Are there any individuals among us yet before our year ahead begins that have not found forgiveness in their hearts towards their neighbors or suppose themselves such sinners that the grace of God is insufficient to absolve them of their own offenses? Let those weak ones quit our company forthwith and find alternative adjustment in our anteroom or otherwise. We would wish them well, because they are not banished, but requested to retire and ask for reconciliation on their own accounts. Any with a strong suspicion of a harbored grudge should go and hope to reach repentance rather than regret remaining as a hypocrite in hiding with the knowledge of another sin upon their souls. Once this is duly done they may rejoin us with rejoicing. Such do not depart in shame, but in sincerity. Now it is needed that they should select themselves for separation, then set forth to find solutions for their personal problems as God guides. Be a Blessing on the outcome.

PRIEST: May our members that have honesty of heart enough to earn respect by an admission that they cannot reconcile themselves with everyone in holy harmony, here depart in dignity while held in honor with our hopes that they will truly come to terms with conscience and come back in blessedness among us when their clearance is complete.

In the name of the **Wisdom**,
    and of the **Love**,
    and of the **Justice**,
    and of the Infinite **Mercy**,
    of the One Eternal **Spirit**,
        Amen.

[Gong]

ALL: Go forth with God and find forgiveness.

[Bells rung and any due departures made swiftly. Preceptor takes up:]

PRECEPTOR: Announce an absolution and command a kiss of peace upon us all remaining to receive it at the hands of Heaven.

ALL: *With all our will, Amen.*

PRIEST: By the Blessed Blood consider old offenses cleared of everything except exact requital as required by cosmic compensation. Be the burden of our debts dismissed by Deity as we do here discharge the human debts we owe to one another from a spiritual standpoint. **Let Love and peace be passed between us and prevail in perpetuity.**

[Here the kiss of peace is passed from one to another according to the custom, with or without musical background. Lastly, the Priest says:]

PRIEST: And be there peace to those beyond our pale at present.

[Priest gestures at door.]

ALL: *With all our will, Amen.*

PRECEPTOR: Be it borne in mind that all of us are exiles and expatriates from the Perfect Presence. Sometimes our Sangreal is termed the stone of exile, since it marks how humankind began to bear the Blessed Blood descended from Divinity in exile on this earth which urges us forever to regain our rightful place in paradise. Until that time of ultimation we will work upon ourselves so that we shall be spiritually fit to live in light forevermore. This means we must be rightly reconciled with our celestial creative origins which are the true beginnings of our beings and hold our only hopes of ending in eternal immortality. Once we cast our sins upon the waters in contrived symbology to represent this. Let that reconciliation be requested now by prayers of purpose and a necessary casting of the waters of regeneration upon us the sinners who repentfully receive them of the Sangreal.

PRIEST: O Thou that art our origin, we would approach Thee with our recognition of thy reasons for creating us as conscious creatures. We turn all our thoughts towards Thee, and we ask for thy reciprocal response. Think Thou through us whatever is thy will within our separate selves. Make us what we must become because of thine intentions in us. Place us properly according to thy plan of ultimate perfection. Do not let us deviate from following the direct line of light that leads to thy Divinity by more than may be tolerable to thy truth. We admit that we are wanderers within the ways of life and often lose ourselves in search of spiritual subjects which can cause confusion with their sheer complexity. So set us straight again and start us yet another year upon the paths which we should plod until we are released into thin ultimate reality. Remember Thou the ones outside that have removed themselves and wait to be restored when they are ready. Mighty one we cast ourselves on thy containing mercy.

> **Receive and reconcile us with thy righteousness, that we shall surely bear the Blessed Blood amongst us always as Thou truly wilt according to thy word in this our world.**

> In the name of the **Wisdom**,
>   and of the **Love**,
>   and of the **Justice**,
>   and of the Infinite **Mercy**,
>   of the One Eternal **Spirit**,
>   **Amen.**

> [Priest scatters lustral fluid over congregation.]

ALL: *With all our will, Amen.*

PRECEPTOR: Now, until the time that we will wait in silent darkness for the dawning of another solar cycle, let us sing or listen to orations with intentions of inspiring us towards the best which we believe or hope will happen if we are allowed to bring it into being. Please be prepared to cease when signalled properly.

> [Here there is an organized interval to take up any spare time until a few minutes before the New Year comes into full effect. This needs to be most carefully calculated, and the Preceptor is responsible for controlling it. The time should not exceed about 20 minutes, and may be cut much shorter if possible. Items may be tape or live talks,

[pure music, but must all be suitable subjects evocative of possible projects for the year ahead. When the time is right, the Preceptor gives signal with gavel and announces:]

PRECEPTOR: Here at this turning point of time we hover at the edge of an extinction and we will pray that perils are averted and that light will once again appear to lead us in our cosmic conflict with the doom of darkness. With firmest faith will we descend into it, and so struggle that it will forever be extinguished in us by that blessed light which shines from the security of our beloved Sangreal blood. Fear not, but fall with full belief that footholds will be found for fighting evils on this earth. **Come Companions of the Quest, fall and fight, descend to darkness and to duty. Battle bravely for the faithful blood. God and goodness save our Sangreal.**

[Crash. Darkness. Silence.]

[At the exact hour, 12 strokes are sounded. If possible the first three are by gavel, second three by bell, third three by gong, and last three by shofar or horn. This may be prerecorded. At the last stroke, Light appears as the yearly candle or Sangreal Symbol is lit and the Priest cries loudly:]

PRIEST: **Arise to Life. Arise to Light. Arise to Learn. Arise to Love.**

In the name of the **Wisdom**,
and of the **Love**,
and of the **Justice**,
and of the Infinite **Mercy**,
of the One Eternal **Spirit**,
Amen.

PRECEPTOR: Rejoice, for we have really won, and darkness is dimissed for yet another year of hope ahead.

ALL: *Glory be to God our Blessed One in whom alone is highest Holiness.*

PRIEST: And every energy that emanates from thence.

PRECEPTOR: Circulate the light that we have lit among us and increase its clarity.

> [Here each individual produces his or her candle. The first one is lit from altar, then the rest around the perimeter lit from each other sunwise until the circle is complete and all face center. Music may be played as a background, but the wording as light is passed around from candle to candle is:]

Light increases light. Pass it in peace.

> [When all is complete and ready, Preceptor says:]

PRECEPTOR: **Centralize and then salute the sun returning in its regal splendor.**

> [Here all candles are carried to the central table or stand and arranged in a close group circularly. After this, all return to places and facing the center give hailing sign on command.]

PRIEST: **Hail Thou the light in us.**

ALL: *Hail Thou the light in us.*

> [All give sign. Gong.]

PRIEST: **Hail Thou the light behind our blood.**

ALL: *Hail Thou the light behind our blood.*

[All give sign. Gong.]

PRIEST: **Hail Thou the light around which we revolve.**

ALL: *Hail Thou the light around which we revolve.*

[All give sign. Gong.]

PRIEST: **Hail Thou the light illuminating our intelligence.**

ALL: *Hail Thou the light illuminating our intelligence.*

[All give sign. Gong.]

[Priest revolves slowly on his own axis sunwise while giving sign.]

PRIEST: **Let our light become a beacon of benevolence that blesses everyone on earth.**

ALL: *Let our light become a beacon of benevolence that blesses everyone on earth.*

[All give sign. Prolonged blast on shofar or horn.]

[Main lights on.]

PRECEPTOR: At last the year of ____[Old Year]____ is definitely dead, while that of ____[New Year]____ is being born. We welcome it with warmth and wonder. May it bring us many blessings and afford us opportunities of action and advancement. [to Doorkeeper] Protector of our portals, see if there is any soul that asks admission. We will greet them gladly.

[Here the doorkeeper attends to duty and admits first whoever is representing the New Year, followed by any returning from the anteroom. The New Year is usually the youngest or latest member to join the temple, or applicant to do so. He/she, carries a coal in one hand and a small piece of black bread in the other. The hands are extended and the right foot must cross the threshold first.]

NEW YEAR: Peace and prosperity to all within this place in the name of ____[New Year]____.

ALL: *And blessed be its bringers*

> In the name of the **Wisdom**,
> and of the **Love**,
> and of the **Justice**,
> and of the Infinite **Mercy**,
> of the One Eternal **Spirit**,
> **Amen.**

NEW YEAR: Here is food and fuel to feed and fire the work that waits.

ALL: *And active is the will that welcomes it.*

[New Year enters fully, followed by any returnees from anteroom, symbolic gifts laid on altar, all go to places and Preceptor calls:]

PRECEPTOR: Let us celebrate our light returning with a cheerful rousing song.

[Here all sing chosen song or hymn.]

PRECEPTOR: Now that we have said and sung whatever we think necessary for the greeting of another year which we are given for pursuit of our life purpose, let us pause for prayer that we shall surely find fulfillment of it, then disperse and duly welcome it in whatsoever way we will.

PRIEST: O Thou to whom a year of time with us is but a breath that barely takes a single second, let us live with peaceful and progressive purposes upon this planet. We know we are not fit and far from ready for removal to a higher habitation than this world that mankind mars with wickedness. Yet in the year to come, perhaps we will have crawled a trifle closer to that mystic mark. Offer us this opportunity O Holiest One and tell us how to take it advantageously. Keep in contact with us by the Blessed Blood of our beliefs, and aid all our adventures in the conscious Quest whereby we seek Thee through our Sangreal. O Thou Totality of Time and Lord of Life, support us with thy strength while we still struggle to survive in this mundane and mortal area of earth expression. Thou knowest all our needs and difficulties as we deliberate how we may work thy will in this our world. Please provide us with the wherewithal to work our Western Way toward Thee as our own inherited Tradition tells us inwardly. All this we ask with confidence in thy complete control of Cosmos. May these blessings be made manifest to those that truly trust.

> In the name of the **Wisdom**,
> and of the **Love**,
> and of the **Justice**,
> and of the Infinite **Mercy**,
> of the One Eternal **Spirit**,
> **Amen.**

ALL: *So mote it be. Amen.*

PRECEPTOR: Another year of hopes and hardships, happiness and happenings with all the vagaries and various events mankind may yet experience upon this earth has come for us to cope with as we can. Who can tell for certain what will happen? Some will suffer, some succeed. Fame for few and shame for some again. Experience for everybody. All amounting to the tests of time which make mankind whatever he will be because of his humanity and how he acts according to the dictates of Divinity that guide him Godwards, or he otherwise accepts the opposite impulses driving him to his insane destruction. One way or the other, man must move. Let us do likewise and attempt to start this solar cycle with a will to work it well for one another, finding fellowship and kindness in our company together for the sake of spirit shared among us all.

· 16 ·

The Seasonal Rituals

Introduction

Periodically, in accordance with the natural tides of nature and the solar/lunar cosmic clocks the people came together in Circles that symbolized their cosmic state, and there and then dedicated themselves and their resources to that which bound them closest to the cosmic wheel of life. They did the things their concept of God commanded. They sacrificed a life from themselves in return. No ordinary, common life, but someone they genuinely loved. Such a privilege belonged to royalty alone, and only royal blood could save the people. The King had to be sacrificed for all the others. Eventually this concept appeared as the mysterious "Sang Real," or "Holy Grail," according to which every member of humanity might ultimately be "saved" through participation.

In order to lift the Rites of basic human beliefs to higher levels of living, the original elements of flesh, blood, seed and sweat became symbolized by bread, wine, water and salt. The Holy Mysteries of old combined these into the most beautiful and uplifting liturgical formulae that might be devised by the mind of man inspired to express its entity through evolution.

At a later stage of development, more especially in the Western evolutions of the Old Faith, the Christian Church attempted to carry on the Mystery procedures and patterns. Because these were fundamentally sound in principle, they endured.

True teachings exist in the Church, but it rests with the will of every single soul to go in and find that truth for itself. Fundamentally our faith is one, and its variations are due to differences in the development of customs and consciousness by which we try to express it.

Time, place and event must be made to coincide for our faith to be relevant and so that all concerned may readily understand when it is, where it is and what it is. Hence the value of seasonal rites.[10]

At the present the Rites are limited to those four which are in keeping with the spirits of the seasons, and are celebrated at about the solstices and equinoxes. The basic pattern of the Rite is the simple Circle Cross of solar Cosmos, and everything relates to its equatorial points and central pivot. There is no set size for the Circle, but since the maximum around the perimeter is ideally twelve, the Circle should not exceed the diameter needed for this number to face center while holding each other's hands at arm's length.

The direction of the Rites falls principally upon the four Officers of the Quarters, who are simply designated by their position at East, South, West, and North. They correspond of course to elements, instruments, and all other quarterly attributes. The action of the Rite takes place around the Circle which symbolizes the cosmic course, and everything taking place is in sympathy with whatever season is being entered in spirit as well as body. There is music, movement, meditation and meaning in the Rites, which add up to magical procedures. A password for the period or key phrase to use during the following three months is chosen, and the mood determination, or will, of all concerned at that particular time is set and dedicated. Divinity is recognized and honored, while humanity relates itself with whatever is best of the two different states of consciousness attempting union of the ultimate Circle.

Since the Rites are designed for those of varying opinions and systems to work together, Divine names, and other references

---

[10] The material in the Seasonal Rituals is not a part of the Sangreal Sodality Series, but has been included in this volume because it is an important contribution to the Western Esoteric Tradition. These rituals originally apeared in *Seasonal Occult Rituals*, published in 1970 by Aquarian Press, U.K., and now out of print.

to specialized branches of the mysteries, are only made in the most general possible way.

The central flame kindled among the Companions of the cosmic Circle does more than symbolize the Divine light which they hope will come in the midst of them both individually and collectively. It must consume their "offerings," which take the practical form of papers on which they have written privately their personal and/or general summations concerning themselves and the seasonal spirit. This is a very important part of the Rites indeed, and unless it is done conscientiously and thoroughly, the Rites will lack an otherwise unobtainable quality. Whatever else may be abridged or altered, the presentation of petitions is morally obligatory for all who participate. What a petiton really amounts to is facing oneself fairly and squarely in the spirit of the season, and having a private showdown on vital spiritual points which regularly need bringing to light. Failure to do this indicates a serious lack of understanding as to the inner nature and operation of the Rites, and anyone unwilling to take the necessary trouble to make out a petition properly is quite unlikely to benefit from them in any marked way.

Having thought about the seasons in a general way, let us consider what sort of people are most likely to typify or "mediate" them individualy as Officiants of the Four Quarters. The best key to their natures is probably their symbolic instruments of Sword, Rod, Cup and Shield. These show the cosmic solar cycle in a very old traditional way, and indicate the kind of person best qualified to bear them.

In the east, associated with dawn and the spring season, the symbol of the sword and element of air are personified by Archangel Raphael. Here is needed (ideally) a young and highly intelligent male, sharp and keen of mind and soul, quick thinking, and alert for signs of trouble threatening the group from external sources. He is incisive and pliant, on the lookout for new projects or interests in which the group might engage if they decide to, and he keeps the rest very much on their toes by his enthusiasm and eagerness to get things right for them. Sometimes they may not be able to avoid an affectionate laugh at his enlivening spirits, which nevertheless keep them active and prevent complacency in the Cosmos all are trying to create together.

In the south, linked with noon and summer, the rod symbol and the element fire personify in Archangel Michael. His human mediator should be the senior male of the group, who could be seen as a father-figure but is more of the commanding officer type. He upholds the conduct of the group, makes most of the rulings, keeps discipline, should set a good example, does the main job of straightening out problems affecting the group, and is perhaps the principal enlightener. He is responsible, with his opposite number, the shield, for making the chief decisions and judgments concerning group activities.

In the west, connected with dusk and autumn, the beautiful symbol of the cup and element water are personified by Archangel Gabriel (pronouned Jiv-ra-ee-el). The human representative here ought to be a young fertile (not pregnant) female. She mediates powerful and beneficial love and compassion throughout the group. If there should be trouble among them, her job is to mollify it, if sorrow, console the sufferers. She must be able to radiate cheerfulness, kindness, good humor and happiness from her quarter. It is she that has to nourish (nurse) things along when they become difficult and, as Guardian of the Grail, keep in touch with the inner nature of this entirely sacred symbol.

At the north, linked with night and winter, the symbol of the shield or mirror and element of earth are personified in Archangel Auriel (Au-ra-ee-el). Here the mediator should be the senior female of the group. She is the one of experience, wisdom, caution, tolerance, patience and all the qualities associated with good, sound, solid sense at its highest level in the human spirit. She helps to show people what they really are, and tries to protect them from over-impulsive propensities. She guards the traditions of the group and teaches the law by which they hope to live.

One last symbol is worth mentioning, if any Officer can be found to mediate it properly. This is the cord, which should be a sort of universal link, able to operate as the periphery of the circle, join it with others, or connect any points within the circle—such an invaluable individual, representing Archangel Savaviel.

It will be notice, and should be emphasized throughout the Rites, that the styles of address vary between sections: some are directed towards humans present and others towards the Inner Ones with whom spiritual contact is sought. The device of addressing these Beings as "Thou" is adopted in order to distinguish between thoughts intended for direction to Divinity, and those meant simply to be shared among intelligent human entities. With these seasonal Rites, the whole trend and approach of each one is in accordance with the cycle being celebrated. In spring, the symbolic time of youth and childhood, the Rite is almost childish in some of its language and terms. Summertime, symbolizing vigorous adulthood, is spoken about from that viewpoint. Autumn, the season of fruitfulness and maturity (despite the preferably young Cup Officer), is dealt with in that sort of tone, and winter, the period of age and wisdom, is ritualized in a serious and quiet fashion. Thus with the Rites we go through an entire natural lifetime in the course of a solar Circle, and relate ourselves with Cosmos as children, adults, mature and old people, regardless of our physical age. They afford a means of making one life provide us with inner experience and evolution which might otherwise take us many incarnations to achieve.

THE RITE OF SPRING

[There is minimum light, as at dawn. If humanly possible this ceremony is best held at dawn. The Companions are seated in their Circle, silent and hooded as if in deep sleep. No sound but that of breathing. When the Officer of the East feels that the right moment has come, he rises, kindles the flame of east, sounds the Call of Life with pipe,

> syrinx or other wind instrument, then trips perimeter deosil, waking each Companion cheerfully, returns to his Station, and declaims as if to quite young people:]

EAST: Awake! Awake! Awake! Awake! Return to life within this mortal world, O Sleeping Ones who wait rebirth from our Great Mother's womb.

Be born again with human hopes, O True Companions of the cosmic light. The shining sun of spiritual strength and splendor wakes and welcomes you to life anew among mankind.

Arise! Arise! Arise! You slumbering children of creation. Here is springtime, and the spirit of eternal youth unquenchably aflame for living and adventure! Accept it and rejoice! Time has turned full Circle, bringing you to birth once more. You are young and fresh again, with every opportunity of life before you. Rise up and claim your birthright, take and use it faithfully according to the cosmic law,

In Perfect Love,
Be What Thou Wilt.

Come into consciousness together, uttering the call of our creation.

I	A	O	M
(EEE)	(YAY)	(OOHH)	(HMMMM)

> [This is the sound of a rising yawn, and also the name of arousing Divinity. All present repeat this vibrantly, rising, stretching arms, etc. as they come to order.]

SOUTH: Blessed be the light arising at our inner dawn to show the way ahead upon our paths.

> [Lights taper from east, and illumine all other lights deosil, returning to Station.]

WEST: Blessed be the word of light above the waters of eternal life that brings us all to being.

NORTH: Blessed be the light delivering our world from darkness and our spirits from despair.

EAST: Companions, it is good to be alive once more together, being as little children with each other, full of wonder and excitement with our new found world. Why should we not enjoy this as all children may, with innocent delight and pleasure?

As we play our games of childhood, so shall we work as adults and evolve as individual souls. Everything arises from our primal patterns, and our best becoming follows on a true beginning. Therefore, if we set our pieces properly at first, the greatest game of life itself is bound to turn out well for us, whatever happens.

Let us try to put this pattern into practice here and now among us. Set up its symbols. Signify it joyfully with fresh fertility of mind and soul. Come forth from weary winter into glorious growing spring with gaiety and gladness. Look at life and laugh! Smile and sing together just because we are alive and full of energy that needs expression. Be happy for the sake of hope alone. To play and pray is one with every child of light. Do both together with a willing heart. Now!

> [Here all decorate the place according to taste with spring flowers, garlands, personal adornments, or whatever has been decided upon. Cloaks and hoods if worn, will be removed. Gay spring dance music played and perfumes diffused. However this may be done, the essential symbol for meditation later on, which must be some arrangement of an egg and seeds artistically combined, has to be either placed on the altar covered with a veil, or ready for production from some convenient place of conceal-

ment. All this is done in the most lighthearted way, there being no reason why people should not chatter and joke like children among themselves if they feel like it. When they are finished and back in their stations, the East calls them to order with three handclaps, as if they were children, and continues:]

EAST: As children of the mysteries ourselves, we realize the power and possibilities of our imagination. Like play-pretense, our thoughts turn into things if we think hard enough for long enough. Let us imagine now that the Divine Ones, whom we honor in our hearts, are asking us what we would ask of them this coming season. How should we answer them?

ALL: *We do not know.*

EAST: That is the truth. Of our own accord we do not know what may be best for us. Therefore in the spirit of sincere simplicity, like little ones that ask with fullest faith, let us approach our primal parents and implore: O Light Divine, be Thou our life, that we may learn thy law of perfect Love, be what Thou wilt.

ALL: *In perfect love, be what Thou wilt.*

SOUTH: Yet suppose our own suggestions were made possible? What ideas among us should we bring to light this springtime? What new notions have we to initiate and start upon their cosmic course? What sort of spiritual seeds do we intend to plant within us so that these may grow to beneficial fruitfulness for everyone concerned? This is the proper time to ask the Holy Ones for help with our endeavors to select and sow what must be rightly chosen and uprightly raised to light by all of us. Let us present our personal petitions to this purpose unto those whose certain aid we confidently ask this instant.

WEST: Who asks for nothing is already answered.

NORTH: Who asks for everything receives the same reward.

EAST: Let us therefore ask no more than due fulfillment of our present needs as human souls upon our pathways to perfection.

> [Here the petitions are collected deosil (clockwise) by South, and presented to East.]

SOUTH: On behalf of our companionship, both present and by proxy, I offer these, our hopes and prayers to the Eternal Ones that They may guide us safely through the gateway of our year ahead.

WEST: May our hopes be truly justified.

NORTH: And may our prayers be heard indeed.

EAST: In the name of the Great Germinator, and the spiritual cultivators of our fields, may these be accepted as good seeds for planting in the garden of the soul, where also may they grow and flourish unto ultimate fulfillment as the fruit and flowers of our most fervent faith. Let their empty husks be burnt to fertilizing ashes by the blessed flame of light among us.

> [Here South takes the petitions again, stacks them in brazier or equivalent saying:]

SOUTH: Blessed be the gentle fire of spring that frees us from the frosts of winter and encourages our new activities.

[Here the Officer of the South lights the fire to burn the petitions, and blesses or consecrates it.]

The Element Fire

Let there be **Light** no darkness may extinguish. Burn evermore, Thou Fire of Love that ripens every spiritual seed. In the separation of thine essence from thy substance lies the work of wisdom. Thou art strongest of the strong, overcoming subtlety and interpenetrating all solidity. In thine adaption is the arcane art, and secret of the sacred science.

We call upon Thee, O Father of All, radiant with thine illuminating rays. O Unseen Parent of the Sun, pour forth thy life-giving power and energize thy Divine Spark. Enter into this flame and let it be agitated by the breath of the Most Holy Spirit.

[Here flame is lit or gestures made.]

Manifest thy power and open for us the hidden temple which is concealed within this flame. May we become regenerated by thy light, and the breadth, height, fullness, and crown of solar radiance appear, so that God within shine forth.

Be Thou consecrated, faithful creature of the fire, through the power, and in the service of, that Supreme Light whose single sparks we surely are. Amen.

[Signify its conclusion to the Officer of the West.]

WEST: Since we are as children, let us sing and dance our way of light around the represented solar point now centered in our Circle.

> [Here a cheerful Circle chant must accompany the tripping peripheral dance around the flame.]

Spring Circle Chant

I am a void and the need of fulfilling.
    EE I O AH-HU, EE I OH HO.
I am a thought and an effort of willing.
    EE I O AH-HU, EE I OH HO.
I am a being and will to begin it.
    EE I O AH-HU, EE I OH HO.
I am a mind and the thinking within it.
    EE I O AH-HU, EE I OH HO.
I am an idea and its utmost abstraction.
    EE I O AH-HU, EE I OH HO.
I am a self for its own satisfaction.
    EE I O AH-HU, EE I OH HO.
I am a force and its centralization.
    EE I O AH-HU, EE I OH HO.
I am a form and its manifestation.
    EE I O AH-HU, EE I OH HO.
I am a light and its ray of reflection.
    EE I O AH-HU, EE I OH HO.
I am a way and its path of direction.
    EE I O AH-HU, EE I OH HO.
I am a word and the sound of it spoken.
    EE I O AH-HU, EE I OH HO.
I am a sign and the truth of its token.
    EE I O AH-HU, EE I OH HO.

I am a voice and the message it utters.
  EE I O AH-HU, EE I OH HO.
I am a breath and the secret it mutters.
  EE I O AH-HU, EE I OH HO.
I am an act and its primal causation.
  EE I O AH-HU, EE I OH HO.
I am a rule and its best regulation.
  EE I O AH-HU, EE I OH HO.
I am a belief and its basic foundation.
  EE I O AH-HU, EE I OH HO.
I am a hope and its realization.
  EE I O AH-HU, EE I OH HO.
I am an aim and its hidden intention.
  EE I O AH-HU, EE I OH HO.
I am a notion and all its invention.
  EE I O AH-HU, EE I OH HO.
I am a soul and the depth of its feeling.
  EE I O AH-HU, EE I OH HO.
I am a hurt and the hope of its healing.
  EE I O AH-HU, EE I OH HO.
I am a deed and the daring that did it.
  EE I O AH-HU, EE I OH HO.
I am a fault and the mercy that hid it.
  EE I O AH-HU, EE I OH HO.
I am a right and a reason for living.
  EE I O AH-HU, EE I OH HO.
I am a wrong and the grace of forgiving.
  EE I O AH-HU, EE I OH HO.
I am a smile and expression of gladness.
  EE I O AH-HU, EE I OH HO.
I am a sigh and sensation of sadness.
  EE I O AH-HU, EE I OH HO.
I am a dream and the solace of sleeping.
  EE I O AH-HU, EE I OH HO.
I am a fear and the sorrow of weeping.
  EE I O AH-HU, EE I OH HO.

I am a prayer and its silent petition.
>EE I O AH-HU, EE I OH HO.

I am a remorse and the deepest contrition.
>EE I O AH-HU, EE I OH HO.

I am a faith and its constant revision.
>EE I O AH-HU, EE I OH HO.

I am a choice and a final decision.
>EE I O AH-HU, EE I OH HO.

I am a life and the will of survival.
>EE I O AH-HU, EE I OH HO.

I am a death and a sense of revival.
>EE I O AH-HU, EE I OH HO.

I am a part of an ultimate union.
>EE I O AH-HU, EE I OH HO.

I am the whole of an inner communion.
>EE I O AH-HU, EE I OH HO.

[Gong]

EAST: **Whoever You are, and however You try, be still and consider, the One that am I.**

> [While the circling proceeds, everyone must try his best to visualize, imagine or feel the presence of the inner entity coming to take its place personally in the midst of the dancing invocants. Should the ashes of the petitions be too hot at the end of the dance, the Officer of the North will take up a small dish of prearranged cold ashes, and presenting them to the East, say:]

NORTH: I bear the ashes of abandoned hopes.

EAST: From these, the faithful seed of spirit springs eternally.

[Takes ashes and places them with a pot of earth, knife, or whatever means will be used for planting the selected seed or bulb later.]

SOUTH: Thanks be for light arising in the east.

WEST: May we perceive with it our pathways to perfection.

NORTH: How stand we this moment?

EAST: We stand before the light of dawn
That greets a human soul reborn
To mortal life again.
Yet how shall we be truly wise
When new occasions now arise
For pleasure and for pain?

SOUTH: Which is the way to wisdom?

WEST: Human trouble mainly springs
From lacking or excess of things
Like two opposing streams.
The art that we should cultivate
Is keeping on a course made straight
Between all such extremes.

NORTH: Blessed be the light that guides our lives, and this, the earth it shines on, that supports our living.

[Here North mixes the ashes with the earth in the pot or pots for seed planting, then blesses or consecrates the earth element.]

The Element Earth

Of slime and clay did the Creative Spirit form the flesh and bones of man, our bodies being of rich red earth and particles of dust. May we manifest through matter with true wills that we shall ultimately rise to be the rightful rulers and adminstrators of this outer kingdom we experience in ordinary living.

We call upon Thee by thine olden and beloved name, O Mother Earth. Thine is our field of present life, and by thine aid do we remain the human beings we are. Enter into this, thine element of earth, and stablize us with thy firm solidity.

[Here the earth is signed, or gestures made.]

Manifest for us the meaning of those special secrets we must learn in order to observe thy laws, and find our purpose on this planet. May we truly grow from being children of creation into loyal and faithful subjects of the Supreme Living Spirit.

Be Thou consecrated, faithful creature of the earth, through the power, and in the service of, that solitary Self-existing One, whose single atoms we most surely are. Amen.

[Finally presents the earth containers or a single pot to East saying:]

As matter has no meaning without mind, so soil has no significance without a seed. Let light breathe forth itself as life.

[East breathes over earth.]

EAST: By the holy breath in us that is our living spirit, be this substance sanctified for service to our souls.

[Here East blesses or consecrates the element of air.]

The Element Air

In the beginning, did the Holy Spirit issue from the void and breathe a vital, living soul into mankind. May we also breathe forth words which act throughout our inner atmosphere, and bring to life our latent spiritual qualities.

We call upon Thee, O Thou Source of inspiration filling us with faith that we shall find our final and immortal freedom in the spheres of spirit. Speak unto our souls that we may hold the echoes of thy harmony. Enter into this, thine ambient element that it may bear for us thy vibrant voice.

> [Here suitable gestures or actions are made.]

Manifest thy meaning for us, that the winds of truth will wake us with thy messages, and may the angels of the air become apparent to our eyes of inner vision.

Be Thou consecrated, faithful creature of the air, through the power, and in the service of, the One Eternal Life whose single breaths we surely are. Amen.

SOUTH: Good is the ground laid open to the winds of truth and radiated by the sun of righteousness.

WEST: Life must come from Love alone. As water was our one-time womb, and moisture is our mother milk on earth, let us approach the spirit set above the waters of compassion and regeneration.

> [Here West blesses or consecrates the element of water, but no salt must be put in that portion of the water intended for moistening the seed pot or pots. Two sorts of cup are useful here, one for the seed, and the other for the people. West will deliver the former to the Officer of East when it is blessed, and

it will be put ready on the altar or whatever surface is otherwise used.]

The Element Water

Let there be a firmament in the midst of the waters so that sea and sky may separate into themselves. That which is above is like to that which is below for the appearance of a single wonder. The Sun is its Father, the Moon its Mother, and the wind has carried it into conception. It ascends from earth to Heaven, and descends to earth again when it is due.

We call upon Thee, O Thou Mighty Mother of whose womb comes everlasting life. Maiden of the Mysteries art Thou, and nurse of all that lives by means of nature. Enter into this, thine element of water, moving it for us by thy compassion.

[Here water is salted or just blessed with a gesture.]

Manifest for us thy potency and open unto us the hidden depths of wisdom. May we savor whatsoever we experience there in with the appreciative salt of good sound sense, and let all tides, waves, and currents of the cosmic ocean bear our consciousness toward the anchorage of our eventual attainment.

Be Thou consecrated, faithful creature of water, through the power, and in the service of, that Universal Sea of Spirit whose particular and scattered drops we surely are. Amen.

NORTH: Blessed be the seed inplanted in a fertile field, for it will ever grow towards the light with strength and splendor.

EAST: Blessed be the seed itself, and all that it implies. The very smallest living seed on earth is infinitely greater in its meaning than the mightiest thing mankind will ever make. Consider this tremendous truth with wonder and humility, yet look upon the symbols of its Holy Mystery with confidence and love, because

> The emblem of a seed
> Shows life Divine indeed.

> [Here a gong should be sounded, and the meditational emblem of an egg and seeds of some sort set out in a pleasing design is placed where it can conveniently be considered by all, or unveiled if it is there already. Everyone now sits quietly and meditates a few minutes either silently or to suitable music. When this is completed, South gives the signal to rise, saying:]

SOUTH: It is written truthfully that as we sow, we shall eventually reap. Now is the season for our sowing. What seed of light is this which we will plant among us?

WEST: Let it be duly named and planted deep within us, so that it will germinate and grow into the flower and fruit of all the faith we here and now place in it.

> [The name of the seed is the "keyword" for the season. As the year progresses, it is changed to suit each phase of the solar cycle accordingly.]

NORTH: May it bring us Blessings of the spirit, manifested through our souls and substance as our minds appreciate this action.

> [East selects seed.]

EAST: Blessed be this chosen seed ____[Name]____ that comes to life among us here and now. May it open unto us the inner ways we search for, and fulfill our present prayers and purpose with its fruits. Be it born of us, and bear within it the intentions of our truest will, that it and we may grow together unto the eternal light whence every living entity emanated.

[Dipping seed in water:]

O Greatest Ocean Mother of all life,
Unfathomed secret sea.
Bless Thou for us this living link
With thine infinity.

[As seed emerges.]

Welcome to our world O ____[Name]____. Blessed be that which comes among us, in the name of the wisdom, the love, the justice, and the infinite mercy of the one eternal spirit, Amen.

[The Cross is made with these words.]

ALL: *So mote it be. Amen.*

SOUTH: A seed unplanted is a word unuttered and a power unproven.

WEST: Blessed be the word that awaits within a willing womb.

[Here North kneels toward East, holding up cupped hands awaiting the pot of earth.]

NORTH: May emptiness be filled, silence hear the word, stillness move, and darkness be enlightened.

[East places earth pot in North's hands, makes hole in earth with dagger point or finger, inserts seed, pours in a little water, then smooths earth over, marking the Circle Cross sign on top.]

EAST: In perfect love,
Let there be life.

[Gong. North stands and elevates pot.]

Behold the miracle of life made manifest among us by the law of light; in perfect Love be what Thou wilt.

ALL: *O Perfect Love, be what Thou wilt.*

SOUTH: Blessed be this day and our devoted deed.

WEST: Blessed be this springtime and our new sown seed.

NORTH: Glory be unto the Greatest One to whom we grow, whose garden has no limits, and whose everlasting season never ends.

[If any other pots are to be planted for a special reason such as other individuals or groups, East does this now, simply repeating a brief blessing over each.]

EAST: O Thou supreme Life Spirit, cause of every change throughout creation, origin of all, and single source of every living soul, of Thee alone is our beginning, and in Thee alone we have no ending. Blessed be thy name and names of us for evermore.

As we have duly sown thy sacred symbol of the seed this springtime, set Thou likewise in our hearts and souls the sacred spark of thine immortal light.

Grant us, we pray, a peaceful season of progression. Let us perceive fresh light upon our Paths and follow this with faith throughout thy plans for our perfection. May this truly be thy will in us and our true will in Thee that we may ultimately unify in everlasting Love.

ALL: *So mote it be. Amen.*

SOUTH: Since we have been brought to light and life, be this our cause for celebration with the cup.

WEST: As springtime before summer, work before reward, and innocence before experience, so should water precede wine. It is right and proper that we should partake of water at this season since without it how could wine exist? With pure water be our primal ancestors remembered, for it was the only wine available to them. Because they were, we are together at this time and place. We live from them, their spirits live in us. Blessed be life for evermore.

NORTH: Whoso refuses water rejects life itself. Be it thankfully accepted by us all.

EAST: Be not bread forgotten so that our descendants may remember us.

SOUTH: And may it become for us a staff of life on earth that raises us to perfect light in Heaven.

WEST: Better is the simplest sustenance with Love and trust than sumptuous fare with hatred and suspicion.

NORTH: Let us share with one another willingly the least we hold, which may be more than we shall ever have.

> [Here the East, as principal Officer of the season, blesses or consecrates the cup of water and platter of bread. These elements may be carried round the circle to each Companion by the Officer of the Cord, or else passed from one to another deosil.]

Blessing the Bread

Blessed be unto Divinity and all of us, our body of belief we share together which unites us unto one another for the sake of loving kindness.

May this special sign with which we seek to feed our faith, sustain our souls to an immortal life in spirit.

> In the name of the **Wisdom**,
>   and of the **Love**,
>   and of the **Justice**,
>   and of the Infinite **Mercy**,
>   of the One Eternal **Spirit**,
>   **Amen.**

Blessing the Wine

Blessed be unto Divinity and all of us, that cup of consciousness wherein the essence of eternal entity and our awareness of it, meet and mingle for the sake of life in one another.

May this special sign by which we hope to realize our true identity, communicate to us the Holy Presence we now humbly seek within our secret hearts.

> In the name of the **Wisdom**,
>   and of the **Love**,
>   and of the **Justice**,
>   and of the Infinite **Mercy**,
>   of the One Eternal **Spirit**,
>   **Amen.**

[When the cup and platter are empty, and recovered by West and North respectively, East says:]

EAST: Companions of the year ahead, be cheerful. The seed is sown, the gates are open, and events await us on the way that we must go. Let us sing and dance the season in.

SOUTH: Companions, come to order cheerfully, for all good times must gracefully become a blessed memory. Happily we met, happily we worked, now happily our ways must part that we may meet in happiness again.

WEST: In what way shall we meet next time?

NORTH: The way for which our word was chosen.

EAST: What is our password of the period?

ALL: [say password]

EAST: Thanks be to the protecting powers that we have worked these Rites in peace, and may we face our future both with confidence and competence. Be a final blessing bidden to us,

>In the name of the **Wisdom**,
>   and of the **Love**,
>   and of the **Justice**,
>   and of the Infinite **Mercy**,
>   of the One Eternal **Spirit**,
>   **Amen.**

Now let us close according to established custom.

THE RITE OF SUMMER

[There is maximum light, everyone is alert and in a state of free motion, miming some task connected with the season. The Officer of the South is Principal. When the moment seems right, South sounds a horn, or raps with a staff to call order. All attend.]

SOUTH: Companions, let us pause a while to rest from all our labors in the light, and celebrate our coming season at this summit of the solar cycle.

WEST: Blessed be the sun that shines at noon upon our inner day and throws no shadow on our paths ahead.

NORTH: Blessed be this time of our enlightenment, and welcome is the warmth with which we ought to live with one another in this world.

EAST: Blessed be the light, the Love, the learning and the life whereby we come together for this work.

SOUTH: High is summer. Let our spirits likewise raise themselves above all clouds of ignorance, so that we may once more regain the heaven of the splendid stars from whence we came to earth as solar seeds.

Work with will and play with purest pleasure, O Ye Men and Maidens of these mysteries. We have work to do together with our fellow mortals in the fields of consciousness which we must cultivate and care for while we are in human form. There is enjoyment to be found in every kind of effort when we learn to look for it with opened inner eyes. However much we may have done already, there is yet far more for us to bring to light within this company, and for the good of all with whom we are concerned.

We need have no fears of failure while the Inner Ones are with us. Are we not employed upon the greatest work of all? Surely we are young and strong enough to forge ahead with perfect faith and confidence that we shall reach the spiritual states we seek if we continue in our cosmic course? However we may lose our way or falter for a moment, can we not recover balance and proceed again whenever we sincerely ask the Holy Ones for their assistance? Let us call upon Them now, and give the ancient greeting from a mortal striving soul to the Immortal Living Spirit.

$$\begin{array}{ccc} \text{I} & \text{A} & \text{O} \\ \text{(EE)} & \text{(YAY)} & \text{(YO)} \end{array}$$

[All repeat this sonic resonantly and loudly.]

WEST: Companions, let us gladly take responsibility for what we are, and all that we may do together. We are no longer helpless children in the mysteries, but old enough to realize and follow out the meanings of man's oldest faith. The sacred seed we sowed at springtime has become a precious plant in flower among us. Now it must be cherished carefully, so that its fruit will be our means of life when we have grown beyond these mortal bodies.

Nature flourishes around us, and so we should flourish also. Since our Great Mother shows her beauty, let these members of her family be beautiful likewise. Put out the pleasant signs of summer with rejoicing and appreciation. Great indeed are They we honor with this happy custom. May They truly link with us through all that lives, and may we learn to link with Them by every leaf upon the tree of life itself.

> [Here the signs, garlands, gauds, etc. are set up or distributed. The veiled solar symbol of a flowering yellow plant and appropriate trimmings is either placed ready, or as suitable for production at the meditation period. Music and full movements. When all is ready, North calls to order.]

NORTH: Blessed are the signs of summer all around us.

EAST: May they show us how to reach the realms of everlasting youth we hope to find within our hearts held high to Heaven.

SOUTH: Let us think about ourselves a while, and wonder what we are accomplishing as willers of the work we claim to care for in the spiritual spheres we are supposed to cultivate. What have we done since spring to earn our living in the state of light, or claim companionship with Cosmos? Are we worthy or unworthy workers? Who can answer us, excepting those whose work is done by using us as instruments, and They speak silently. If They spoke with human words, and asked us now what we are doing in their names, how should we answer Them?

WEST: With faith in confidence.

ALL: *With faith in confidence.*

NORTH: This is the true tongue of the Holy Ones. If we communicate with Them by our beliefs, They will reply in language that enlightened souls may understand. Let their aid be asked upon our present undertakings.

EAST: O Thou Single Source of light and life whose scattered seeds we are on earth, thanks be that we have grown and flourished as we stand within thy garden. Prosper Thou, we pray, whatever further efforts we must make in thy Divine direction.

SOUTH: We expect so much from Inner Ones, and now They only ask in gentle ways what we have done on their behalf, or would accomplish if we could. How have we worked since seed time? What are we doing now? What are our hopes of harvest? Who is ready with a reasonable answer?

> [Here the Officer of the West collects the written petitions and hands them to South.]

WEST: On behalf of our companionship, both present and by proxy, I present before these portals the petitions from the hearts and souls of all among us who believe in the essential goodness of the Great Eternal Ones behind our being.

NORTH: Blessed be their steadfast light beyond all darkness. Now does night pay homage unto everlasting day.

EAST: Let these emblems of our secret thoughts and prayers be sent through fire to highest light. May reflection upon what has passed illuminate our present, that our future may be clearer to us.

[South stacks petitions in brazier or as for burning.]

SOUTH: Blessed be the faithful fires of summer kindled on the hilltops of the outer world and deep within our hearts in honor of the High Ones we would work for and enjoy existing with. During ages past, we offered blood upon our altars, then progressed to sacrificing fruits of earth or precious gifts. Now we have learned to dedicate our living souls to light, instead of mere material possessions. Here we stand stonefast within our cosmic Circle, offering ourselves as an oblation. May we be accepted in the spirit moving us to make this true **At-one-ment**. May the Blessed Ones enlighten us this summer season, and throughout our time for evermore.

[Here South consecrates and lights the fire.]

The Element Fire

Let there be light no darkness may extinguish. Burn evermore, Thou Fire of Love that ripens every spiritual seed. In the separation of thine essence from thy substance lies the work of wisdom. Thou art strongest of the strong, overcoming subtlety and interpenetrating all solidity. In thine adaption is the arcane art, and secret of the sacred science.

We call upon Thee, O Father of All, radiant with thine illuminating rays. O Unseen Parent of the Sun, pour forth thy life-giving power and energize thy Divine Spark. Enter into this flame and let it be agitated by the breath of the Most Holy Spirit.

[Here flame is lit or gestures made.]

Manifest thy power and open for us the hidden temple which is concealed within this flame. May we become regenerated by thy light, and the breadth, height, fullness, and crown of solar radiance appear, so that God within shine forth.

Be Thou consecrated, faithful creature of the fire, through the power, and in the service of, that Supreme Light whose single sparks we surely are. Amen.

WEST: Blessed be the sun that comes among us as a friendly fire.

NORTH: Let us dance the measure of this mystery around and through the flame of faith that we have kindled in the name of light within our circle.

EAST: And may our spiritual links with inner life become true partners of our progress.

> [Here the Circle dance is performed, while the human participants endeavor to "dance down" the invisible companions among them. They try to dance through the fire in some way, even if a hand is only rapidly passed across the flame. At the conclusion, order is called by South.]

SOUTH: Thanks be for light increased among us.

WEST: Shining at the sun of summer overhead.

NORTH: Overcoming all deceits of darkness.

EAST: How stand we at this moment?

SOUTH: We stand between the day and night
When darkness has been lost in light,
Being neither curst nor blest.
Betwixt this way of wrong and right,
Our choice is clear through black and white.
The middle path is best.

ALL: *Show us the Way and we will follow.*

WEST: The way is straight, the path is long,
While flesh is weak, but spirit strong,
We need to **Be** and **Know**.
Who enters life is past recall,
For none may rise save we that fall,
Above is reached **below**.

NORTH: How blows the wind of summer?

EAST: It blows our blossoms into their full flowering. Blessed be the light revealing their true beauty to beholders by the inner sight. Blessed also be the wholesome air that brings us inspiration as we breathe it with belief.

> [Here Officer of the East blesses and consecrates the element of air. Flower petals may be scattered during this.]

The Element Air

In the beginning, did the Holy Spirit issue from the void and breathe a vital, living soul into mankind. May we also breathe forth words which act throughout our inner atmosphere, and bring to life our latent spiritual qualities.

We call upon Thee, O Thou Source of inspiration filling us with faith that we shall find our final and immortal freedom in the spheres of spirit. Speak unto our souls that we may hold the echoes of thy harmony. Enter into this, thine ambient element that it may bear for us thy vibrant voice.

[Here suitable gestures or actions are made.]

Manifest thy meaning for us, that the wind of truth will wake us with thy messages, and may the angels of the air become apparent to our eyes of inner vision.

Be Thou consecrated, faithful creature of the air, through the power, and in the service of, the One Eternal Life whose single breaths we surely are. Amen.

SOUTH: A miracle has come among us as an answer to our prayers. Here is a work of wonder wrought by the Creative Ones themselves, and utterly beyond our human hands to make, or mortal minds' design.

Behold might manifest as mercy in the lovely form of flowers. Contemplate the blessing of such beauty both with reverence and rapture. None but Divinity itself would dare conceive simplicity in such a supreme way as this.

[Here the floral emblem is produced and contemplated in silence or to suitable music. At the conclusion West speaks:]

WEST: From what seed sprang this bloom before us?

NORTH: From ____[Name]____ that was sown last spring.

EAST: How shall we name the flower among us?

SOUTH: Let us agree to call it ____[Name]____.

ALL: *So mote it be. Amen.*

SOUTH: Blessed be this flower that has been brought to bloom within our cosmic Circle as a symbol of the spirit in whose beauty we believe with our whole hearts. May we flourish faithfully and grow to grace the gardens of eternal glory,

> In the name of the **Wisdom**,
> and of the **Love**,
> and of the **Justice**,
> and of the Infinite **Mercy**,
> of the One Eternal **Spirit**,
> **Amen.**

ALL: *So mote it be. Amen.*

WEST: Whoso plucks a flower prevents a fruit.

NORTH: Let us continue with its cultivation, that the fruit may form.

EAST: Be it so with water and with willing work.

SOUTH: May the waters of the west work well with us.

> [West here blesses or consecrates the element of water in a ewer, basin or pool, as the case may be.]

The Element Water

Let there be a firmament in the midst of the waters so that sea and sky may separate into themselves. That which is above is like to that which is below for the appearance of a single wonder. The Sun is its Father, the Moon its Mother, and the wind has carried it into conception. It ascends from earth to Heaven, and descends to earth again when it is due.

We call upon Thee, O Thou Mighty Mother of whose womb comes everlasting life. Maiden of the Mysteries art Thou, and nurse of all that lives by means of nature. Enter into this, thine element of water, moving it for us by thy compassion.

[Here water is salted or just blessed with a gesture.]

Manifest for us thy potency and open unto us the hidden depths of wisdom. May we savor whatsoever we experience therein with the appreciative salt of good sound sense, and let all tides, waves, and currents of the cosmic ocean bear our consciousness toward the anchorage of our eventual attainment.

Be Thou consecrated, faithful creature of the water, through the power, and in the service of, the Universal Sea of Spirit whose particular and scattered drops we surely are. Amen.

Only over water may the greatest name of all be uttered. Though no mortal mouth may give this forth, we offer up our call above the water to the winds of Heaven hoping that we may be heard by that which brought us into being.

I   A   O
(EE)   (YAH)   (YOH)

[The call is sounded over the water to the four quarters by West:]

NORTH: Let an echo of this universal utterance reach everyone within our world.

EAST: May it be borne by every breath of air.

SOUTH: May it be flashed by every form of fire.

WEST: May it be written with each wave of water.

NORTH: May the word of will in us be felt as firmly as this earth beneath our feet.

[Here the Officer of North consecrates the element of earth.]

The Element Earth

Of slime and clay did the Creative Spirit form the flesh and bones of man, our bodies being of rich red earth and particles of dust. May we manifest through matter with true wills that we shall ultimately rise to be the rightful rulers and administrators of this outer kingdom we experience in ordinary living.

We call upon Thee by thine olden and beloved name, O Mother Earth. Thine is our field of present life, and by thine aid do we remain the human beings we are. Enter into this, thine element of earth, and stabilize us with thy firm solidity.

[Here the earth is signed, or gestures made.]

Manifest for us the meaning of those special secrets we must learn in order to observe thy laws, and find our purpose on this planet. May we truly grow from being children of creation into loyal and faithful subjects of the Supreme Living Spirit.

Be Thou consecrated, faithful creature of the earth, through the power, and in the service of, the solitary Self-existing One, whose single atoms we most surely are. Amen.

EAST: How shall our purely human hands not tire of everlasting toil with this, or any other sort of earth?

SOUTH: By refreshing them with radiance from our immortal sun of spirit and by plunging them within the pool of *Peace Profound*.

WEST: Come then, Companion, wash away with will our weariness from work or worry in this world. Be rested and regenerated by the waters of compassion, in the depths of which the Supreme Spirit of Surpassing Love renews the life of every single soul.

> [Here the whole company of the Circle ablute. They file around the circle past the west point, dipping their fingers and drying them. As each ablutes, the West says:]

WEST: Be purity and peace upon you.

> In the name of the **Wisdom,**
> and of the **Love,**
> and of the **Justice,**
> and of the Infinite **Mercy,**
> of the One Eternal **Spirit,**
>   **Amen.**

NORTH: As water opens up the way for wine, now let perfume mark our pathways to perfection.

EAST: What must we give to gain perfection?

SOUTH: A flower gives out its perfume to the atmosphere of all the world, and yet retains its own perfections for itself. So does the goodness of the Great Ones come to all of us without diminishing the single source of its supply.

As our animals communicate by means of scent, and flowers by fragrance, so has the human soul an odor of its own, pervading worlds most proper to itself.

Therefore we should learn to live so that we may make a pleasant perfume for the Inner Ones as we approach Them. To this end let us anoint ourselves in honor of the Blessed Ones whose company we seek this season and for evermore.

[Blesses anointing oil, saying:]

Blessed be the fragrance of this oil wherewith both light and beauty may be manifest about us. By sharing its aroma, may we truly be of one accord as a most welcome savor to the High Ones unto whom we now aspire in spirit. May it help to cover our remaining human imperfections with its perfume as we present ourselves before the Holy Presence,

> In the name of the **Wisdom**,
> and of the **Love**,
> and of the **Justice**,
> and of the Infinite **Mercy**,
> of the One Eternal **Spirit**,
> **Amen.**

Come then, Companions, let us be anointed with the sacred scent by which true dedicants to light and beauty are made known to one another, and the single spirit that all serve together. May the fragrance of the simplest flower provide us with sufficient faith to lead us into *Peace Profound* for evermore.

[Here the Companions either file past the Officer of the South, who anoints them, or he goes around the circle, depending on convenience. As he anoints each, he says:]

SOUTH: May light and beauty be upon you

In the name of the **Wisdom,**

[touches forehead]

and of the **Love,**

[chin]

and of the **Justice,**

[right cheek]

and of the Infinite **Mercy,**

[left cheek]

of the One Eternal **Spirit,**

[encircle face]

Amen.

[under nose]

[South anoints himself last.]

WEST: Let the cup be circulated, that we may be cheered upon our ways of light. Of olden times our ancestors used ale to celebrate this season, since it seemed to them the blood of that beneficence which brought them barley bread. Let us share this symbol gladly in our company with that same spirit which commenced the custom and continues it among us at the present time.

NORTH: As ale is liquid, bread is solid grain. Let the cakes of bread be not forgotten. They make good bodies for a willing soul to live in.

EAST: Be a blessing bidden upon both.

> [Here the Officer of the South, as Principal, blesses the cup, which may have barley wine in it if ale is not wanted, and also the bread cakes. These are passed round the circle first, and the cup last.]

SOUTH: Blessed be this season of the summer sun, and all it shines on visibly or inwardly. Even though it may be hidden from us by the darkest clouds, let us ever keep its glorious light undimmed within us, shining in our hearts and radiating warmth around us unto every other soul.

WEST: Be the season started with a cheerful song. Let us make melody among us:

1. Now is high midsummer sun,
    hay down, hi down, ho down, hu-u down.
   But living time is never done,
    hay down, ho down, deri down day.

2. Cease all sorrow, stop all strife,
    hay down, hi down, ho down, hu-u down.
   Come hopeful hearts and a happy life,
    hay down, ho down, deri down day.

3. If you mind midsummer day,
    hay down, hi down, ho down, hu-u down.
   Luck and love will come your way,
    hay down, ho down, deri down day.

4. Joy and gladness, good and true,
    hay down, hi down, ho down, hu-u down.

SOUTH: May light and beauty be upon you

> In the name of the **Wisdom,**
>
>> [touches forehead]
>
> and of the **Love,**
>
>> [chin]
>
> and of the **Justice,**
>
>> [right cheek]
>
> and of the Infinite **Mercy,**
>
>> [left cheek]
>
> of the One Eternal **Spirit,**
>
>> [encircle face]
>
>> **Amen.**
>
>> [under nose]
>
>> [South anoints himself last.]

WEST: Let the cup be circulated, that we may be cheered upon our ways of light. Of olden times our ancestors used ale to celebrate this season, since it seemed to them the blood of that beneficence which brought them barley bread. Let us share this symbol gladly in our company with that same spirit which commenced the custom and continues it among us at the present time.

NORTH: As ale is liquid, bread is solid grain. Let the cakes of bread be not forgotten. They make good bodies for a willing soul to live in.

EAST: Be a blessing bidden upon both.

> [Here the Officer of the South, as Principal, blesses the cup, which may have barley wine in it if ale is not wanted, and also the bread cakes. These are passed round the circle first, and the cup last.]

SOUTH: Blessed be this season of the summer sun, and all it shines on visibly or inwardly. Even though it may be hidden from us by the darkest clouds, let us ever keep its glorious light undimmed within us, shining in our hearts and radiating warmth around us unto every other soul.

WEST: Be the season started with a cheerful song. Let us make melody among us:

1. Now is high midsummer sun,
     hay down, hi down, ho down, hu-u down.
   But living time is never done,
     hay down, ho down, deri down day.

2. Cease all sorrow, stop all strife,
     hay down, hi down, ho down, hu-u down.
   Come hopeful hearts and a happy life,
     hay down, ho down, deri down day.

3. If you mind midsummer day,
     hay down, hi down, ho down, hu-u down.
   Luck and love will come your way,
     hay down, ho down, deri down day.

4. Joy and gladness, good and true,
     hay down, hi down, ho down, hu-u down.

Come to me and go to you,
   hay down, ho down, deri down day.

5. Who is older than the sun?
   hay down, hi down, ho down, hu-u down.
   That in whom all lives are one,
   hay down, ho down, deri down day.

6. Who is wiser than the rest?
   hay down, hi down, ho down, hu-u down.
   Only who knows what is best,
   hay down, ho down, deri down day.

7. Who is greatest of the great?
   hay down, hi down, ho down, hu-u down.
   That which stays the hand of fate,
   hay down, ho down, deri down day.

8. Who is higher than the sky?
   hay down, hi down, ho down, hu-u down.
   Whoso outgrows the tallest lie,
   hay down, ho down, deri down day.

9. If you would have every right,
   hay down, hi down, ho down, hu-u down.
   Follow on the way of light,
   hay down, ho down, deri down day.

10. Here is common sense to try,
    hay down, hi down, ho down, hu-u down.
    Do as you would be done by,
    hay down, ho down, deri down day.

11. Here is counsel to fulfill,
    hay down, hi down, ho down, hu-u down.
    If you harm none do what you will,
    hay down, ho down, deri down day.

12. Now be gladsome, light and gay,
        hay down, hi down, ho down, hu-u down.
    On this good midsummer day,
        hay down, ho down, deri down day.

NORTH: Companions, come to order cheerfully, for all good things must sometimes be a blessed memory. Happy did we meet, now happy let us part, that happily we all may meet again together.

EAST: In what way shall we meet again?

SOUTH: The way for which our word was chosen. What is that word?

ALL: [Repeat password.]

SOUTH: In that way of light let us proceed in peace with thanks to the Eternal Ones that we have worked our Rite according to our will. Now let us close in our accustomed manner.

> In the name of the **Wisdom**,
>   and of the **Love**,
>   and of the **Justice**,
>   and of the Infinite **Mercy**,
>   of the One Eternal **Spirit**,
>   **Amen.**

THE RITE OF AUTUMN

[The place is lit as for sunset. Harvest signs evident. The principal Officer is West. Everyone has taken on an air of being middle-aged and prosperous, cheerful to a degree and relaxed in character. When the time seems ripe, West calls to order:]

WEST: Companions, here at last comes harvest time that we have worked for. Blessed be the fruits of our endeavors and the generosity of the Immortal Ones that gave us grace to gather them.

NORTH: Let all be safely stored against the waiting days of winter when the longest shadows lie across the land.

EAST: As carefully collected provender protects us from the full effects of famine upon earth, so may the contents of our minds and souls provide against our spiritual starvation.

SOUTH: Hearty be our harvest, and in highest honor held the willing hands that bring it home for us.

WEST: Nothing is for nothing in all worlds. As we sowed and tended, so must we now reap. At this season of requital and reward we have to ask the Great Ones for our due returns from service in their fields. We shall be fairly and most fully paid for what we have accomplished, and even granted credit for our good intentions. Nothing will be held from us that we deserve, nor can we possibly be cheated by, or cheat ourselves, the All Aware Accountant of our actions. Let us call attention from the Inner Beings of our beliefs by uttering the ancient cry,

       I   A   O
   (EE) (YAY) (YOH)

ALL: [Echo call vibrantly.]

NORTH: May we ourselves become the welcome harvest of the Blessed Ones upon this earth.

EAST: Companions, what sort of harvest have we any right to hope for in exchange for our endeavors of the past? If we claim rewards for what we did that was worthwhile, we must risk retribution for our less deserving deeds. Who is sure enough of how they stand in spiritual status to make definite demands for what Divinity may owe them?

Now that night and day are equal, we have this brief opportunity for balancing the best against the worst in us, and asking the Eternal Ones to compensate the difference as lightly as may be.

Let us set out the signs and symbols of this autumn season, so that we may honor with due forms the spiritual power providing what is due to us.

> [Here the signs, garlands, etc. are set out according to will. The emblem of meditation is crucial and must include stems of ripe wheat or barley. There should be a dish of assorted fruits, at least one fruit per person. A small sickle or shears of the ritual type should be available. Music of an autumnal sort.]

SOUTH: Blessed be the hearty signs of autumn gathered pleasantly around us.

WEST: Companions, let us try and realize what we are worth intrinsically as individual living souls. We obviously cannot know our value to the Highest One, nor should we ever set too low an estimate on our most irreplaceable and precious legacy of light.

How can we honestly put prices on ourselves, and say sincerely what we should receive as due returns for what we think we have accomplished on behalf of those from whom we claim our recompense? We are worth no more nor less to the Eternal Ones than They are worth to us as spiritual standards which we value as the fundamental basis of our beings, behavior and beliefs. Who dares declare what this may be in each of us?

   Yet our time has come within this solar cycle when we have the right and privilege to ask the Holy Ones for our fair share of what we are entitled to, by what we have become within ourselves since we began to earn our self-existence. If They asked us in return what we consider our true compensation ought to be, how should we answer Them?

NORTH: In absolute sincerity, not fearing the Requiting Ones nor favoring ourselves.

EAST: As we deal with Them, so may They duly deal with us.

SOUTH: Be a Blessing bidden upon us and on our harvest work that waits our hands.

WEST: O Thou Perfect Power of Providence, from whom proceeds all we shall ever be, bless Thou what we may gather of thy bounty and beneficence from every source supplying our spiritual needs. Let the level of our measure be according to the balance of thy might and mercy.

>In the name of the **Wisdom**,
> and of the **Love**,
> and of the **Justice**,
> and of the Infinite **Mercy**,
> of the One Eternal **Spirit**,
>   **Amen.**

NORTH: Naught pays for naught on inner, as on outer, levels of our lives. If we set no value on ourselves, then how may we expect the Holy Ones to value us? Let us at least present our personal petitions to those Mighty Beings. They will deal with us according to the way we deal with them in honesty and honor.

EAST: May our offerings from earth be found of good account by Heaven.

> [Here the South collects accounts, or the Officer of the Cord may do so, and these are presented to the West Portal.]

SOUTH: On behalf of our companionship, both present and by proxy, I present these true petitions of our hopes this harvest time among us all who work with will in spiritual fields of inner cultivation.

WEST: May these be accepted in the spirit they are offered, and according to the asking may the answers be received in recompense for what has been requested. Let us submit these estimations of ourselves to the decisive test of fire, from whence the burning light of truth alone emerges. This should be sufficient for each honest soul to recognize his proper payment.

NORTH: Blessed be the careful fire of autumn, ripening the fruits of earth, and separating good from worthless growth.

EAST: May what we sow on earth be reaped by Heaven, and the seeds which we have sown in spirit come to wholesome harvest in this world.

SOUTH: O Thou Eternal One from whom our lives originate, and by whose grace we grow to what is best we should become, take Thou our thoughts and turn them into things, as we take things and turn them into thoughts.

Here are the tokens of our self-esteem on earth. We only offer them as a sincere attempt to bring ourselves before Thee for whatever we are worth as souls who seek to serve thy cause of Cosmos. Measure these against thy boundless Love in which we trust completely, then—be it As Thou Wilt with us forever.

May the light of sunset shine resplendently on us this autumn equinox, that the surpassing glory of the heavens might enfold us for a single moment here and now on earth.

> [Here the petitions are stacked, the fire lit and consecrated by South.]

The Element Fire

Let there be light no darkness may extinguish. Burn evermore Thou Fire of Love that ripens every spiritual seed. In the separation of thine essence from thy substance lies the work of wisdom. Thou art strongest of the strong, overcoming subtlety and interpenetrating all solidity. In thine adaption is the arcane art, and secret of the sacred science.

We call upon Thee, O Father of All, radiant with thine illuminating rays. O Unseen Parent of the Sun, pour forth thy life-giving power and energize thy Divine Spark. Enter into this flame and let it be agitated by the breath of the Most Holy Spirit.

> [Here flame is lit or gestures made.]

Manifest thy power and open for us the hidden temple which is concealed within this flame. May we become regenerated by thy light, and the breadth, height, fullness, and crown of solar Radiance appear, so that God within shines forth.

Be Thou consecrated, faithful creature of the fire, through the power and in the service of, that Supreme Light whose single sparks we surely are. Amen.

WEST: Blessed be the sun of autumn bringing heavenly beauty to the edges of this earth.

NORTH: Let that same sun be danced among us down into our Circle.

EAST: That we may receive our due rewards with gladness and rejoicing.

> [Here the Circle dance is done to appropriate seasonal chanting. The dancers look in centrally and inwardly build up their figure among them as powerfully as they can.[11]]

SOUTH: Glory be unto the golden light by which we shall ourselves be glorified.

WEST: Thanks be for light descending to this level of our lives.

NORTH: That we may be illuminated by its richest rays.

EAST: Blessed be light so wonderfully shown to us upon its path of power.

---

[11] These are the principles behind the practice of Circle dancing. Naturally the actual rhythms and steps of a dance will vary according to season or purpose. In springtime, a light skipping movement; in summer a firm, tapping tread; in autumn a hearty jog; and in winter a slow and steady measure.

SOUTH: How stand we on that path this moment?

WEST: We stand between the light and shade
Upon the middle path we made
Where day and night divide,
As we have lived and worked and prayed,
We now expect to be repaid
With neither shame nor pride.

ALL: *How shall we find our true fulfillment?*

NORTH: Fire and water bring to birth
With air, the outcome of this earth.
For this we know without a doubt,
Our seed goes in, and fruits come out.
So bless the earth on which we stand
For harvests of the sea and land.

EAST: How fare the fields of autumn?

SOUTH: Roots below, fruits above, ripe and ready for our reaping.

WEST: Blessed be the earth supporting life, and air that brings the breath of life to earth. Let us keep our feet well grounded on our earth however high we hold our heads to Heaven. So shall we live as upright souls between both ends of our existence.

NORTH: In ancient times, mankind approached the earth as our own mother, from whose womb we came to incarnation, by whose breasts we lived, and whose loving mouth devoured us at our deaths. Why should we deny the basics of this beautiful belief, by which we once enjoyed the closest possible relationship between ourselves and the Creative Spirit that conceived us? Blessed be our Mother Earth indeed, and every single soul evolving with her.

[Here the North blesses or consecrates the element of earth.]

The Element Earth

Of slime and clay did the Creative Spirit form the flesh and bones of man, our bodies being of rich red earth and particles of dust. May we manifest through matter with true wills that we shall ultimately rise to be the rightful rulers and administrators of this outer kingdom we experience in ordinary living.

We call upon Thee by thine olden and beloved name, O Mother Earth. Thine is our field of present life, and by thine aid do we remain the human beings we are. Enter into this, thine element of earth, and stabilize us with thy firm solidity.

[Here the earth is signed, or gestures made.]

Manifest for us the meaning of those special secrets we must learn in order to observe thy laws, and find our purpose on this planet. May we truly grow from being children of creation into loyal and faithful subjects of the Supreme Living Spirit.

Be Thou consecrated, faithful creature of the earth, through the power, and in the service of, that solitary Self-Existing One, whose single atoms we most surely are. Amen.

SOUTH: What is the most we may expect on earth?

WEST: Our highest hope of harvest is to grow beyond necessity of being embodied, and exist in fuller freedom by the means of finer forces than are practical to us at present. Since we are not ready for such reaping, here is our symbolic substitute in shape of fruitful forms which none but nature may mature for our consumption, that we may continue on our cosmic course. Let us be conscious of its inner content.

> [Here the meditation symbol is produced. It has stems of ripe corn at the center and assorted fruits or vegetables round the edges. Music as suitable.]

NORTH: How did all these fruits develop?

EAST: They matured from ____[Name]____ that flowered in summer.

SOUTH: What shall we name it now?

WEST: Be it named among us ____[Name]____.

ALL: *So mote it be Amen*

WEST: Blessed be our harvest fairly earned by all the efforts we have made to grow more perfectly toward our light this solar cycle. May it be sufficient to sustain our souls throughout the coming seasons. Let us remember it by name as ____[Name]____.

> In the name of the **Wisdom**,
> and of the **Love**,
> and of the **Justice**,
> and of the Infinite **Mercy**,
> of the One Eternal **Spirit**,
> **Amen.**

NORTH: Whoso eats a fruit will surely sacrifice a seed.

EAST: Who eats not lives not. Sacrifice selects the seed that should survive to spread its species in their finest forms.

SOUTH: May we ourselves be chosen to continue as evolving entities when the instant of Divine decision is upon us.

WEST: Whatever comes to us of any lasting value should be well and truly earned by our own efforts to become the sort of spiritual beings our true wills realize we ought to be. Such a heavenly harvest lies within our hands on earth, so here and now let willing hands be dedicated to this duty.

[Symbolic spitting on right hand:]

Blessed be the Hand put forth with might. [All repeat.]

[Symbolic spitting on left hand:]

Blessed be the Hand put forth with meaning. [All repeat.]

[Rubbing both hands vigorously:]

Blessed be what we must do with might and meaning, that our hands may hold the harvest of our highest hopes. [All repeat.]

WEST: Companions, out of all that we have been, a seed must be selected out of which will grow the souls and selves we shall become. This is a constant process, and the favored moment for our choice is always **now**.

Every instant brings our re-becoming in some way. We die and are reborn with every breath. Let us only save the very best in us for seeds to plant more perfectly at every step we take upon the spiral of the solar seasons leading upwards to the ultimate of highest light. With all the will which we may bring to bear on this most special stroke of our selective sickle, let us now in Sacred Silence.

    Choose. Cut. Cherish.

> [Here Officer of West raises sickle or shears, and reaps a single ear of wheat or grain. This is elevated and borne to the altar in silence. Momentary pause for individual intentions to be made. A soft clap of hands may terminate this period.]

NORTH: Blessed be that attaining what it wills to be in *Peace Profound*.

EAST: What shall we attain unless we eat what providence has ripened for us on the tree of life? In with the harvest!

SOUTH: Which way is best for us to gather it?

WEST: With willing hands, happy hearts and singing souls. Let the season be sung in.

> [Here a seasonal song is sung, such as the following selected verses from the Harvest Song. The complete song is on pages 307-308.]

Harvest Song

1. The fruits of the earth may be sent from above,
And we should improve them with wisdom and love.
If apples and grapes are both products divine,
Who prefers water to cider or wine?

> *Chorus: Up with a ladder and down with the fruits,*
>   *In with a shovel and out with the roots.*
>   *The Gods may provide us with life from the land,*
>   *But the harvest we hold is the work of our hand.*

3. The wheat and the barley as much as the corn.
   Have kept us alive ever since we were born.
   But unless we had turned them to flour and bread,
   Few would be living, and many be dead.

   Chorus: *Up with a ladder and down with the fruits,*
   In with a shovel and out with the roots.
   The Gods may provide us with life from the land,
   But the harvest we hold is the work of our hand.

6. So here's to the Gods and the men of this earth.
   Who take one another for what they are worth.
   Each of them doing what has to be done,
   In order to live altogther as **one**.

   Chorus: *Up with a ladder and down with the fruits,*
   In with a shovel and out with the roots.
   The Gods may provide us with life from the land,
   But the harvest we hold is the work of our hand.

NORTH: Here is harvest. Be the call of celebration sounded.

EAST: Loud and clear above the water of the wise.

SOUTH: What is the water of the wise?

WEST: The essence of experience, or juice of judgment, likened to a fermentation from that fruit which grew upon the tree of knowledge. This is what we really harvest from our human lives on earth, and that is why we choose an apple ale or cider for potation at this solar season. May it indeed sustain us through out times of trial, refresh us when occasions for rejoicing arise, and be as the waters of eternal life, by which we grow to highest light in *Peace Profound*. Let our call be clearly heard by all that listen in the compass of complete compassion.

[Here the Officer of the West blesses the cup of cider which is the element of water for this season.]

The Element Water

Let there be a firmament in the midst of the waters so that sea and sky may separate into themselves. That which is above is like to that which is below for the appearance of a single wonder. The Sun is its Father, the Moon its Mother, and the wind has carried it into conception. It ascends from earth to Heaven, and descends to earth again when it is due.

We call upon Thee, O Thou Mighty Mother from whose womb comes everlasting life. Maiden of the Mysteries art Thou, and nurse of all that lives by means of nature. Enter into this, thine element of water, moving it for us by thy Compassion.

[Here water is salted or just blessed with a gesture.]

Manifest for us thy potency and open unto us the hidden depths of wisdom. May we savor whatsoever we experience therein with the appreciative salt of good sound sense, and let all tides, waves, and currents of the cosmic ocean bear our consciousness toward the anchorage of our eventual attainment.

Be Thou consecrated, faithful creature of the water, through the power, and in the service of, that Universal Sea of Spirit whose particular and scattered drops we surely are. Amen.

Blessing the Cider

Blessed be unto Divinity and all of us, that cup of consciousness wherein the essence of Eternal Entity and our awareness of It, meet and mingle for the sake of life in one another.

May this special sign by which we hope to realize our true identity, communicate to us the Holy Presence we now humbly seek within our secret hearts.

>In the name of the **Wisdom**,
>and of the **Love**,
>and of the **Justice**,
>and of the Infinite **Mercy**,
>of the One Eternal **Spirit**,
>**Amen.**

[The call must be sounded over it to the Four Quarters. I. A. O. is most generally given, but the call may be given by sounding a horn above the cup.]

NORTH: Let the cakes of fruit and bread be shared among us who have surely earned them by our efforts. Bread for work, fruit for refreshment, salt for sense, and spice for pleasure. Such are the ingredients of life on earth we mix together. We must combine the right proportions properly, if we would eat enjoyably the bread of our own baking. Blessed may it be for us.

Blessing the Bread

Blessed be unto Divinity and all of us, our body of belief we share together which unites us unto one another for the sake of loving kindness.

May this special sign with which we seek to feed our faith, sustain our souls to an immortal life in spirit.

>In the name of the **Wisdom**,
>and of the **Love**,

and of the **Justice**,
and of the Infinite **Mercy**,
of the One Eternal **Spirit**,
Amen.

[Here the bread is blessed by West and circulated round the Companions by the way of light. The cup follows. There may be music during this if time seems to justify it.]

EAST: As we have willed and worked with one another, so may we ever reap the benefits of all we have attempted in our common cause of Cosmos.

SOUTH: Are we fully satisfied? Has everyone sufficient for his present needs until we are provided for again?

WEST: Companions, by the Love that binds us in the Circle Cross of Cosmos at all solar seasons, let us freely share our spiritual assets with each other, as and when necessity directs. None should lack what Love can well afford to give most willingly. If we care nothing for conditions of imbalance and disharmony in this immediate Circle of companionship, how shall we dare demand assistance from superior spiritual sources? We only have the right to ask for inner aid when humanly available supplies are insufficient to support our souls. Our petitions otherwise are purely a privilege which we should not presume to demand. Let us therefore help each other very willingly in every way that leads to our eventual enlightenment.

NORTH: No unsought aid must be imposed on any soul. All should be free to ask and answer as they will.

EAST: Blessed be they that set no price upon themselves nor make undue demands for anything they do in spiritual spheres. They shall surely reap the harvest of a heart in harmony with Heaven.

SOUTH: May our lengthening shadows in the setting sun become most perfect pointers on our paths ahead, and lead us steadily to hidden light beyond our present horizons.

WEST: Companions, let us cheerfully complete the purpose of this pleasant circle. Willingly we came together, and with will we worked. Now we must willingly part company, that in goodwill our ways will meet again. What is our word of will for this occasion?

ALL: [repeat password]

WEST: Thanks be that we have worked our Rites in peace. Let us go forth upon our ways according to the will within the word uniting our intentions, and may happy harmony prevail among us from this time as long as light may let it last. Now let us close in our accustomed manner.

> In the name of the **Wisdom**,
>   and of the **Love**,
>   and of the **Justice**,
>   and of the Infinite **Mercy**,
>   of the One Eternal **Spirit**,
>   **Amen.**

[Here the fruits may be divided among the company, and individual ears of grain reaped if required. There should certainly be some kind of harvest feast afterwards, and suitable singing. A good seasonal action song during which miming is possible, especially in the chorus, is as follows:]

Harvest Song

1. The fruits of the earth may be sent from above,
   And we should improve them with wisdom and love.
   If apples and grapes are both products divine,
   Who prefers water to cider or wine?

   Chorus: Up with a ladder and down with the fruits,
   In with a shovel and out with the roots.
   The Gods may provide us with life from the land,
   But the harvest we hold is the work of our hand.

2. Dame Nature's a wonder, we all do agree.
   Who knows our necessities better than she?
   Yet though she is doing as well as she can,
   She answers her best to the touch of a man!

   Chorus: Up with a ladder and down with the fruits,
   In with a shovel and out with the roots.
   The Gods may provide us with life from the land,
   But the harvest we hold is the work of our hand.

3. The wheat and the barley as much as the corn
   Have kept us alive ever since we were born.
   But unless we had turned them to flour and bread,
   Few would be living, and many be dead.

   Chorus: Up with a ladder and down with the fruits,
   In with a shovel and out with the roots.
   The Gods may provide us with life from the land,
   But the harvest we hold is the work of our hand.

4. We pray for the seasons to be as they should
   Dry or wet weather may do our crops good.
   Though if sunshine is needed to ripen the grain,
   Who risks rheumatics by working in rain?

Chorus: *Up with a ladder and down with the fruits,*
In with a shovel and out with the roots.
The Gods may provide us with life from the land,
But the harvest we hold is the work of our hand.

5. Whatever the task, and wherever the field,
We reap our reward with the sickles we wield,
For if all things grew from their numberless seeds,
The whole of our world would be covered in weeds.

Chorus: *Up with a ladder and down with the fruits,*
In with a shovel and out with the roots.
The Gods may provide us with life from the land,
But the harvest we hold is the work of our hand.

6. So here's to the Gods and the men of this earth
Who take one another for what they are worth.
Each of them doing what has to be done,
In order to live altogether as **one**.

Chorus: *Up with a ladder and down with the fruits,*
In with a shovel and out with the roots.
The Gods may provide us with life from the land,
But the harvest we hold is the work of our hand.

THE RITE OF WINTER

[The place is as dimly lit as possible, while still allowing scripts to be read. All color is very sober, and everyone is in an elderly and tolerant mood as if at the end of long and well-spent lives. The principal Officer is North. The Companions are seated quietly when North brings them slowly to their feet by four knocks or stamps on the ground.]

NORTH: Companions, it is time we rested from our labors for a season, and reposed with nature through the winter night to come.

EAST: What shall we do while we are separated from the sun?

SOUTH: Recuperate our strength, and rectify our past mistakes as far as we are able. Let us be well rid of all our rubbish in the solstice fire, and sleep a while to find the future in our dreams, then wake and realize them in the world of light.

WEST: Let us indeed seek slumber with our Mother Nature. She will be kind to us, with her soft songs reminding us of wonders in the past and promises of paradise to come. She alone will try to teach us wisdom while we wait within her womb before we are reborn to active living in the light.

NORTH: Whatever we have been has made us what we are this very moment. All we shall ever be commences at this very moment. Now is always the best moment for reflection on the past in order to project our purpose into future and much finer forms. This is the proper time and season of the solar cycle to be free from whatsoever hinders us from making progress, and for clearing up completely all obscurities which might prevent our passage on the path of light. Such an opportunity should not slip by unnoticed or unused by us. Let us call upon the Old and Wise Ones in the hope that They will hear and help us.

>   I   A   O
>   (EE)   (YAY)   (YOH)

[All echo the call with deep resonance.]

EAST: We are passing rapidly enough towards the closing of our lives for this past solar cycle. When human beings grow old, we tend to think too much about the past because we fear, or cannot find a welcome way to face our future. Surely in this Circle our experience of life has led us to expect far more than mere cessation at the ending of our earth existence? Let us look forward to continuance in Cosmos. Why should we be always bound to mortal bodies, when we might express ourselves as entities in many better ways, away from this one world, in one of all the others there are for us to find? Having done our duty here, we should be glad to go elsewhere in order to enjoy existing otherwise. Meanwhile, we ought to be as happy and harmonious as our humanity occasionally allows on this earth. Let the signs and symbols of the season be set out among us, so that we may celebrate our closure of the solar cycle cheerfully.

> [Here the signs and symbols are placed—the traditional evergreens, garlands, etc. The meditation symbol is some kind of a platter with earth on it and dead leaves, twigs and so forth in random patterns. These are set fire to, so ought to be dry. Music as suitable. South calls to order.]

SOUTH: Blessed be these signs of winter unto us that wait with patience in this world to find our way into another.

WEST: We should not look back upon the outworn old, except for guidance to the needed new.

NORTH: Companions, we are at the ending of our solar year, and what have we accomplished in that period to bring us spiritual satisfaction with a clear conscience? Are we content with our past service in the cause of Cosmos? How otherwise would we behave, if our last set of seasons lay before, instead of being, as they lie, behind us? This is the final opportunity among ourselves for thinking of these things, and meeting our reflections in the mirror of our memories. Whether we enjoy this self-encounter or endure it, the experience should certainly be undergone by every soul in search of spirit. If the Lords of Life should ask us at this instant what defects of character or imperfections in ourselves we would be free from, if their will and ours agreed, how should we reply?

EAST: With true humility and highest hope.

SOUTH: As we allow for others' faults, so may allowances be made for ours.

WEST: Be a Blessing bidden on us so that we may pass this winter season peacefully.

NORTH: O Compassionate and Understanding One, in whom our endings are but new beginnings of another way of life, be merciful to we who wait before the gates of winter with anxiety or apprehension. Temper Thou for us the bitter winds and biting frosts we fear to face in spiritual solitude. May the welcome warmth of thy eternal

Love envelop and protect us from the perils of this period, comforting our souls and caring for their safety.

> In the name of the **Wisdom**,
> and of the **Love**,
> and of the **Justice**,
> and of the Infinite **Mercy**,
> of the One Eternal **Spirit**,
> **Amen.**

EAST: None are secure in idleness. Outer rest and inner action serve each other's purpose in the surest way. Let us now consider how we seem as individual souls, and then approach the Mighty Ones with our ideas about improving our integrity by altering our attitudes with their assistance.

> [Here the petitions to that effect are gathered by South or by Officer of Cord, and presented to North.]

SOUTH: On behalf of our companionship, both present and by proxy, I present before these portals our petitions for the faults we find with our own natures to be dealt with by Divinity according to the will made one between us.

WEST: May we never mourn our former failures, but anticipate far more success with our achievements in the future.

NORTH: O Ancient and Eternal Spirit unto whom our entities are simply energies to be emanated into existence As Thou Wilt, Thou alone art perfect power. Take Thou our offered imperfections and convert them As Thou Wilt to whatsoever forms of force we might most carefully control upon a cosmic course.

Let not thy light depart from us forever at this solstice, leaving us to end despairingly in darkness and extinction. Permit us to continue round the circle of creation, and complete what Thou commenced with our original conception in thy likeness brought to independent life by thine imaginative will.

[Petitions stacked for burning.]

EAST: Blessed be the fire of faith that burns on earth this season, shining forth in friendly substitution for the sun.

SOUTH: Leave us not, O Light on whom our spiritual lives depend for their direction.
 Take thyself not from us, O Thou Torch of Truth and sole illuminator of our ignorance.
 Forsake us not, O Flame of Freedom to proceed the way we will to thy perfection.
 Be Thou for each and every soul the sacred spark of spirit, round which they revolve unceasingly in their cosmic circles of thy living light.

[Here the South blesses or consecrates the fire, lights petitions.]

The Element Fire

Let there be light no darkness may extinguish. Burn evermore, Thou Fire of Love that ripens every spiritual seed. In the separation of thine essence from thy substance lies the work of wisdom. Thou art strongest of the strong, overcoming subtlety and interpenetrating all solidity. In thine adaptation is the arcane art, and secret of the sacred science.

We call upon Thee, O Father of All, radiant with thine illuminating rays. O Unseen Parent of the Sun, pour forth thy life-giving power and energize thy Divine Spark. Enter into this flame and let it be agitated by the breath of the Most Holy Spirit.

[Here flame is lit or gestures made.]

Manifest thy power and open for us the hidden temple which is concealed within this flame. May we become regenerated by thy light, and the breadth, height, fullness, and crown of solar Radiance appear, so that God within shines forth.

Be Thou consecrated, faithful creature of the fire, through the power and in the service of, that Supreme Light whose single sparks we surely are. Amen.

WEST: Let us enjoy the bright and blessed beauty of a friendly fire.

NORTH: May the faith and friendship that we share in spirit round our fireside never fail this Circle of companionship, or any other in the world this coming season. However cold and bitter it may be elsewhere, may we always welcome one another in our hearts and homes with warmth enough to overcome the very worst of winter. Now let us see if we have sufficient strength for our feet to follow the returning solar rays around the symbol by which we represent them.

[Here the Circle dance is performed. This is somewhat slow and steady, in the manner of old people enjoying unusual activity.]

EAST: Thanks be for warmth and close companionship with kindred souls.

SOUTH: May we continue so forever in the kindest light.

WEST: How stand we on its Path this moment?

NORTH: We stand in the perplexing night,
With insufficiency of light
To see what lies ahead.
So now with skyward gaze, we plead
All Heaven for one star to lead
The living—and the dead!

ALL: *What will happen while our sun is hidden from us?*

EAST: The deepest night no one need dread
Who finds safe guiding light ahead.
Within us glows a sacred spark
Which we should follow through the dark
With perfect faith its starlike ray
Will lead us to a better day.

SOUTH: How is it with the earth in winter?

WEST: Bleak and barren above, rich and resting below. Hands find what eyes see not.

NORTH: Blessed be the earth at rest beneath our feet, as we have hope of rest in peace one day with earth above our heads. Be it remembered peace is a static state, but is the perfect poise of power. Not cessation, but completion and continuation. May there be peace on earth to all mankind that bear goodwill to one another.

> [Here North blesses or consecrates the element of earth, while Companions tread the ground as if warming feet on an icy day.]

The Element Earth

Of slime and clay did the Creative Spirit form the flesh and bones of man, our bodies being of rich red earth and particles of dust. May we manifest through matter with true wills that we shall ultimately rise to be the rightful rulers and administrators of this outer kingdom we experience in ordinary living.

We call upon Thee by thine olden and beloved name, O Mother Earth. Thine is our field of present life, and by thine aid do we remain the human beings we are. Enter into this, thine element of earth, and stabilize us with thy firm solidity.

[Here the earth is signed, or gestures made.]

Manifest for us the meaning of those special secrets we must learn in order to observe thy laws, and find our purpose on this planet. May we truly grow from being children of creation into loyal and faithful subjects of the Supreme Living Spirit.

Be Thou consecrated, faithful creature of the earth, through the power, and in the service of, that solitary Self-existing One, whose single atoms we most surely are. Amen.

[At conclusion, the meditation emblem is produced and displayed. It is simply a small heap of dead combustible twigs and leaves. North continues:]

NORTH: Behold what dead disorders and what muddled minds we may encounter if we live in human bodies long enough to meet them. How sad it is that we might come to such confusion of our consciousness if we outstay our welcome in this world. Surely it is best for our outworn beings and bodies to return to earth for their renewal rather than remain imprisoned uselessly by human incarnation. Nature never wastes such opportunities in her economy, for she changes chaos into Cosmos by the redistribution of disintegrating force forms. We can work this alchemy of alteration for ourselves if we so will. Let us attempt to learn whatever lesson contemplation may communicate to us on this occasion.

> [Here the symbol is contemplated either silently or to suitable music.]

EAST: Where did all this debris fall from?

SOUTH: From ____[Name]____ of the autumn.

WEST: What shall we name it now?

NORTH: Be it known to us henceforth as ____[Name]____.

ALL: *So mote it be. Amen.*

NORTH: Blessed be the end of our endeavors on this earth for the past solar cycle. May we face our future through the season set before us with calm confidence that we are following with fearless faith the cosmic course that we have chosen to call ____[Name]____.

> In the name of the **Wisdom**,
> and of the **Love**,
> and of the **Justice**,
> and of the Infinite **Mercy**,
> of the One Eternal **Spirit**,
> **Amen.**

EAST: What shall we do with all the residue remaining with us here and now?

SOUTH: Let us burn it into beauty that it may become a beacon of deliverance from darkness, and finally a fertilizing ash to aid arising growth in future fields.

ALL: *So mote it be.*

[South lights pyre.]

SOUTH: By the light of the past be the future perceived.

WEST: By what we have learned be new teaching received.

NORTH: By that which is left, may we find what is right.

EAST: By the fire that is spent, may we come to fresh light.

SOUTH: What is keener than the worst of winter winds?

WEST: The bitter blow to self-esteem exposing all the difference between the sort of soul we ought to be, and those we are as actualities.

NORTH: Surely we should equalize these two extremities, and look between them both to recognize a middle path of poise that leads to light above the pillars of opposed opinions. So may we reach a reasonable measure of respect for what we surely will be, if we seek real inspiration from our inner sources of intelligence and spiritual strength.

EAST: O Infinite Intelligence in whom all inspiration is, tell us the truth about ourselves in whatsoever ways we best may bear without being broken by that burden. Deal lightly with us, O Divine Directing One, that we may learn our lessons of this life through Love, yet with an unassuming air of absolute and utter confidence in thy complete command of Cosmos.

> [Here the Officer of East blesses or consecrates element of air.]

The Element Air

In the beginning, did the Holy Spirit issue from the void and breathe a vital, living soul into mankind. May we also breathe forth words which act throughout our inner atmosphere, and bring to life our latent spiritual qualities.
 We call upon Thee, O Thou source of inspiration filling us with faith that we shall find our final and immortal freedom in the spheres of spirit. Speak unto our souls that we may hold the echoes of thy harmony. Enter into this, thine ambient element that it may bear for us thy vibrant voice.

> [Here suitable gestures or actions are made.]

Manifest thy meaning for us, that the winds of truth will wake us with thy messages, and may the angels of the air become apparent to our eyes of inner vision.
 Be Thou consecrated, faithful creature of the air, through the power, and in the service of, the One Eternal Life whose single breaths we surely are. Amen.

SOUTH: There is no best or worst to find or fear within us saving that which we have made ourselves.

WEST: Even as most welcome water is withheld from eager earth by freezing up its flow with chilling cold, so does spiritual bitterness inhibit our most needed waters of compassion, isolating souls in icy solitude by lack of Love. Let us not allow such coldness in our Circle that might cause our cup to freeze and fail its function of supplying the free and friendly spirit we should seek to share among us. As ordinary ice will melt within a cup held closely to our hearts, so may the slightest chill within our souls be banished by the spirit of surpassing Love itself, through all the willing warmth we ought to hold towards each other from our truest heart of hearts.

> [Here the Officer of West blesses or consecrates the element of water in the form of ice, suitably contrived either in a cup not needed later, or in the same cup which will presently be used for iced spirits or other chilled drink, depending on which symbol is willed.]

The Element Water

Let there be a firmament in the midst of the waters so that sea and sky may separate into themselves. That which is above is like to that which is below for the appearance of a single wonder. The Sun is its Father, the Moon its Mother, and the wind has carried it into conception. It ascends from earth to Heaven, and descends to earth again when it is due.

We call upon Thee, O thou Mighty Mother of whose womb comes everlasting life. Maiden of the Mysteries art Thou, and nurse of all that lives by means of nature. Enter into this, thine element of water, moving it for us by thy compassion.

> [Here water is salted or just blessed with a gesture.]

Manifest for us thy potency and open unto us the hidden depths of wisdom. May we savor whatsoever we experience therein with the appreciative salt of good sound sense, and let all tides, waves, and currents of the cosmic ocean bear our consciousness toward the anchorage of our eventual attainment.

    Be Thou consecrated, faithful creature of the water, through the power, and in the service of, that Universal Sea of Spirit whose particular and scattered drops we surely are. Amen.

NORTH: Come then, O Companions, that each soul of us may find what he amounts to as an individual, by looking for his image in the magic mirror which reflects reality according to the light emitted by that soul itself. A taper, to be lit by everyone, is representative of revelation which has been or is to be received. As we look our last upon the fading face of the past period, let us see ourselves reflected from it, and consider how we might improve that image in the season set before us with this opportunity.

> [Here the companions file past the North point. First, a dark reflector is presented before their faces, then a white one, after which they are given a taper or candle, which they must light from the North flame, before they continue circling back to their places. The words said by North during this action are:]

NORTH: Behold the one you were [Black reflector].
          Behold the one you might be [White reflector].
          Behold the one you are to light [Lighted flame].

> [When this circling is concluded, East says:]

EAST: May our true reflections be revealed to us most brightly by the welcome wine of wisdom.

SOUTH: Let the cup of our companionship be circulated in the way of light around our Circle.

WEST: From hand to hand, mouth to mouth, mind to mind, and heart to heart among us all.

NORTH: Be this season celebrated with the symbol of good wine, like that of life itself, pressed from us by experience at first, and then maturing as we mellow with it, to become much better beings than we were at birth. Nothing else than aging rightly makes a wine worthwhile, nor will the savor of our souls seem right for us til we are old enough and able to appreciate the taste of truth.

EAST: May this never be too strong for us to bear with benefit, but only serve to stimulate our search for spirit.

SOUTH: Consider well the rich rewarding cakes with which this solstice is remembered. They represent the only realistic wealth within us, which belongs of right unto our souls alone, all else being left behind us with our bodies. These cakes remind us that our finest qualities in life are left until the last on earth, when what is best in us begins to live in Heaven. May all that we remember of our earth lives afterwards be as sweet and satisfying as the richness of these symbols.

WEST: Be a Blessing bidden on them both.

NORTH: Blessed be the forms of flesh and blood which we must share together, since we are but individual atoms of the body which belongs to Universal Spirit. This is the mystery of light made manifest as living man. Whether in or out of human incarnation, may each single soul be guided to its proper place within the perfect plan, and live in ultimate enlightenment with *Peace Profound*.

[Here the wine and cakes are blessed or consecrated by North and distributed around the circle.]

Blessing the Bread

Blessed be unto Divinity and all of us, our body of belief we share together which unites us unto one another for the sake of loving kindness.

May this special sign with which we seek to feed our faith, sustain our souls to an immortal life in spirit.

> In the name of the **Wisdom**,
> and of the **Love**,
> and of the **Justice**,
> and of the Infinite **Mercy**,
> of the One Eternal **Spirit**,
> **Amen.**

Blessing the Wine

Blessed be unto Divinity and all of us, that cup of consciousness wherein the essence of Eternal Entity and our awareness of It, meet and mingle for the sake of life in one another.

May this special sign by which we hope to realize our true identity, communicate to us the Holy Presence we now humbly seek within our secret hearts.

> In the name of the **Wisdom**,
> and of the **Love**,
> and of the **Justice**,
> and of the Infinite **Mercy**,
> of the One Eternal **Spirit**,
> **Amen.**

EAST: May we truly pass beyond our bodies by the blessed bridge that leads to *Perfect Peace* in living light.

SOUTH: Let us sing the passing season of our lives to sleep.

> [Here the Sleeping song is sung. The tone of the Rite becomes very quiet and hushed from this point on, the few remaining lines being taken somewhat *sotto voce*, as if for fear of waking someone.]

Sleeping Song

1. The last year of life has gone past our recalling,
   Except for our feelings of pride or regret.
   Of all that was dreadful, just dull, or enthralling,
   What should we remember, and how much forget?

   > *Chorus: Sleep! Deep! Hoping to wake with the Blest.*
   > *Dream! Scheme! How we may live for the best.*
   > *Our past left behind leaves a future to find,*
   > *So now let us thankfully rest.*

2. Is a Beneficent Being above us?
   Or nothing whatever concerned with our fate.
   Are there good spirits that care for and love us?
   Or none but ourselves to consider our state.

   > *Chorus: Sleep! Deep! Hoping to wake with the Blest.*
   > *Dream! Scheme! How we may live for the best.*
   > *Our past left behind leaves a future to find,*
   > *So now let us thankfully rest.*

3. What is the meaning of human existence?
   And may we become any more than mere man?
   Such vital enigmas demand with insistence,
   We seek their solutions however we can.

> Chorus: Sleep! Deep! Hoping to wake with the Blest.
> Dream! Scheme! How we may live for the best.
> Our past left behind leaves a future to find,
> So now let us thankfully rest.

4. If reincarnation should ever restore us
   To birth beyond reach of a blessing or curse,
   And we had our lives once again set before us,
   Should we do better, or might we do worse?

   > Chorus: Sleep! Deep! Hoping to wake with the Blest.
   > Dream! Scheme! How we may live for the best.
   > Our past left behind leaves a future to find,
   > So now let us thankfully rest.

5. Blessed be life beyond all need of dying
   And happy the soul with no burden to shed,
   Yet who knows, without any thought of denying,
   Whether it's best to be living or dead?

   > Chorus: Sleep! Deep! Hoping to wake with the Blest.
   > Dream! Scheme! How we may live for the best.
   > Our past left behind leaves a future to find,
   > So now let us thankfully rest.

6. Our questions are answered by living and learning
   Whatever comes next on the path we must plod,
   Between birth and death while we have means of earning
   The wisdom that makes man become like a God.

   > Chorus: Sleep! Deep! Hoping to wake with the Blest.
   > Dream! Scheme! How we may live for the best.
   > Our past left behind leaves a future to find,
   > So now let us thankfully rest.

WEST [gently]: With whom lies the last word?

NORTH: With that by whom the first was uttered. In the beginning was the word of power. At the ending comes the word of peace. With that word let us pass according to the will within. What is our present word?

ALL: [password]

NORTH: Peacefully we met, and peacefully we worked, now let us part in peace, that we may meet once more that blessed way. Closed be the Rite according to custom.

        In the name of the **Wisdom**,
            and of the **Love**,
            and of the **Justice**,
            and of the Infinite **Mercy**,
            of the One Eternal **Spirit**,
                      Amen.

· Appendix ·

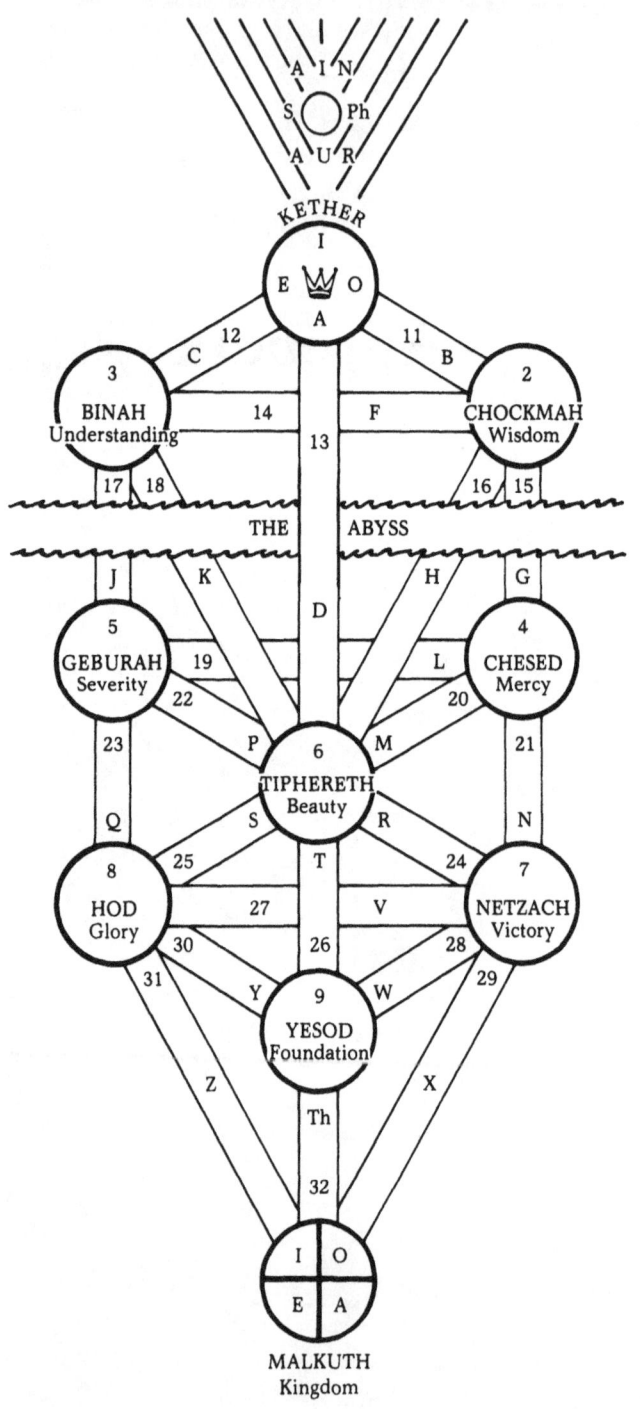

The Office of the Holy Tree of Life

Introduction

This Appendix contains *The Office of the Holy Tree of Life*, which is not a part of the Sangreal Sodality Series, but is an important contribution to the Western Tradition. It consists of a separate prayer section for the Ain Soph and all ten Spheres, plus a special Path invocation for each of the 22 Paths or connections between the Spheres as outlined by the Tree-Glyph itself. There are also a short series of statements and responses for relating the required Spheres and Paths together so as to make a useful devotional practice.

The general plan for use of the Office is to take a single Path each day, and work steadily from top to bottom of the Tree, then back again in a continuous prayer plan. Although the script has been very carefully arranged for ordinary Gregorian chanting as a complete short ceremony either alone or in company, it may also be read or recited in silence or aloud as required. This Office is best worked last thing before sleeping, so that the soul is able to meditate and live with that particular Path during physical repose.

It will be seen that each Sphere and Path invocation is built by associate linkage through the Four Worlds, and other connective concepts including sensory symbology of colors, scents, and various conventional attributions of God Names, Archangels, Angels, planetary personifications, Telesmic figures and so forth. The customary way of connecting Spheres is by their proper Paths. Therefore the general procedure is to lead in with the introductory phrases, select and read or chant the first of whichever pair of Spheres lies at the proximal end of the chosen Path, then work the Sphere at its distal end, and finally pronounce the Path invocation itself. After this, observe a few moments of meditation upon that particular Path. Whatever may be cut or curtailed in the Office, the Path meditation of the day should be regarded as obligatory, for this is the inner contact of the Life Spirit vivifying all our Tree concepts. When this meditation has been completed, the valedictory chants and responses are given, and the daily Office has been duly offered up to the Living Spirit it should serve.

In ceremonial form, an Office may be as simple or elaborate as demanded. Conventional costume consists of plain habit and girdle with no special ornamentation. Hoods are to be worn up as with meditational work. Lights at low level, signals by numbered raps for the Spheres, a handclap to announce the Path, otherwise soft gong strokes. Musical background or otherwise at will, but meditation period should be silent. The leader, who chants the statements in Gregorian style and should proclaim the Path also, is responsible for terminating the meditation time. Otherwise the Spheres are worked between everyone in chant style or by rhythmic recitation with low resonance. It is usual to stand for the introduction, valediction, and proclamation of the Path, but be seated for the Spheres and, of course, the vital meditation.

The true function of this, or any Office, is to open and develop in souls who use them a spiritual sense of their own existence and continuity in a state of inner Cosmos on levels of life which extend far beyond the boundaries of manifested matter. This will certainly eventuate providing that regular and rhythmic use is made of an Office. That is the most important factor of all, which may be summed up as: constancy in conscious contact with inner Cosmos and its concepts.

Full ritual usage of an Office is unlikely to be a practical proposition every day for many modern people. Nevertheless, the least that can be done is to carry the Office book somewhere about the person in pocket or handbag. If daily use of this consists of no more than a single opening, brief glance through even one paragraph, then returning the book to its place until next time, this constitutes an Office of a sort which is bound to lead souls lightwards. It is better to do a faithful and regular minimum, than sporadic and disjointed splurges of performance. If, say, a daily minimum and a weekly expanded effort is possible, that would be a sensible and helpful usage.

Every major faith has an Office of some description, and in offering this present Office for use by those relatively few souls who follow the Qabalistic system of human-Divine associations, it is felt that a long missing link has at last been forged in the great chain of consciousness joining God with man in the spirit of eternal life. May this be truly so indeed.

THE OFFICE

[Standing]

In the name of the **Wisdom**,
    and of the **Love**,
    and of the **Justice**,
    and of the **Infinite Mercy**,
  of the **One Eternal Spirit**,
          Amen.

Blessed be the light by which we learn the laws of life.

Response: *Holy is the Tree thereof whose fruits fulfill for us the faith we place in all its powers.*

Blessed be the principles and paths throughout the Tree that constitutes our conscious Cosmos.

Response: *Tenfold is the truth of our beloved Tree while two and twenty are the ways between its blessed branches.*

From mere mortality among mankind, our Tree leads up to infinite extension past existence as identity in *Perfect Peace Profound*.

Response: *Let us therefore find and follow faithfully our present Path upon the Holy Tree of Life between the principles of...and...*
So Mote It Be. Amen.

[Knocks of the starting sphere]
[Seated]

Blessed be Thou unto us, O Thou First Principle of...

In the name of the **Wisdom**,
and of the **Love**,
and of the **Justice**,
and of the **Infinite Mercy**,
of the **One Eternal Spirit**,
Amen.

[Invocation of the sphere concerned]
[Seated]
[Knocks of the completing sphere]
[Seated]

Blessed be Thou unto us, O Thou Last Principle of...

In the name of the **Wisdom**,
and of the **Love**,
and of the **Justice**,
and of the **Infinite Mercy**,
of the **One Eternal Spirit**,
Amen.

[Invocation of the sphere concerned]
[Seated]
[Single Handclap]
[Standing]

Blessed be Thou unto us, O welcome middle way that we must walk between extremities of our existence in this present instance.

In the name of the **Wisdom**,
and of the **Love**,
and of the **Justice**,
and of the **Infinite Mercy**,
of the **One Eternal Spirit**,
Amen.

[Invocation of the path]
[Standing]

Blessed be the information and enlightenment we shall experience through mediation of this potent path.

In the name of the **Wisdom**,
and of the **Love**,
and of the **Justice**,
and of the **Infinite Mercy**,
of the **One Eternal Spirit**,
Amen.

[Short Meditation]
[Seated]
[gong or knocks]
[Standing]

Chant

Glory be to Thee
O living one of light
May we forever be
Upon thy path of right.

Direct us from above
According to thy law,
And may thy boundless Love
Be with us evermore.

Let thy sublime design
The Tree of God and man
Both human and Divine
Prove our most perfect plan. *Amen.*

Thanks be that we are better for the will which has been worked within us.

Response: *Let us now change consciousness from inner Cosmos to our normal living levels.*

Because of what has happened in ourselves, may we impart some benefit to other souls.

Response: *Blessed be what has been done with us, and so may everyone experience Divinity in whatsoever way they will.*

In the name of the **Wisdom**,
and of the **Love**,
and of the **Justice**,
and of the **Infinite Mercy**,
of the **One Eternal Spirit**.
Amen.

INVOCATIONS OF THE SPHERES

Ain Soph Aur

Principle of Light beyond all Being

O Perfect Peace Profound beyond all being; Thou that art not what Thou wilt not-be.

O Cosmic Cipher infinitely inexisting; Zero-Zenith of transcendent truth.

Unidentifiable art Thou; and utterly apart from anything Thou art.

Naught would exist as anything; unless thy universal nucleus of nil began its being.

Thou art pre-primal first and final factor of emerging and equating energy.

Limitless art Thou that livest not; bornless and unbounded is thine unilluminated light.

We reverence in Thee our whole unmanifested universe; Thou art parabeing and pure potential.

We know we know Thee not; and only thus we know Thee.

We know no symbol for Thee; nor have we any name for Thee except necessity of nothing.

In gaining life we lose Thee; and by our loss of life Thou gainest us.

Our solitary means of recognizing thy reality is inwardly through silent stillness of our senses.

With awe do we accept thine actuality; and now await Thee with due worship.

So Mote It Be. Amen.

Kether

Principle of the Summative Crown

O Thou Solitary Spirit of Entire Existence; Begetter of All Being and Light of Every Life.

Thou art what Thou wilt be within thyself; O Ancient of the Ancient Ones.

Concealed art Thou of the concealed; thine end and origin is with thyself alone.

Thou art the source and sum of every soul; O Perfect Point of everyone and everything.

Thou first emerging entity upon the Holy Tree of Life; Crown of Consciousness and apex of awareness.

O Light of Lights we are thy separated sparks; who seek for our fulfillment in thy sacred flame.

May our searching souls arise toward Thee; until we rejoin thy ruling radiance.

Most Mystical Intelligence beyond the comprehension of created beings; inspire in us a sense of thy true actuality.

So at last in striving to attain Thee; we may surely come to know ourselves.

O Highest Holiness of the Originative World; thy still small voice breathes forth thy name — Eheieh.

Blind us not by thy surpassing brilliance; but encourage us to live by whatsoever light enables us to recognize thine absolute reality.

Most mighty Metatron, thou privileged Archangel of the Only Perfect Presence; mediate for us in the creative world that power none other than thyself may deal with face to face.

Shine Thou before the blessed throne of truth; like purest light outpoured in benediction.

Chaioth ha Qadesh Thou art Holy Living Creatures and the first formative angels; uphold the dignity of life before all lesser dignities.

Uplift also our hearts and take our prayers to heaven; like an offering of ambergris arising from our earthly altars.

Shine Thou as a spiritual beacon; and become our welcome watchfires of the inner way.

O Primal Motion of our matter with the swirling nebulae expressed into existence; be unto us the sign of Cosmos coming forth from chaos. Let the light in darkness of thy golden sparklings set in space awaken us to look above ourselves and find illumination.

Thou art pre-primal first and final factor of emerging and equating energy.

Limitless art Thou that livest not; bornless and unbounded is thine unilluminated light.

We reverence in Thee our whole unmanifested universe; Thou art parabeing and pure potential.

We know we know Thee not; and only thus we know Thee.

We know no symbol for Thee; nor have we any name for Thee except necessity of nothing.

In gaining life we lose Thee; and by our loss of life Thou gainest us.

Our solitary means of recognizing thy reality is inwardly through silent stillness of our senses.

With awe do we accept thine actuality; and now await Thee with due worship.

So Mote It Be. Amen.

Kether

Principle of the Summative Crown

O Thou Solitary Spirit of Entire Existence; Begetter of All Being and Light of Every Life.

Thou art what Thou wilt be within thyself; O Ancient of the Ancient Ones.

Concealed art Thou of the concealed; thine end and origin is with thyself alone.

Thou art the source and sum of every soul; O Perfect Point of everyone and everything.

Thou first emerging entity upon the Holy Tree of Life; Crown of Consciousness and apex of awareness.

O Light of Lights we are thy separated sparks; who seek for our fulfillment in thy sacred flame.

May our searching souls arise toward Thee; until we rejoin thy ruling radiance.

Most Mystical Intelligence beyond the comprehension of created beings; inspire in us a sense of thy true actuality.

So at last in striving to attain Thee; we may surely come to know ourselves.

O Highest Holiness of the Originative World; thy still small voice breathes forth thy name — Eheieh.

Blind us not by thy surpassing brilliance; but encourage us to live by whatsoever light enables us to recognize thine absolute reality.

Most mighty Metatron, thou privileged Archangel of the Only Perfect Presence; mediate for us in the creative world that power none other than thyself may deal with face to face.

Shine Thou before the blessed throne of truth; like purest light outpoured in benediction.

Chaioth ha Qadesh Thou art Holy Living Creatures and the first formative angels; uphold the dignity of life before all lesser dignities.

Uplift also our hearts and take our prayers to heaven; like an offering of ambergris arising from our earthly altars.

Shine Thou as a spiritual beacon; and become our welcome watchfires of the inner way.

O Primal Motion of our matter with the swirling nebulae expressed into existence; be unto us the sign of Cosmos coming forth from chaos. Let the light in darkness of thy golden sparklings set in space awaken us to look above ourselves and find illumination.

Thou Oldest One of the Vast Countenance Eternal, *Amen*; in Thee is nothing left but only right remains.

Ancient of Days be Thou our whole significance; and only point of our becoming separated selves within Thee.

Blessed be thy symbol of the spinning cross and central stillness; around thy point of poise all powers revolve forever.

Let thy light in us reveal thy real intention with us; that by its aid we shall accomplish what Thou wilt through our continuance in Thee forevermore.

So Mote It Be. Amen.

Chockmah

Principle of the Eternal Wisdom

O Supernal Spirit of our Primal Procreation; Father force of Life art Thou, projected into people.

Send forth the living stream of thy most sacred seed; that every soul alive proclaims thy parenthood.

May each and every one of our humanity acknowledge the authority of thy Divinity.

Thou second sphere upon the Holy Tree of Life; praise be to thy paternal principle of wisdom.

True wisdom was brought forth before all other attributes; and its beginning lies in our perception of Thee as our Supreme Patriarch.

O Thou Omnipotent Omniscience; may we be wise within Thee.

Intelligence of true illumination manifesting the most high magnificence; be exalted over us eternally.

Allow us to achieve immortal entity; existing with Thee everlastingly.

Name of Names within the world of origins; that never may be said by mortals save through substitution.

Tetragrammaton! Thou made us in thy mind; make us more mindful of Thee in ourselves.

Thou art the spirit of our sapience; be thy beneficence around us like a soft blue sky.

Archangel Ratziel Thou herald of the Holy Wisdom throughout all creation; Thou speakest from the summit of thy mystic mountain.

Proclaim aloud to us the word we lost on earth; so that we shall remember how to regain Heaven.

Protect us with thy good grey cloak from all the perils possible upon this path.

Angel Order of the Auphanim, trueturning ones of the formative world; work well with us through our life cycles on the ceaseless wheel of cosmic changes.

O pearly iridescent ones take Thou our thoughts into the holy presence; like the stimulating scent of musk makes meaning for our senses.

Mazloth, Thou mysterious influence appearing in expression as our zodiac; be thy solar cross and circle a significance of our salvation.

Let thy soft white light so shine around us that we shall see all cosmic colors in our spiritual spectrum.

Almighty Abba our first father; Thou hast bred us of thy being.

Sacred be to us on earth thy symbol of the standing stone; or staff erect and strong in its significance.

Thou art our most trustworthy tower of truth; set Thou us at the top of it with thy straight scepter.

Take our left shoulders and direct us in the upright way; that lies along the line of light from our unworthiness to thy Divinity.

So Mote It Be. Amen.

Binah

Principle of the Omniscient Understanding

O Thou Mysterious Mother from whose womb all lesser entities emerge; from Thee our souls set forth as selves upon their paths of progress.

Thou art Aima darkly waiting impregnation by the seed of light; Aima art Thou as it burns within Thee on its way to birth.

O Spiritual Sea supporting life as space supports a universe, let us be borne in Thee with utmost safety and security.

Third upon the Holy Tree of Life art Thou O Understanding One; thy total comprehension covers complete Cosmos.

From Thee, O Mother, we inherit intuition; and Thou art the instinct of all conscious creatures.

We would consider ourselves as thy chosen children; cherish us as we have confidence and trust in Thee.

O Sanctifying Intelligence in whom begins primordial perception; Thou art the fount of faith and fostermother of fidelity.

Teach us to accept Thee absolutely; believe in us as we have reason to rely on Thee.

O Matriarch of all Mankind within the world of origins Evoi Elohim; Thou art Mother to the greatest gods themselves.

Only Thou art mistress of the mighty ones; crimson is thy clothing with the blood of all becoming.

Archangel Tzaphkiel who watches over every entity from the creative world; guide and guard us through gestation and in excarnation.

May we find a blessed sanctuary beneath thy black concealing cloak; when we would hold communion with most sacred silence.

Angel Order of the Aralim, Thou seats of sapience in the formative world; uphold us as we try to understand the meanings of the Holy Mysteries.

As we sometimes send ourselves into a deep brown mood of study; so send our meanings to the universal mind as myrrh is offered in the way of worship.

Thou sphere of Saturn in expressive terms be not to us a sign of sadness; but a symbol of stability and sensible behavior.

Thou art the counterbalance of creation; and the certain test of every truth.

May we recognize within thine ashen grey; those rosy tints that tell of an impending golden resurrection.

O Supernal Mother, we depend on thy Divinity for life and our perception of its purpose; in Thee do we perceive a promise of eternal entity.

Sacred be thy symbol of a stone outspread on earth; and honored be the cup of celebration or the cauldron of a consecrated circle.

Take Thou firmly and securely our right shoulders; then complete thy cosmic course with us forevermore.

So Mote It Be. Amen.

Chesed

Principle of the Perpetual Compassion

O Thou Good Governor of Life with an affectionate authority; Thou givest thine attention to us with a generous amusement.

Since we were created with a shout of laughter; let spiritual happiness and holiness be truly one.

We pray that we may always please Thee; affording Thee the highest form of any entertainment.

Fourth upon the Holy Tree of Life art Thou O Kindly King of Cosmos; thy beneficence extends to every being.

Magnanimity and mercy are thine attributes; Thou art concerned with care and consolation for thy creatures.

Boundless are the blessings of thy bounty; and we are comforted by thy compassion.

O Thou receiver of intelligence, Thou holdest all the holy powers; from Thee emanates the essence of exalted virtues.

Cohesive is thy special consciousness; send Thou a share of this into our souls.

Thy name is singularly simple in the world of origins; El alone art Thou, the only one from evermore to evermore.

Violet seems to us the veil before thy face; be Thou good and gracious unto us forever.

Archangel Tzadkiel most righteous art Thou in the creative world; guide us gently in whatever way we ought to go.

Be Thou forbearing of our frequent failures; and correct our courses with thy beams of brightest blue.

O Angel Order of the Chasmalim with thine especial gift of cheerful speech in the formative world; welcome unto us are all thy words of faithful friendly feelings.

Bear our thoughts to heaven like the scent of cedar on a sea-born breeze; and may a pleasant place await us in the purple shadows of thy secret shades.

Thou expressive sphere of Jupiter supply us with thy joviality; prosper us upon this planet.

Help us to earn and afterwards enjoy; the rich rewards of our endeavors on our earth.

Lead us ahead by thy deep azure light; which hints at happiness to come for every soul.

Thou art the recompenser of the righteous; may we be recognized within thy realm.

May we be glad to share thy gifts; with those who truly need them in thy name.

Blessed be thy symbol of the fourfold form; and spiritual scepter of sovereignty.

Take our left arms and guide us graciously; throughout thy path that leads toward perfection.

So Mote It Be. Amen

Geburah

Principle of the Almighty Justice

O Thou Spirit of Severe Economy throughout existence; Thou art the eternal enemy of evil.

In making man observe obedience of thy divine decrees; Thou also makest us amenable to thine authority.

Deal not with us on purely past deserts alone; but because of what we shall become when we have learned our lessons.

Fifth upon the Holy Tree of Life art Thou O Ever-Winning Warrior; Thou art the certain champion of Cosmos.

Inflictions of injustice are avenged by Thee; nor will wickedness prevail against thy power.

On Thee do we rely for restitution of our rights; and we obey thine orders with respect and reverence.

Radical is thine intelligence, being rooted in the depth of reason; thy principles of retribution are entirely free from passion.

Sensible is thy sincere severity; may we realize its strict impartiality.

Elohim Gebor the Overcoming One art Thou within the world of origins; may we be worthy of inclusion with thy holy hosts.

Let us always act with confidence and constant courage; defending our beliefs in thy Divinity beneath thine orange banner.

Archangel Khamael Thou burning one of the creative world; cleanse corruption from us with thy torch of truth.

Free Thou our souls from every filthy falsehood; by thy most faithful fire that melts our fetters with its searing scarlet flames.

O Angel Order of the Seraphim, Thou Fiery Serpents of formation; burn out of us ideas of rage, revenge, or any rash behavior.

Sterilize Thou such infections of the soul like an ammoniacal antidote dispels all acid dangers; and be thy brilliant scarlet badge an honored pledge of health and purity.

Thou mighty one expressed as Mars, spare us from stupid strife; may we not waste this world with savage wars.

Let us learn instead to fight the enemies within ourselves; without inflicting injuries upon each other.

Be thine ensign of exacting red and black; our best reminder of this all-important issue.

O Thou prevailing power whose symbols are the sword and scourge; be unto us a surgeon, not a slayer.

Help us realize the reasons why we must find fortitude; and face faithfully the dangers and disasters on our Paths to peace.

Take us by our right arms and make us resolute; that we may conquer all adversities against thy cosmic cause.

So Mote It Be. Amen

Tiphereth

Principle of the Transcendent Beauty

O Thou Central Cosmic Spirit of the Living Light; entire existence hangs upon thy perfect point of equilibrium.

May we receive thy radiance into our souls; according to our state of readiness for such intense illumination.

Let us not demand more light from Thee than we may hold; with dignity and honor for thy high Divinity.

Sixth upon the Holy Tree of Life art Thou O Beautiful and Blessed Being; thine image is like immolated innocence.

Priest-King and Risen Son of rightful royal blood art Thou; perpetuated through thy line of light forever.

May we who sacrifice ourselves in spirit; become related with Thee in reality.

Thine intelligence is interceding as a mediator; issuing influences through itself that offer inspiration to entire mankind.

Thou bringest what is best to bear on everyone; may we experience thy true enlightenment.

Thou art Aloah Va Daath the Knower of All Life within the world of origins; let us also be aware that we live in Thee.

May we recognize thy rosy rays of rising; that the radiance of thy Divinity will surely dawn upon us.

Godlike art Thou Archangel Michael in the creative world; we pray for thy protection.

Free us from a fiery fate; and liberate us with thy shaft of light from every evil.

Send Thou thy golden ones of grace to guard and guide us; past all the pitfalls that prevent our progress on our Paths.

Angelic Order of the Malachim, Thou art the regulating ones of the formative world; help us rule ourselves before we seek control of others.

Correct our conduct carefully; with thy roseate reminders.

Take Thou our thoughts unto the eye of Heaven; like finest frankincense arising from our earthly altars.

O Solar Center of the expressed Cosmos; Thou art our oldest sign of spiritual order.

Thy seasons show our passing Paths of progress; and Thou art the point round which we pivot on this planet.

Lead us by thy golden-amber light; into thy secret inner system.

Thou art the lesser countenance which hides the holy face no mortal may behold; let our waking inner vision be unclouded by a veil of willful ignorance.

Honored be thy cross and cube together with the six-pointed star; thine is the harmony that holds the spheres together as a whole.

Let thy sacred sign of LVX shine forth; from every single living breast forever.

So Mote It Be. Amen.

Netzach

Principle of the Unceasing Victory

O Thou Amiable Spirit of Achievement; thy truth must triumph over all in time.

Thou dost not win thy way with wicked wars; but slowly gains supremacy by gentleness of soul.

May we also come to share in thy success; conquering conditions set against attainment of thy potent peace.

Seventh on the Holy Tree of Life art Thou; O Force of Feminine and Virtuous Victory.

Thou art She in whom brutalities become abated; and absorbed by thine amative sense-subduing softness.

Reform our rudeness and our bad behavior; that lust becomes in us an ardent love instead.

Hidden from humanity is thine intelligence by its concealment; courtesy and charm come to those souls who cultivate Thee.

Only deepest insight will discern Thee; in ecstasy alone art Thou experienced.

Yahwe Tzabaoth is thy name within the world of origins; Thou wilt be to every one of us as thy whole entity.

Let us realize thine ambience with every amber ray attracting our attention; and may we become aware of Thee with all our spiritual senses.

Archangel Auriel in the creative world art Thou; who like a lamp upheld on earth exemplify the light of Heaven.

Shield us safely and securely with thine emerald aegis; defend our sensitivities of soul from desecration.

O Angelic Order of the Elohim in the formative world; Thou art the godlike inner images mankind may look upon and live.

Be gracious to us in thy groves of golden-green; where moving music makes us glad to be alive.

Send our supplications like the scent of sandalwood to Heaven; that we may hope for happiness in earth existence.

Thou Brilliant One of dawn and dusk expressed behind the veil of Venus; shine upon us with sweet sympathy for our aspiring souls.

May thine olive-golden garments give us goodly grace; and signify a stimulating life of peaceful plenty.

O Lovely Lady of Divine Delight, Thou art the deep necessity of our divided natures; satisfy our spiritual senses so that we are conscious of complete contentment.

Thou whose sacred symbols are the girdle and the lamp; lead us lightly by thy tender touch on our left loins.

Let us love Thee always and show unto us thy true affection; when we come to Thee for comfort, counsel, or in search of consolation.

So Mote It Be. Amen.

Hod

Principle of the Surpassing Glory

Thou Splendid Spirit of Sagacity and Honor; in thy hands are held the works of hidden wisdom.

Thou art the instructor of our intellects; and mentor of our mental movements.

Thy special secrets are revealed to us by reason; initiate our minds into the meaning of the Holy and Hermetic Mysteries.

Eighth upon the Holy Tree of Life art Thou; O Glorious Hermaphrodite of Heaven.

Male and female talents meet in Thee with clever caution; Thou combinest in thyself the best of both.

At thine instigation we inquire into the laws of life; with thy willing aid do we investigate enigmas of existence.

Perfect is the inner path of thine intelligence; it prepares us to perceive the principles behind our beings.

Thou showest us the splendid sorts of souls we may become; we take our best encouragement from thine example.

Thou art Elohim Tzabaoth in the world of origins; Maker of Multitudes and Lord of Legions.

O Thou who livest always in the thoughts of everyone; awake thy people's vision with thy purple-violet light.

Archangel Raphael art Thou in the creative world; healing hurts sustained in swordlike situations.

Invest us also with the air of thine authority; and may our entire organisms be invigorated by thine orange emanations.

O Angelic Order of the Beni Elohim in the formative world; Thou art the descendants of Divinities.

Let thy likeness lighten up our lives; like children of our consciousness.

Send our thoughts into the spheres of spirit as an interesting scent of storax; and may we remember Thee with every shade of russet-red that we shall ever see.

Thou art expressed as Hermes of the Heavens; silver speech is thine with scintillating wit.

Be thy black and yellow whipped with white; a secret sign to us of subtlety and commonsense combined.

O Thrice Great One, be our trusted teacher in thy spiritual schools and temples; make our minds achieve thy mutability and motion.

Thou whose sacred symbols are the written Rites concealed within the ancient craft-adornment of an apron; take Thou and train us in the rules of ritual and magic methods.

Lead us skillfully by our right loins along the special inner lines; which we must follow for initiation sponsored by the spirit.

So Mote It Be. Amen.

Yesod

Principle of the Infallible Foundation

O Thou basis of our living beings and fount of our fertility; Thou art the softly shining one of the Shekinah.

Thy reflection shows us safely what we dare not look directly at as mortals; Thou art the link between our ignorance and true illuminations.

In Thee appears the cause of our continuance as human creatures; for Thou art the reality our reproduction represents.

Ninth upon the Holy Tree of Life art Thou, O Vision of Virility; Thou art the firm foundation of our faith in life itself.

While thy potent force prevails, we surely shall not perish from this planet.

We evolve through Thee into much more than mortal entities; our inner destination lies with thy Divinity.

Thine intelligence is termed the purified; it prevents imagination from distorting or destroying thine intention.

Thou art the systematic savior of our sanity; through Thee do we discern the basic truth behind our dreams.

Shaddai el Chaiim the Lord of Lives art Thou in the creative world beginning every birth; of Thee do we emerge into embodiment and end our days on earth.

Dark as deepest indigo is thy profundity of purpose; may thine intentions come to light among mankind.

Archangel Gabriel art Thou in the creative world; awake us all to life on every level.

Call and awaken us across the holy water held within thy cup; that we may hear thy voice through thy thin violet veil.

O Angelic Order of the Aishim in the formative world; thy powers are adequate to found the families of fit and proper people.

Let us experience the taste of life enjoyably like jasmine; and protect us from its perils with thy purple panoply.

Elusive light of night art Thou, expressive Moon of many meanings; may thy bright beams become a bridge for us to cross the chasms of confusion.

Let us not be lost amid thy maze nor tangled with thy thorns; but live to share the secrets of thy silver castle in its citrine-azure setting.

O Thou mighty and majestic mystery; how shall our souls seek thy solution?

Deceive us not nor let us doubt unduly; may we make some sense of what we see within thy magic mirror.

Thy sacred symbols are perfumes and sandals; when employed for proper ritual reasons.

Guard Thou our genitals that life may only come of Love; and free us from all forms of falsehood into living light forevermore.

So Mote It Be. Amen.

Malkuth

Principle of the Life throughout the Kingdom

O Thou Kingdom of all evident and obvious existence; Thou art the special sphere in which we start our spiritual searchings.

Here as humanity we are thy cosmic children; formed by thy forces out of living flesh and blood.

Forgive us for our frequent failures; in recognizing our relationship with thy reality.

Tenth upon the Holy Tree of Life art Thou; O Ruling One whose rightful name is Nature.

The entirety of evolution is thine empire; it extends all through our earth existence.

Blessed art Thou as a blissful bride; bestowed on honored human husbands.

Resplendent is thy royal intelligence; exalted over everyone as the immortal way of wisdom.

Thou art the persuasive power of prayer; and by thy grace are we delivered from the gates of death.

Adonai ha Aretz art Thou in the orginative world; O King of Kings and the unequalled master of our manifested universe.

May we always yield ourselves to thy Divine authority; displayed by thy bright yellow banner of obedience.

Archangel Sandalphon art Thou in the creative world; thy feet are firmly on the floor of our far-flying cosmic chariot.

Steer straight our course throughout creation; O Close Companion cloaked with the sequential colors of the seasons.

O Thou Angelic Order of the Kerubim in the formative world; thine is the fourfold force of mobile matter.

We recognize thy special signs of sable russet graced by golden points of power; may they be discerned through screens of smoke as dense as those of cretan dittany.

Thou art the elements of earth expressively; O physical phenomena within our working world.

We rely on Thee for proofs of our reality as people; give us golden hints of higher meanings in the blackest of our basic matter.

O Thou Mighty Daughter of Divinity and Lesser Mother of Our Lives; we value thy virginity as a most sacred secret which must be maintained inviolate.

Thou whose symbols are the altar cubes and cosmic Circle Cross, we seek to serve the spirit of thy cause.

Lead Thou our faithful feet forever on the line of light; that lies between all human beings and their highest everlasting entity.

So Mote It Be. Amen

INVOCATIONS OF THE PATHS

Path 0-33

Connecting Ain Soph Aur with Sphere 1

O Thou that wilt or wilt-not-be entirely as Thou wilt. Be or unbe thy will with us.

Thou art our infinite impossibility. Of Thee alone is inspiration to be anything we will within Thee other than thine unidentity.

Thou art the void, yet breathest forth vitality and being as Eheieh.

Thou art uncreate, yet cause of all creation mediated through Archangel Metatron.

Thou art silence, yet the Holy Living Creatures sing in praise of thy perfection.

Thou art motionless, yet every moving nebula proclaims thy power made manifest through nature.

Blessed unto us be what Thou wilt or wilt-not-be forevermore.

So Mote It Be. Amen

Path 11 — B

Connecting Sphere 1 with Sphere 2

O Ruling Spirit of Summative Wisdom, grant in us that we may likewise know ourselves in Thee.

May we become true pontiffs of thy power, and bridge with spiritual skill the distance that divides our state from thine.

Thou Breath of Life! Be in us what Thou wilt.

Mediate our cause before the crown of our creation O Thou Metatron, and proclaim our purpose to the Highest One, O Ratziel.

Thou living elements, sustain us through all cosmic cycles which we must complete.

As the nebulae, so may we come to life in light, and thence continue till the ending of the twelvefold Circle that contains our consciousness as separated entities within existence.

So Mote It Be. Amen

Path 12 — C

Connecting Sphere 1 with Sphere 3

O Thou Crown of Understanding, let us comprehend what we shall be in Thee above all else.

Let thy solitary single spirit be the only light in us that leads us into everlasting liberation.

Breathe Thou forth from Thee our souls that we may live.

Archangel Metatron uphold humanity unto the being that Thou beholdest, and teach us truth, O Tzaphkiel when we are ready to receive it.

Thou Holy Living Creatures, set us most securely on our seats of sensibility.

From our first movement, may we gain sufficient gravity to proceed steadily like Saturn on our cosmic courses, holding thy most precious secrets safely in our souls til time reveals to all, thy total and most radiant golden truth.

So Mote It Be. Amen.

Path 13 — D

Connecting Sphere 1 with Sphere 6

O Thou Supreme Crown and Beauty of all being, may we live forever in the state of thy perfection.

May every single star of Heaven be for us a sign of thy most holy spirit and a pointer of our ways upon the path of light.

Breathe Thou in us that we may know Thee in ourselves.

Be mindful of us, O Thou Mighty Metatron, who dares to face Divinity directly, and do Thou, O Michael, intercede on our behalf before the highest throne.

O Holy Creatures, be our active elements of life, and may the rightly ruling ones make straight our inner lines of light.

Like unto the nebulae may we bestir ourselves so that the sun of truth may surely come to light in us, and dissipate all doubts and darkness from us evermore.

So Mote It Be. Amen.

Path 14 — F

Connecting Sphere 2 with Sphere 3

O Thou Spirit of All Understanding Wisdom, be aware of us in Thee who art the total truth of us in living light.

May thy judgment ever be the safeguard of our souls, arousing our abilities to comprehend our spiritual purpose and position in thy Cosmos.

Thou life of all! Be Thou our will to live in light.

O Archangel Ratziel declare Divine intentions to us, and do Thou Archangel Tzaphkiel help us to observe them.

Crush not our souls, O Circling Angels, but surround us with security upon our thrones of reasonable rulership.

Be Thou not too seriously heavy in our human hearts, O Saturn. Let us sometimes leave the solemn side of life, and dance for sheer delight within the solar circle of our Cosmos.

So Mote It Be. Amen.

Path 15 — G

Connecting Sphere 2 with Sphere 4

O Thou Spirit of Beneficence and Wisdom, be magnanimous to us who may not live without thy mercy.

Be Thou to us an emperor of gracious government, so that we may attempt to emulate thy ways of ruling on our earth.

Thou that wilt be what Thou art, be Thou unique in us.

Proclaim this perfect power, O Ratziel, and do Thou Archangel Tzadkiel, preserve our rightful pathways leading us to light.

Encircle us with careful counsel Thou Auphanim, and be kind to us, O Chasmalim with thy most welcome warmth within our souls.

May we indeed be jovial and generous throughout the twelvefold cycle of the solar seasons, so that we may ever claim compassion at the hands of earth or Heaven with a clear conscience.

So Mote It Be. Amen.

Path 16 — H

Connecting Sphere 2 with Sphere 6

O Thou Supremacy of Beautiful Omniscience, may we become aware of Thee through wisdom and with wonder.

Teach us temperance with every way of life, that we may cross our chasms carefully, in firm control of every spiritual situation.

O Thou that knowest what Thou wilt, let us become enlightened in Thee.

Reveal to us Archangel Ratziel, thy holy secrets, and deliver us O Michael from doubts and dangers.

Assist us, O Thou Angels of the Malakim, to rule ourselves with reason in the living circles of the Auphanim.

May our secret sun behind the sun shine forth in glory through the signs of heaven, so that every soul may likewise live in light forevermore.

So Mote It Be. Amen.

Path 17 — J

Connecting Sphere 3 with Sphere 5

O Thou Strictest Spirit of Controlled Severity, we pray that we may learn to understand Thee.

Let thy decree of death deter us in no way from living, but encourage us to alter as we will within Thee for the better.

O Mighty Life of Lives! Thou livest for us ever.

Archangel Tzaphkiel, observe what is unworthy in us, so that Khamael the burner may remove it from us beneficially.

Support us steadfastly, O Thrones, so that the purifying seraphim may purge us of corruption.

Saturn, be Thou our protective shield against all martial dangers of destruction, so that our surviving souls may live immortally in purest golden light forevermore.

So Mote It Be. Amen.

Path 18 — K

Connecting Sphere 3 with Sphere 6

O Thou Most Beautiful of Beings, grant us sufficient understanding to become aware of thine existence.

In the sign of man suspended from the Tree of Life may we find our salvation and those secrets which our souls are ever seeking.

Thou art everyone! Thou knowest all we are.

Watch over us Archangel Tzaphkiel and Michael be Thou our mediators as our souls are called to their account before Divine authority.

O Thou Angelic Thrones and Rulers, guide and establish us with law and learning.

May our spiritual operation of the Sun and Saturn be successful in transmuting our base natures into souls of highest value to ourselves and the Eternal One in whom we live.

So Mote It Be. Amen.

Path 19 — L

Connecting Sphere 4 with Sphere 5

O Most Compassionate Severity, may both extremes in us be balanced with the edge of thine exactitude.

Let us be delivered from afflictions and disasters by thy faultless justice, and the point of all we shall experience made plain to us.

Almighty One, Thou livest by thy laws alone.

Archangel Tzadkiel stimulate our sense of rightness, and do Thou Khamael, warn us from wrongdoing with thy fiery finger.

Angelic Flames of Fusion and of Fission, weld us firmly unto what is good, and separate our souls from evil.

May martial might and jovial mercy make us into finely balanced beings, completely compensated by whatever laws of life correct the errors of existence.

So Mote It Be. Amen.

Path 20 — M

Connecting Sphere 4 with Sphere 6

O Most Merciful and Beautiful of Beings, thy powers alone are perfectly proportioned.

Thine is the strongest spirit in existence. All is accomplished by thine actions. Thine energy is inexhaustible.

Omniscient One, the whole of life is thine experience.

Archangel Tzadkiel, make thy right our might, and Michael, preserve our souls from peril by potency of thy protection.

O Warmhearted Angels, and our ruling guides to goodness, be Thou kind and kingly unto us forever.

May the spiritual sun of our illumination shine eternally within us, and the magnanmity of Jove incline our feelings to be generous toward our fellow creatures of this Cosmos.

So Mote It Be. Amen.

Path 21 — N

Connecting Sphere 4 with Sphere 7

O Thou Victorious One of all Achievements, may thy truimphant life be also ours to share with Thee eternally.

Be Thou like unto an empress, governing with grace, and let us similarly gain control of our emotions with a fair and firm benevolence.

Thou ruling one of everyone, may we reign with Thee in ourselves.

Archangel Tzadkiel, encourage us upon our way of right, and Auriel enlighten us, so that we may be led with loyalty and love toward our ultimate attainment.

Thou Shining and Celestial Spirits, help us to uphold the good opinions we should have for one another.

May our Lord and Lady, symbolized as Jove and Venus, signify to us true spiritual loving kindness, which alone will make our lives worth living in this world or any other evermore.

So Mote It Be. Amen.

Path 22 — P

Connecting Sphere 5 with Sphere 6

O Beautiful Severity, lay not the lash of thy most holy discipline too heavily upon us.

Break Thou our selfish strongholds of stupidity as Thou must surely blast the towers of those defying thy Divine authority.

Thou Mightiest of Mind, may we be strongly sensible.

Archangel Khamael, be Thou our finest flame of spiritual freedom, and do Thou, O Michael, become our leading liberator into light.

Thou Burning and controlling Angels, help us hold our tempers from becoming out of hand or overheated.

May the might of Mars be balanced by the poising power of solar strength, so that by equalizing energies peace will prevail throughout all actions on this path.

So Mote It Be. Amen.

Path 23 — Q

Connecting Sphere 5 with Sphere 8

O Glorious Severity, try Thou us not beyond our spiritual strength, nor send us sufferings we are ashamed to bear.

Thou tempting one, whose tests make us torment ourselves, we shall be delivered from thine influences by our inner sense of discipline and duty.

Mighty One of Multitudes, may all mankind mean most to Thee.

Archangel Khamael, be Thou the fire and Raphael, the sword which conquers whatsoever would corrupt our consciousness, or send our souls to senseless slavery.

O Flaming and Appearing Angels, help us to be forceful and apparent, utterly without ferocity, unkindness, or aggression.

By the help of Hermes, and the might of Mars, may all actions be averted which would lead to wicked wars. Let good counsel overcome the very worst of serious situations, so that peaceful power prevails with honor evermore.

So Mote It Be. Amen.

Path 24 — R

Connecting Sphere 6 with Sphere 7

O victorious Beauty, Thou art winner of the cosmic contest. May we win this world of ours with Thee.

Beloved unto everyone are lovers, and blessed be the bond between our living legions. Let us Love each other through our lives on every level.

Thou Experience of all, may Thou be shared by every single soul.

Archangel Auriel, enlighten us on earth, and lead us Michael, to our illumination in the living spirit of eternal Love. May we satisfy our spiritual sense with success.

O Thou Governing and Guiding Angels, help us to achieve a genuine affection for each other's entities.

Thou Lord of Light and Lady of our Love appearing unto us as Sol and Venus, give us cause to conquer all conditions of confused antagonisms. May entire humanity, released from hates, rejoice within thy happy radiance forevermore.

So Mote It Be. Amen.

Path 25 — S

Connecting Sphere 6 with Sphere 8

O Glorious Beauty, manifest thyself in all mankind. May our minds be made aware of thy magnificence.

Thou art the chariot that carries consciousness through cosmos. Take us with Thee on thy travels so that we will also come to comprehend thy truth.

Thou knowest every issue of intelligence. Perfect Thou our perception.

Archangel Raphael, instruct us rightly on our inner way, and Michael, point out for us the proper paths, which we must find and follow for attaining ultimate awareness.

O Thou Controlling and Contriving Angels, help us to cleverly command ourselves with cheerful confidence.

Thou Solar and Hermetic Spirit of all hidden science, initiate our intellects into the holy inner secrets. May our searching souls be made full members of thy mysteries, and thus achieve admission to thine adytum therein forever.

So Mote It Be. Amen.

Path 26 — T

Connecting Sphere 6 with Sphere 9

Thou Basic Beauty of all Being and firm foundation of our faith, let us never doubt thy true Divinity.

Thou art the centralizing Sun of Cosmos. Thy spirit is the light of every life. Let us exist through Thee eternally, for thine illumination indicates our true identity.

All life is thine to know. Make known thyself through us.

Archangel Michael, send Thou thy sacred staff for our support, and communicate to us, O Gabriel, the contents of thy consecrated cup.

O Thou Ruling and Reflective Angels, help us to believe that Deity knows what is best for us.

As Sun and Moon appear within the sky to man on earth, so may the souls of humankind be seen with their own light by the discerning spirit of Divinity in Heaven. May we be worthy of the will that works in us.

So Mote It Be. Amen.

Path 27 — V

Connecting Sphere 7 with Sphere 8

O Glorious Victory of Love and Learning, Thou makest our mortality worthwhile. We pray and practice for thy sake.

Events fall as Thou wilt, exactly as thy wheel of fate decrees our destinies. May we find favor from thy holy hand that casts our living lot into creation.

Thou art everything to everyone. Blessed be our share of Thee in spirit.

Archangel Auriel, assist us to make light of life, and Raphael, reveal some really suitable behavior to adopt in order to obtain the best of any situation.

O Thou angelic Ones of Items and Ideas, tell us what we should think of things to make the most of them.

May hermetic wit and aphroditic winsomeness be with us when we will. Let us not be lost for lack of instinct or imagination, but be always ready with the right response in every chance or circumstance.

So Mote It Be. Amen.

Path 28 — W

Connecting Sphere 7 with Sphere 9

O Victory of Life, Thou art the spirit that inspires each soul to seek its individual existence. Let us become thy best-born beings.

Thou art like unto a pure priestess who prays for the perfection of all people. May we also mediate thy will in us which makes us more than merely mortals.

Our Overlord of Life are Thou. May we truly recognize thy rulership.

Archangel Auriel, shield Thou our sentient souls, and Gabriel, arouse our finer feelings so that we are capable of contact with Divinity through our devotions.

O Representing and Reflecting Angels, make us meditate upon the inner meaning of initiation. May we be worthy members of the Holy Hidden Mysteries.

May the Moon and Venus bring before our minds that Virgin-Mother concept which connects a high identity with human incarnation. Let us also live to be illuminated in this mystic manner.

So Mote It Be. Amen.

Path 29 — X

Connecting Sphere 7 with Sphere 10

O Kingdom of Established Victory, in Thee does man discover his essential meaning. May we preserve thy peace entirely.

Thou art our complete Cosmos, and the world wherein we work thy will within our words. May we always live according to the laws of light and Love.

Ruler of reality in everything art Thou. Remember us eternally.

Archangel Auriel, enlighten us on earth, and do Thou stand by us, O Sandalphon, when we strive to rise beyond its barriers toward a higher spiritual habitation.

O Thou Angelic Ones of Living Likenesses, show us what we should be like, so that at least we shall attempt to live aspiringly.

May earth existence be made very comfortable when it is combined with ways of Venus. May all the arts of life become more lovely as mankind develops indications of Divinity, evincing true intentions of achieving immortality.

So Mote It Be. Amen.

Path 30 — Y

Connecting Sphere 8 with Sphere 9

O Ever Glorious Foundation, in Thee begins belief by which we have our hopes of Heaven. May this be true for all humanity.

Thou art the Magician who makes man continue to seek more than mortal consciousness. Inspire us likewise with some spiritual interests in our lives.

Lord of Life art Thou and its intentions. Live Thou thy will within us.

Archangel Raphael, remind us of the reasons we should stay alive, and Gabriel, supply us with the strength we shall require for our survival.

Thou Angel Orders of Well-bred and Worthy Ones, help us honor our most holy heritage. May we deserve our destiny.

May mercurial resilience and lunar relaxation be a secret spring behind our lives. Let us never be despairing nor depressed beyond recovery, but restore ourselves to rights again with a recuperative will.

So Mote It Be. Amen.

Path 31 — Z

Connecting Sphere 8 with Sphere 10

O Glorious Kingdom, Thou art the provider of that paradise on earth which we expect humanity to earn from Heaven.

Innocence alone art Thou, and guiltless of all guile. May we also place a childlike confidence in Thee, trusting in thine inner guidance for our everlasting good.

Monarch of thine endless multitudes art Thou. Consider us thy children.

Archangel Raphael, reveal to us the meanings of the Holy Mysteries, and Sandalphon, support our search for the solution of their secrets.

O Thou Angelic Families and Fourfold Forces, aid and assist our actions in our spiritual struggles. We welcome Thee at work.

May hermetic help and earth experience evolve the souls of them that strive to live in light. Let every life that we endure within this world be worthy of the will that caused us to be creatures of this Cosmos.

So Mote It Be. Amen.

Path 32 — Th

Connecting Sphere 9 with Sphere 10

O Thou Firm-Founded Kingdom, in Thee is life established and expressed within the compass of our living consciousness.

Mankind is like the Moon, held back by earth while hoping for escape to final freedom. May our first steps in spiritual space be dedicated and directed to Divinity.

Lord of Life extended unto earth art Thou. Be as Thou wilt with us.

Archangel Gabriel, be Thou the heavenly mediator of that message meant for all humanity, and Sandalphon, make us see what lies before us by the highest light of life.

O Angelic Orders of the Friendly Flames and Forces, help us see and serve the cosmic cause. Aid Thou our efforts to obtain enlightenment.

Thou Light of Luna, representing upon earth reflections of humanity on higher holy subjects, shine Thou so strongly in our souls, that we shall seek the spiritual side of everyone and everything forevermore.

So Mote It Be. Amen.

www.ingramcontent.com/pod-product-compliance
Lightning Source LLC
Chambersburg PA
CBHW022059150426
43195CB00008B/196